W9-CLI-827

Crusader Archaeology

In 1099 the Crusaders conquered Jerusalem. For several hundred years, large areas in the Eastern Mediterranean were under Latin rule. This unique volume describes the fascinating story of an invading society transplanting itself into completely new surroundings, providing comprehensive coverage of all aspects of life in the area they occupied.

Crusader Archaeology draws together recently excavated material from Israel, Cyprus, Syria, Lebanon and Jordan to examine what life was like for the Crusaders in their new territory, and how they were influenced by the local population. Chapters discuss urban and rural settlements, surveying agriculture, industry, military, church, public and private architecture, arts and crafts, leisure pursuits, death and burial, and building techniques.

This highly illustrated volume creates an intriguing portrait of the period, which will make fascinating reading for all those interested in the Middle Ages, and particularly in the Crusaders.

Adrian J. Boas is Lecturer in medieval archaeology at the Hebrew University, Jerusalem, and at Haifa University. He has directed excavations at a Crusader village and a number of castles in Israel.

Crusader Archaeology

The Material Culture of the
Latin East

Adrian J. Boas

London and New York

First published 1999
by Routledge
11 New Fetter Lane, London EC4P 4EE

Simultaneously published in the USA and Canada
by Routledge
29 West 35th Street, New York, NY 10001

Routledge is an imprint of the Taylor & Francis Group

© 1999 Adrian J. Boas

Typeset in Garamond 3 by
Keystroke, Jacaranda Lodge, Wolverhampton
Printed and bound in Great Britain by
Biddles Ltd, Guildford and King's Lynn

All rights reserved. No part of this book may be reprinted or
reproduced or utilised in any form or by any electronic,
mechanical, or other means, now known or hereafter
invented, including photocopying and recording, or in any
information storage or retrieval system, without permission in
writing from the publishers.

British Library Cataloguing in Publication Data
A catalogue record for this book is available from the British Library

Library of Congress Cataloguing in Publication Data
A catalogue record for this book has been requested

ISBN 0–415–17361–2

For my wife Yochi,
and sons Jonathan, Amir and Daniel

Contents

Illustrations

Plates

Preface and acknowledgements

There are few historical topics more intriguing than that of a foreign society transplanted into completely new surroundings. The struggle to adapt to a strange environment, and the degree to which that environment influenced and was changed by the newcomers, are amongst the more fascinating aspects of historical research. From the end of the eleventh century there were Christian states in the Levant which shared many similarities with their counterparts in western Europe but in many ways were quite different. The kingdoms of Jerusalem and Cyprus and the Latin principalities in Syria were very much products of the soil in which they took root, hybrids that resulted from the meeting of quite different cultures. In every area we look we see a blending of Eastern and Western cultures.

For many people romantic images conceal much of the reality of the Crusader period. They tend to view it through myopic eyes that see little more than the popular images of armed knights and fortified castles. If we look beyond these images however, it is possible to perceive something of the reality of Frankish life in the East. For close to a century archaeologists have worked at removing the accumulated dust and rubble from the remnants of this period. Although motivation and method have not been consistently adequate, our knowledge of the material culture of the Frankish period in the East has advanced considerably and is no longer confined to the more impressive monuments of the past. Alongside major publications of castles and churches, a growing number of scholars have produced a considerable body of information on urban and rural settlement, daily life, arts and crafts, burial customs and so on. All of these studies contribute to our knowledge of the period and expand what we know from written sources about life in the Latin East.

The theme of this book is the archaeological research of the Latin East. A wealth of modern historical literature on the Crusades has enabled us to dispense with many preconceptions regarding the Crusading movement and Frankish settlement. Although many people have a better idea of what the Crusades were about, comparatively few are aware of how the Franks lived in *Outremer* ('the lands beyond the sea' as the Frankish states in the East were known), how they built their castles, churches and houses, what their possessions were, how they fought their battles and what weapons they used, what food they ate and how they raised their crops – in short, how they lived their daily lives. In this book I intend to answer some of these questions and to make available part of the considerable but often obscurely located and occasionally unobtainable information that archaeological research has brought to light.

Much of the archaeological activity concerned with the Crusader period has concentrated in the modern State of Israel, which covers most of the territory of the kingdom of Jerusalem. Frankish Cyprus has been discussed, since the ground-breaking work of Camille Enlart, in a number of important publications describing amongst other things castles, sugar mills, fine arts, numismatics and ceramics. However, apart from some important architectural studies of the monuments of Syria and Lebanon, the remainder of the Latin East is poorly represented in publications and very little fieldwork has been carried out in recent years. This deficiency, together with my own intimate knowledge of the archaeological developments in Israel, has resulted in a disproportionate emphasis on the kingdom of Jerusalem at the expense of the other areas under Latin rule. I can only express the hope that in the future there will be a greater interchange of knowledge between scholars working in the region, and that in the meantime my own shortcomings will cause less harm than the good served by publishing even so limited a study.

My interest in Crusader history developed when I attended lectures given by the late Professor Joshua Prawer of the Hebrew University in Jerusalem. I was immensely fortunate in being able to continue in this field under Professor Benjamin Ze'ev Kedar. I have been equally fortunate in the guidance and encouragement of Professor Yoram Tsafrir of the Institute of Archaeology at the Hebrew University of Jerusalem. I am grateful to Professor Tsafrir and my good friend and colleague Dr Ronnie Ellenblum, who agreed to read the first draft, and to others whose expertise kept me from major blunders including Professor Bianca Kühnel, Robert Kool, Orit Shamir and Danny Syon. Amongst the many archaeologists who advised me and aided me in research for this book I would like to mention Dr Dan Bahat, Dr Ze'ev Goldmann, Dr Yizhar Hirschfeld, Gabi Laron, Ayalah Lester, Dr Denys Pringle, Katie Raphael, Eliezer Stern and Edna Stern. If this book is readable it is due in no small part to Sue Gorodetsky, who vastly improved my occasionally rusty English. I would like to express my appreciation of the assistance of the staff at Routledge, namely Andrew Wheatcroft, Victoria Peters, Nadia Jacobson, Alan Peterson, Lynne Maddock and Ann King. I am grateful for the kindness and helpfulness of the staff of various institutions including the Israel National Library, the library of the Institute of Archaeology at the Hebrew University of Jerusalem, the library of Haifa University, the British School of Archaeology in Jerusalem, the convent of St Anne, Jerusalem, the Ecole Biblique et Archéologique Française (Saint-Etienne), the library and archives of the Israel Antiquities Authority at the Rockefeller Museum, the library of Yad Itzak Ben-Zvi in Jerusalem and the

Cyprus American Archaeological Research Institute in Nicosia. Research for Chapter 3 was carried out while I was on a Lady Davis Post-Doctorate fellowship. I am greatly indebted to my sister-in-law Batsheva Kohai who worked long and hard at preparing the plates and maps, and to Buki Boaz, Michele Piccirillo, Dr Jonathan Phillips, the Israel Antiquities Authority and the Ha'aretz Museum for supplying me with many of the photographs. The Institute of Archaeology at the Hebrew University covered part of the cost of the illustrations.

On a more personal level, I am grateful to my parents and family for their continued love and support. My greatest debt of gratitude is to my wife and sons who bore the burden of this work and to whom this book is dedicated.

A. J. Boas
Jerusalem, June 1998

A note on the use of place-names

Place-names are inevitably a problem in a book of this nature. In order not to confuse the reader with a medley of Latin, French, Hebrew and Arabic names I have generally used the modern rather than the Frankish form – Yoqne'am rather than Caymont, Beit She'an rather than Baisan, Haifa rather than Caiphas, Beit Govrin rather than Betgibelin – and on its first appearance I have given the more commonly used Frankish name in parentheses. However in cases where the Frankish name is well known I have used it throughout.

Abbreviations

AB	Art Bulletin
ABSA	Annual of the British School at Athens
ANSMN	American Numismatic Society Museum Notes
ATN	Archaeological Textiles Newsletter
BAIAS	Bulletin of the Anglo-Israel Archaeological Society
BAR	British Archaeological Reports
BASOR	Bulletin of the American School of Oriental Research
BMB	Bulletin du Musée de Beyrouth
BSFN	Bulletin de la Société française de Numismatique
BZ	Byzantinische Zeitschrift
CNI	Christian News from Israel
DOP	Dumbarton Oaks Papers
DRHC	Documents relatives à l'histoire des croisades
EAEHL	Encyclopedia of Archaeological Excavations in the Holy Land
IEJ	Israel Exploration Journal
INJ	Israel Numismatic Journal
JGS	Journal of Glass Studies
JWCI	Journal of the Warburg and Courtauld Institutes
JPOS	Journal of the Palestine Oriental Society
LA	Liber Annuus
NEAEHL	The New Encyclopedia of Archaeological Excavations in the Holy Land
PEFA	Palestine Exploration Fund Annual
PEFQS	Palestine Exploration Fund Quarterly Statement
PPTS	Palestine Pilgrims' Text Society Library, 13 vols. London (1890–97)
QSAP	Quarterly of the Department of Antiquities of Palestine
RB	Revue Biblique
RDAC	Report of the Department of Antiquities of Cyprus
RN	Revue Numismatique
RZ	Römische Quartalschrift für Christliche Altertumskunde und Kirchengeschichte
ZDPV	Zeitschrift des Deutschen-Pälestina Vereins

Chronology

Dates	Events
1095	Byzantine Emperor *Alexius II Comnenus* appeals to the West for aid against the Seljuks
27 November 1095	At Clermont *Pope Urban II* preaches the Crusade
June 1096	The 'People's Crusade' led by *Peter the Hermit* sets out for the East, massacring Jewish communities, and is destroyed by Seljuk leader Kilij Arslan
August 1096	The First Crusade departs from western Europe
1097	Fall of Nicaea (19 June) and of Dorylaeum (1 July)
20 October 1097	The Crusader army reaches Antioch
March 1098	First Crusader state established in Edessa by *Baldwin of Boulogne*
3 June 1098	Crusaders take Antioch
7 June 1099	Crusader army arrives at Nebi Samwil within sight of Jerusalem
15 July 1099	Conquest of Jerusalem
22 July 1099	*Godfrey of Bouillon* elected ruler of Jerusalem
18 July 1100	Death of Godfrey. His brother *Baldwin of Edessa* is elected as the first king of Jerusalem (1100–18)
1101	Capture of Caesarea and Haifa
1104	Capture of Akko
4 December 1110	Capture of Sidon
1113	Papal recognition of the Hospital of St John in Jerusalem
1119	Founding of the Order of Knights Templar
1118–31	Reign of *Baldwin II*, king of Jerusalem
7 July 1124	Tyre captured by the Franks and Venetians
1131–43	Reign of *Fulk of Anjou*, king of Jerusalem
1143–63	Reign of *Baldwin III*, king of Jerusalem
1144	Fall of Edessa to the Muslims
1147–49	Second Crusade
15 July 1149	Consecration of reconstructed Church of the Holy Sepulchre

22 August 1153	Fall of Ascalon to the Frankish army
1163–74	Reign of *Amalric*, king of Jerusalem
1174	Following death of *Nur al-Din*, *Saladin* takes Damascus
1174–86	Reign of *Baldwin IV*, king of Jerusalem
1185–86	Reign of *Baldwin V*, king of Jerusalem
1186–92	Reign of *Guy of Lusignan*, king of Jerusalem
4 July 1187	Battle of Hattin
2 October 1187	Jerusalem falls to *Saladin*
1189–92	Third Crusade led by *Richard I of England* and *Philip Augustus of France*
May 1191	*Richard I* conquers Cyprus
12 July 1191	Akko falls to the Crusaders
7 September 1191	Battle of Arsuf
2 September 1192	Treaty between *Richard I of England* and *Saladin* (Treaty of Jaffa)
1192–94	Reign of *Guy of Lusignan*, king of Cyprus
1196-1205	Reign of *Aimery of Lusignan*, king of Jerusalem and Cyprus
1202–4	Fourth Crusade
1204	Crusaders sack Constantinople
1205–18	Reign of *Hugh I*, king of Cyprus
1210–25	Reign of *John of Brienne*, king of Jerusalem
1217/1218	Construction of Château Pèlerin ('Atlit)
1218–21	Fifth Crusade
1218–53	Reign of *Henry I*, king of Cyprus
1225–43	Reign of Emperor *Frederick II*, king of Jerusalem
1229	Jerusalem restored to the Franks under the terms of a treaty
1242–54	Nominal reign of *Conrad*
1244	Jerusalem falls to the Khwaresmians
1251	Construction of the defences of Caesarea by *Louis IX*
1253–67	Reign of *Hugh II*, king of Cyprus
1254–68	Nominal reign of *Conradin*
1256–68	War of St Sabas between the Italian merchant communes in Akko
1263	Nazareth destroyed by *Baybars*
1265	Arsuf and Caesarea fall to Baybars
1266	Safed falls to Baybars
1267–84	Reign of *Hugh III*, king of Cyprus
1268	Antioch, Belfort and Jaffa fall to Baybars
1269–84	Reign of *Hugh III*, king of Jerusalem
1271	Chastel Blanc, Montfort and Crac des Chevaliers fall to Baybars
	Crown sold by *Maria of Antioch* to *Charles of Anjou*

1284–85	Reign of *John I*, king of Jerusalem and Cyprus
1286–1324	Reign of *Henry II*, king of Jerusalem and Cyprus
1287	Latakieh falls to *Qalawun*
1289	Tripoli falls to *Qalawun*
18 May 1291	Fall of Akko to *al-Ashraf Khalil*
July 1291	Fall of Sidon and Beirut
August 1291	Departure from Château Pèlerin ('Atlit)
1312	Suppression of the Order of the Knights Templar
1324–59	Reign of *Hugh IV*, king of Jerusalem and Cyprus
1359–69	Reign of *Peter I*, king of Jerusalem and Cyprus
1369–82	Reign of *Peter II*, king of Jerusalem and Cyprus
1385–98	Reign of *James I*, king of Jerusalem and Cyprus
1398–1432	Reign of *Janus*, king of Jerusalem and Cyprus
1489	End of monarchy in Cyprus
1570–1	Cyprus falls to the Turks

1 Background

The Crusades and Outremer

On 27 November 1095 at Clermont in the Auvergne Pope Urban II spoke before a crowded audience of clerics and laymen. He called for the formation of a Christian army to come to the aid of the Eastern churches and the Christian communities suffering under Muslim rule. This was partly in response to an appeal from the Byzantine emperor, Alexius I Comnenus, that had reached the pope nine months earlier. The emperor had requested Western aid against the Seljuk armies that were threatening the truncated Eastern Empire. Alexius' letter to the pope had helped set in motion an unprecedented development in which thousands of Europeans voluntarily tore up their roots to set out on what must, in their more sober moments, have seemed at the very least a daunting enterprise. The remarkable success of Urban's call lay to no small degree in the renewed spirituality that had embraced Western Christianity since the approach of the second millennium. Many of the followers were certainly motivated by the fact that the Crusade had taken on the form of a holy pilgrimage, with indulgences given by the Church as a reward for participation. There were also various social and economic factors that contributed to the success of Urban's call.[1]

The response generated by his speech was immediate and of a magnitude that must have surprised the pope himself. In the first wave an estimated 20,000 followers of the hermit preacher, Peter of Amiens, set out; this number had risen to about 25,000 by the time they reached Asia Minor. This was only one of the contingents taking part, and possibly as many as 40–50,000 followed in the second wave. This must have been not only beyond the expectations of the pope but also beyond those of Alexius, who had hoped for a limited force of Western mercenaries who would aid him in staving off Seljuk attacks. Instead the enterprise begun at Clermont was one of history's great popular movements. What came to be known as the People's Crusade was an undisciplined rabble mainly comprised of the non-knightly classes, including many non-combatants. It is perhaps best remembered for the terrible massacres of Jews carried out by many of the followers in the Rhineland before they were wiped out in Hungary. Peter the Hermit and some of his followers managed to reach Constantinople and cross the Bosphorus before they were routed by the Turks outside their camp at Civitot in October.

Map 1 The Latin East

The first organized crusade, led by Raymond of St Gilles, count of Toulouse, Godfrey of Bouillon, his brother Baldwin, Hugh of Vermandois, Bohemond of Taranto and his nephew Tancred, set out in August 1096 by various routes, reaching Constantinople in April and May 1097. After swearing oaths of homage and fealty to Alexius, the Crusaders crossed the Bosphorus. The Byzantine troops accompanying them took Nicaea on 19 June and the first Frankish victory occurred at Dorylaeum on 1 July. The

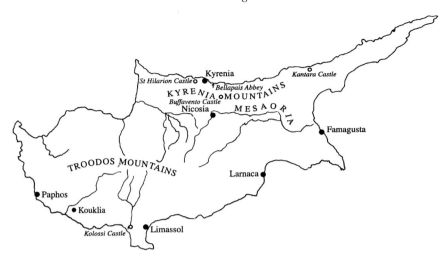

Map 2 The kingdom of Cyprus

army then crossed Anatolia, taking Iconium (modern Konya), and arrived at the Taurus Mountains, where they divided into two groups; one led by Baldwin crossed the mountains and took Cilicia, while the other skirted around Anatolia to Caesarea and hence to Antioch.

The first major Frankish territorial gain and the establishment of the first Frankish state in the East came in March 1098 following the death of Thoros, prince of Edessa (Urfa), who after asking for Baldwin of Boulogne's aid against the Seljuk attacks had adopted him as co-ruler and heir. With Thoros' death during an uprising, timely from the point of view of Baldwin and perhaps instigated by him, Baldwin became count of Edessa. Prior to this, in the previous October, the Crusaders had gathered outside the walls of Antioch and a seven-month siege of the city began. Antioch was still protected by its remarkable fortifications built by Justinian and repaired in the tenth century. The long wall had over 400 well-placed towers. It surrounded not only the built-up area of the town but also its gardens and fields, and it climbed up Mount Silpius, making an effective siege almost impossible. Raymond of Toulouse was in favour of a direct attack on the walls. Such a strike might have succeeded, but instead a decision was made to try to encircle the city. In the end it was only through the treachery of one of the defenders, an Armenian named Firouz, that on 3 June 1098 Bohemond gained access to the city. With the capture of Antioch, the second Frankish state, the principality of Antioch, was established. After much delay, the march to Jerusalem commenced on 13 January 1099. Skirting the coastal towns, the Crusaders moved south to Jaffa and then turned inland to Lydda, Ramla and Nebi Samwil where on 7 June they encamped before the Holy City. After a six-week siege, on 15 July 1099 the wall was breached near the north-eastern corner by troops under the command of Godfrey of Bouillon. A week later Godfrey was elected ruler of the newly established kingdom of Jerusalem.

During the reign of Baldwin I (1100–18) the kingdom of Jerusalem expanded as the coastal cities fell one by one to the Franks. Jaffa and Haifa had already been occupied in 1099. Caesarea and Arsuf fell in 1101, Akko in 1104, Sidon and Beirut in 1110, Tyre in 1124 and Ascalon in 1153. At its peak in the twelfth century, the kingdom occupied an area extending from slightly north of Beirut to Darum in the south on the Mediterranean coast, and inland to several kilometres east of the Jordan valley and the Arava Desert, down to the Gulf of Eilat.

The county of Tripoli, last of the mainland states, was founded by Raymond of Toulouse between 1102 and 1105, although the city of Tripoli itself fell to the Franks only in 1109. The northern principalities of Antioch, Tripoli and Edessa were essentially dependencies of the kingdom of Jerusalem, though they often acted independently. In 1191 Cyprus also came under Frankish rule.

Division amongst the Muslims enabled the Frankish states to maintain a degree of stability; but towards the middle of the twelfth century the Franks suffered a major blow when in 1144 Zangi, master of Aleppo and Mosul, took Edessa. This county, which had been the first territorial gain of the Crusades, now became its first major loss and Zangi became known by his followers as the leader of the *Jihad* (Holy War). After his death and following the humiliating failure of the Second Crusade which had attacked Damascus rather than Edessa, Zangi's son Nur al-Din took Damascus. In order to strengthen his position Nur al-Din sent Shirkuh, a Kurdish general, together with Shirkuh's nephew, Saladin, to occupy Egypt. Shirkuh took Cairo in January 1169 and on his death Saladin became vizier of Egypt. Although formally he was under the overlordship of Nur al-Din, Saladin was in practice sultan of Egypt. When Nur al-Din died in 1174, Saladin occupied Damascus and united Egypt and Syria, thereby establishing himself as the leader of the *Jihad* against the Franks.

At the time when Muslims were finding unity under Saladin, Frankish rule was falling apart. After the death of King Amalric in 1174, the 13-year-old Baldwin IV, who suffered from leprosy, ascended the throne of Jerusalem. Despite his youth and illness Baldwin proved to be an able ruler, but as his disease progressed it became clear that he would have to delegate rule to a regent until the coming of age of his heir, the future Baldwin V, who was the son of his sister Sibylla and William of Montferrat. The king reluctantly appointed as regent Guy of Lusignan, who had married the recently widowed Sibylla, but shortly thereafter replaced him with Raymond III of Tripoli. Baldwin IV died at the age of 24 in 1185, and Baldwin V died in the following year.

Whatever Raymond's expectations may have been, it was Guy of Lusignan who became king. In the meantime Saladin had consolidated his hold over the region and in 1187 events came to a head. A truce which Saladin had signed with the Franks in 1181 was broken by Reynald of Châtillon, who even attempted to attack Mecca itself. A subsequent four-year truce signed in 1185 was broken two years later when Reynald attacked a caravan on its way to Mecca, capturing Saladin's sister. Saladin prepared for war. A huge Muslim army that has been estimated at 30,000 with 12,000 cavalry prepared for battle. First Saladin attacked Reynald's fortresses of Montréal and Kerak. Then in June 1187 he crossed the Jordan and on 2 July his troops laid siege to Tiberias. The Frankish army marched to Saffuriya (Tsipori) and on the morning of 4 July met the Muslims in battle at the Horns of Hattin. The Frankish army was encircled and destroyed.

Within a few months most of the castles and towns of the kingdom, including Jerusalem, fell to Saladin and by the end of 1189 only Tyre remained in their hands. Much of the territory to the north was also lost, though Antioch and the castles of Crac des Chevaliers, Margat (Marqab) and Qusair remained in Frankish hands, as did Tripoli. Even with the reoccupation of the coast by the Third Crusade (1189–92) and the short-lived recovery of Jerusalem, Bethlehem, Nazareth, Toron and Sidon following a treaty reached in 1229, the Franks never really overcame this defeat. One of the few lasting consequences of the Third Crusade was the occupation of the island of Cyprus, which fell to Richard I of England in 1191. He sold it to the Templars and it was eventually granted to the deposed king of Jerusalem, Guy of Lusignan.

In the thirteenth century the Latin East was in a state of decline that accelerated with the ascendancy of the Mamluk dynasty in Egypt, united under its leader Baybars. After he became sultan in 1260 Baybars began a systematic attack on the Frankish possessions. In 1263 he sacked Nazareth and two years later he launched a major offensive, capturing Caesarea, Haifa, Toron and Arsuf. Baybars adopted a scorched-earth policy to prevent the reoccupation of the coastal towns by the Franks. In 1266 he took Safad and in 1268 Jaffa and Antioch.

As Baybars made his advances the Franks were under the imminent threat of invasion by the Mongols from the north. As if this were not enough, internal divisions within the Frankish states were coming to a head with the outbreak of open war between the Italian communes in Akko in 1256. Baybars died in 1277, but by that time all that remained of the Frankish possessions on the mainland was a strip of coastline between 'Atlit Castle and Latakieh. Latakieh fell to the Mamluks in 1287 and Tripoli in 1289. In 1290 Baybars' successor, Qalawun, attacked Akko and in the following May it fell to his son, al-Ashraf Khalil. Tyre, Sidon, Beirut and Tortosa followed, and in August the last of the Franks evacuated 'Atlit Castle, bringing to an end nearly two hundred years of Frankish rule in the Levant.

Constantinople, which had become a Frankish possession during the Fourth Crusade in 1204, was lost in 1261. After the collapse of the kingdom of Jerusalem and of the principalities in Syria, many of the Franks fled to

Cyprus. For nearly another three hundred years the island remained under Christian rule. In that period it knew prosperity, but it went into decline from 1373 when the Genoese invaded the island and exacted a heavy ransom as the price for their departure. Cyprus remained a Frankish possession and an independent monarchy, but in 1426 the Egyptians invaded the island and it became a vassal state of the sultanate. In 1489 it was acquired by the Venetians, and finally in 1571 the island was occupied by the Turks. This brought to an end the Frankish presence in the eastern Mediterranean.

Geography and climate

At their peak the Crusader states extended from Cilicia in the north to the northern edge of the Sinai peninsula in the south; until the collapse that followed the Battle of Hattin, they included the whole of western Palestine and the eastern edge of Transjordan. After the Third Crusade the island of Cyprus also came under Frankish rule. Rarely are the blessings and curses of nature so heavily concentrated in one fairly small region, although the blessings perhaps outweigh the curses. In the north, from the Taurus Mountains to the east, the countryside is fertile and well watered. So too is the Lebanon and the coastal plain as far south as Rafiah. The Golan, and beyond it the Hauran, are highly fertile basaltic lands. To the south and east, however, aridity sets in, broken here and there by springs and oases. The climate varies over this region but generally falls into a pattern of an extended dry season commencing in April and continuing until late October, tempered only by occasional morning mists. It is followed by a wet season during which heavy but erratic showers occur, often of short duration but occasionally lasting for several days. Most of the towns are situated along the Mediterranean littoral. In the Crusader period these included Tripoli, Beirut, Sidon, Tyre, Akko, Caesarea, Arsuf, Jaffa and Ascalon. Several secondary and some important towns lie inland: Antioch on the River Orontes, Tiberias and Nazareth in the lower Galilee, Sebaste, and Nablus in the Samaria Hills, Lydda and Ramla in the inland plain, Jerusalem, Bethlehem and Hebron in the Judean hills.

The island of Cyprus is physically little different from the mainland. It is often coarse, dry countryside with narrow, seasonal streams, but it is also remarkably fertile. The well-watered Troodos Mountains rise at the island's centre to a height of over 1800 m. To the north is the lower, Kyrenia range (1067 m). Between them is an extensive plain, the Mesaoria, and to the south of the Troodos are the plains of Paphos and Limassol. The principal towns and districts are Nicosia, Larnaca, Limassol, Famagusta, Paphos and Kyrenia. Under the Lusignans Cyprus was divided into twelve districts: Nicosia, Salines (Larnaca), Limassol, Famagusta, Paphos, Kyrenia, the Mesaoria, the Karpas Peninsula, the Masoto, Avdimou, Chrysokhou and Pendayia.

The native population

The native population of the territories that came under Frankish rule included Sunni and Shi'ite Muslims, Jews, Samaritans and a number of Christian sects: Armenians, Copts, Greek Orthodox (Melkites), Jacobites, Maronites and Nestorians. The early Frankish conquests were accompanied by widespread slaughter of the local urban population, Muslims, Jews and even the Eastern Christians, a policy which left the Franks facing a significant demographic problem. The population of Jerusalem dropped to a few hundred knights and footmen (Fulcher of Chartres 1913: 2.6; William of Tyre 1986: 9.19). Non-Christians were not allowed to return to Jerusalem, but this was not the case elsewhere. In general, after the initial slaughters and expulsions the Franks came to terms with the existence of the local communities, particularly once the majority of the Crusaders had returned to Europe. Except in the case of Jerusalem there was probably never any intention of entirely eliminating the non-Frankish population from the cities, and the Franks must have soon become aware of the need to rely on the local peasantry for food and many other necessities. Thus most of the rural population remained in place, retaining a near-serf status little different from that which they had held under the Fatimids. The depopulated capital was resettled, not with the remnants of the previous population but with Frankish and Eastern Christians. On the whole the Franks appear to have been reluctant to remain in Jerusalem. It became necessary to pass legislation aimed at making settlement in the city more attractive by easing the tax burdens: tariffs were removed from certain goods entering the city gates. In order to put an end to the widespread absentee landlordship, a law was passed whereby an estate whose owner was absent for a year and a day would become the property of the tenant. An additional means of increasing the city's population was by the organized settlement of local Christians from Transjordan. They were housed in what had previously been the Jewish quarter, *Juverie*, in the north-east of the city.

The Frankish settlers

'Crusader' – the popular label used to describe anything or anyone connected to the Frankish presence in the East – is a somewhat misleading term. If we limit its use to people who participated in a Crusade we are on safe ground, but what about those who were born in the East and never took part in a Crusade? Strictly speaking, 'Frank' is not much better. A large part of the Western population settled in the East was certainly not of Frankish origin: Normans, Germans, Italians and other nations made up much of the permanent population. However, 'Frank' (*Franj* in Arabic) has a certain legitimacy in that it was the name used by the local population at the time to refer to Westerners, both new arrivals as well as *pulani* (those who were born in the East), whatever their ethnic origins.

The Frankish population included a minority of nobles and a large class of burgesses consisting of shopkeepers and artisans, many of whom were probably of peasant origin. In the countryside there seems to have occasionally been voluntary downward social mobility, when men who had previously been burgesses chose to become peasants. William of Tyre hints at this when he suggests that it was easier for men of limited means to make a living in these settlements than in the towns (William of Tyre 1986: 20.19).

The Italians

The role played by the Italian maritime cities of Venice, Genoa and Pisa in the occupation of the coastal towns cannot be overestimated. The inability of the Frankish armies to lay siege successfully to the fortified coastal towns became apparent as early as 1101 during the abortive first attempt at occupying Akko. The utilization of Italian naval power subsequently became, at no little expense to the Frankish rulers, a precondition of the Crusader expansionist strategy. As an outcome of this role the Italians established their position as one of the main landowning groups in the Latin East and thus both achieved their desired key position in the trade between Europe and the East and at the same time emerged as an important element in the population of the Frankish states. The cities of Genoa, Pisa and Venice founded merchant quarters known as communes in Akko, Tyre, Tripoli and Antioch. In return for the part they played in the conquest of the coastal towns they were granted large quarters in the occupied cities and agricultural lands around them. By granting them substantial commercial and judicial rights in their quarters, the king gave the Italian communes a virtual autonomy which, together with the gains made by the landed nobility, eroded the hegemony of the king. The impact of Italian mercantile activity was widely felt both in the Latin East and in Europe, where previously unknown goods, notably sugar and certain tropical fruits like the banana, were introduced.

Frankish administration and institutions

Following a brief leadership contest during which Raymond of Toulouse was offered the title but in such a reluctant manner that he refused it, Godfrey of Bouillon was elected to rule over the newly established kingdom. For reasons of piety he refused the title of king, but to all intents and purposes that is what he was. He ruled until his untimely death on 18 July 1100, when his brother Baldwin of Edessa ascended the throne and took the title of king of Jerusalem. After its nominal establishment the kingdom of Jerusalem began to emerge as a physical reality. The conquest of inland areas coincided with the progressive occupation of the coastal cities. Command of the coast was vital to the survival of the kingdom and of the northern principalities. Despite the gains of the First Crusade, the overland route was not a viable alternative to the maritime connection with Europe, a fact that became particularly obvious when Zangi, the ruler of Mosul and Aleppo, retook Edessa in 1144. From the outset the coastal towns served as the only route of contact with the West. Thus their conquest was a priority that was dealt with immediately after the conquest of Jerusalem and the defeat of the Fatimid army at Ascalon in the summer of 1099.

The king of Jerusalem headed what was in theory an elective monarchy but in practice a hereditary one. Baldwin I's successor, Baldwin de Burg was elected to the position by a council of clergy and nobles, but he was also the king's nephew and, according to Albert of Aix, one of his choices as heir. On his deathbed Baldwin II had his eldest daughter Melisende married to the barons' choice of his successor, Fulk of Anjou. On Fulk's death Melisende, who ruled jointly with the king, was crowned together with her eldest son Baldwin. Thus in fact the monarchy had dropped its elective facade and openly become a hereditary one. Subsequently, with a few exceptions, the succession remained hereditary.

In the early years of the century the king was prepotent, his power stemming largely from the possession of extensive tracts of land in the interior and from the commercial revenues deriving from the port cities. His strength declined, however, as the royal domains diminished in the twelfth century and much of the port revenues were siphoned off by the Italian merchant communes. Displaying perhaps lack of foresight but clearly also lack of choice, the kings of Jerusalem granted extensive lordships from the royal lands in Judea, Samaria and the coastal plain. In this manner the king's holdings were depleted until what remained consisted of little more than areas around the cities of Jerusalem, Akko, Tyre and Nazareth, and the region of Darum in the south. The increasingly independent class of nobles who received these land grants thereby acquired considerable political authority at the king's expense and exercised an expanding role in the decision-making of the *Haute Cour* (High Court). By the later twelfth century the king was largely dependent on the barons.

In the other Frankish states the situation was rather different. The principality of Antioch was ruled by the prince, who was theoretically a vassal not of the king of Jerusalem but of the Byzantine emperor. However, Bohemund II of Antioch married the daughter of Baldwin II and after Bohemund's death in 1130 Baldwin became guardian of Antioch and the principality became a dependency of Jerusalem. The count of Tripoli was vassal of the king of Jerusalem, while the count of Edessa was vassal of both the king of Jerusalem and the prince of Antioch. As for Cyprus, in 1192 Guy of Lusignan became ruler of the island but adopted the title *dominus*, rather than assuming the status of king. On his death two years later his brother Aimery (1194–1205) became the first of the Frankish kings of Cyprus. Although the new governing body, the High Court of Nicosia, was empowered to choose the king or if necessary regent; as in Jerusalem this was a hereditary kingdom. The position of the king in relation to the barons was much more advantageous than on the mainland. One reason for this was that in Cyprus, unlike the kingdom of Jerusalem, the hereditary fiefs received by the barons reverted to the Crown if there was no direct heir. Thus the king retained considerable landed property and there were no great baronies that could pose a threat to him. The seigneuries were generally limited to a few villages at the most. All the walled towns and castles were held by the king; the only exceptions were the fortresses of Kolossi and Gastria, which were held by the Hospitallers and Templars.

The Church

Although it did not achieve its expectations of establishing theocratic rule in the East, the Church maintained a certain influence throughout the two centuries of Frankish rule. The political strength of the patriarchate was never very great, and in comparison to its position in the West the Church in the Latin East was neither influential nor wealthy. However, individual ecclesiastical establishments did become important property owners. Notable amongst these were the Church of the Holy Sepulchre, the Convent of St Anne, St Mary of Mount Zion, and St Mary in Jehoshaphat in Jerusalem, the Church of the Annunciation in Nazareth, the Church of the Nativity in Bethlehem and the Abbey of St Lazarus in Bethany. Their holdings were varied; the Church of the Holy Sepulchre, for example, possessed houses in the major cities as well as in many of the smaller towns, whole villages (both those of the indigenous peasantry and the newly established villages of Frankish settlers), mills, bakeries and other institutions.

The military orders

The military order was a new and uniquely Crusader institution combining the concepts of knighthood and monasticism. The orders became an important element in Crusader society, the principal means of maintaining organized and well-equipped armed forces in the Latin East. The possession of numerous castles added to their weight in the defence of the Latin East. The Order of the Hospitallers or the Knights of St John, which had its beginnings in the monastery hospital of St Mary Latin in Jerusalem established around 1070, was recognized in 1113 by the pope and became a military order around 1130. Its principal aim was to care for the sick. The second military order was the Order of the Templars, so called because they had their headquarters in al-Aqsa Mosque, which was known to the Franks as the *Templum Salomonis*. It was founded in 1119–20 by a knight named Hugh of Payns with the aim of defending pilgrims on the roads. Both orders developed into huge organizations with vast holdings both in *Outremer* and in Europe. There were other military orders, notable amongst them the German Teutonic Order founded in 1190 which had its headquarters in Akko, the Order of St Lazarus and the Order of St Thomas.

Note

1 The rising European population and the system of primogeniture, which made the eldest son the sole inheritor of property and left the other sons with no choice but to enter the Church or take on a military career, were factors which played no small part in the popularity of the Crusades amongst the knightly class.

2   The city and urban life

There was no need for the Franks to establish new cities in the East. They occupied the existing cities, expanding them beyond their walls as the need arose and sometimes extending the walls to include the newly settled areas. Within the cities they built new public and private buildings and converted others to suit their own needs. In short they imposed certain changes, many of which are still very much in evidence today. With the introduction of Latin populations into the cities several mosques were converted into churches, existing churches were expanded or rebuilt and new churches were constructed. In the larger cities the military orders established new quarters and in the major port cities Italians from Venice, Genoa and Pisa established their own independent colonies.

After occupying a city one of the first needs that arose was the restoration or strengthening of the fortifications. A number of the cities were already walled when they were occupied in the first half of the twelfth century. During their rule the Franks refortified them, in some cases several times, and occasionally expanded them to cover a larger area than had been enclosed in pre-Frankish times. Thus, for example, in Caesarea the walls were rebuilt at least three times and in Akko they were expanded to cover a far greater area than they had in the Fatimid period (Kedar 1997: 157–80). Some of the cities were enhanced with new citadels, double gates, moats, outer walls and new towers.

It is, however, rather surprising to find that under Frankish rule many cities had rather poor defences. Some cities lacked walls altogether and four of them did not even have towers, so that the inhabitants could find shelter only in the fortified churches (Pringle 1995: 71).[1] The importance of the coastal cities was not lost on the Franks however, and they were defended with walls and citadels. The importance of these cities lay not only in the trade that passed through them but also in the fact that they were their only link to the West, which also made them favourite targets for the Muslims. In the kingdom of Jerusalem only Tyre and Akko were important ports and the harbours south of Akko were of little value. Tripoli had a good harbour and the port of St Symeon served the needs of Antioch. Cyprus was well provided for, with ports at Limassol, Kyrenia, Paphos and Famagusta; and after the loss of Akko in 1291, Famagusta became the main port for trade between Syria-Palestine and Europe.[2]

Other than fortifications and ports, the Franks left their mark on the cities by the construction of a number of public and private works including churches, covered and open markets, hospices, hospitals, bathhouses, aqueducts, open pools, sewers and graveyards. In the coastal cities that were destroyed at the end of the thirteenth century many houses have survived, being buried under the rubble. In Famagusta and Nicosia several fine Gothic houses survive almost intact and more fragmentary remains of private dwellings have been found at Caesarea, Caymont (Yoqne'am), Arsuf and Jerusalem. No doubt many more lie buried under rubble in other Frankish cities. Urban houses fall into a number of basic types: courtyard houses, two- and three-storey apartment houses, merchant houses and tower houses.

Urban industries and crafts of which archaeological remains have been found, or of which we know from written sources, included mints, gold- and silversmiths, blacksmiths, bakeries, abattoirs, tanners, furriers and soap-makers. Many of these occupations were restricted to the peripheral areas within the walls, which in medieval cities were often open areas. Pottery, glass and sugar manufacture and some other industries were probably conducted outside the town walls.

Major cities

Jerusalem

When on 7 June 1099 the army of the First Crusade arrived at the outskirts of Jerusalem, the city was no doubt very much as the Persian traveller Nasir i-Khusrau described it fifty-two years earlier: a great city with strong walls, iron gates, high, well-built bazaars, paved streets and a population of 20,000 (Figure 2.1). Under Seljuk rule since 1071, the city was retaken by the Fatimids in August 1098. A large, well-trained army defended the city in 1099. With the approach of the Franks the Muslims poisoned the wells, destroyed the crops and burnt the trees in the vicinity. They also strengthened the walls, particularly to the north where they built a barbican (*antemurale*) in preparation for the siege. The barbican possibly already existed in the vulnerable north and on Mount Zion. The residents of surrounding villages took refuge within the walls, causing a considerable increase in the popu-lation. Part of the Christian population was expelled, as it was considered unreliable in the face of an approaching Christian army. Because they were not easily distinguishable from the non-Christian inhabitants, wearing the same dress and speaking Arabic, many of the Christians who remained in the city were slaughtered together with the Muslims and Jews when the Crusaders took Jerusalem.

The approaching Frankish army numbered perhaps 40,000. They passed through Ramla and on 7 June arrived at Mons Gaudi (Nebi Samwil). The

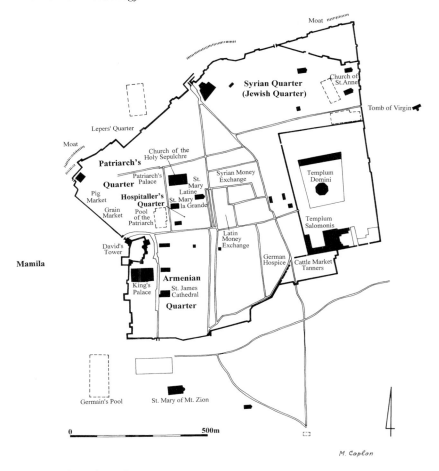

Moat

Syrian Quarter
(Jewish Quarter)

Church of
St.Anne

Tomb of Virgin

Lepers' Quarter

Moat

Church of the
Holy Sepulchre

Patriarch's

Patriarch's
Quarter Palace

Syrian Money
Exchange

Templum
Domini

Pig
Market

Hospitaller's
Quarter

St.
Mary
Latine
St. Mary
la Grande

Grain
Market

Pool
of the
Patriarch

Latin
Money
Exchange

Templum
Salomonis

David's
Tower

Mamila

German
Hospice

Cattle Market
Tanners

King's
Palace

Armenian
St. James
Cathedral

Quarter

Germain's Pool

St. Mary of Mt. Zion

0   500m

M. Coplan

Figure 2.1 Plan of twelfth-century Jerusalem

next day they began an assault on the city. Since Jerusalem was too large to be surrounded, the Franks aimed at taking it by storm and planned to attack the weaker points. The steep topography around much of the city made it possible to launch a successful attack only from a limited number of positions. An initial, unsuccessful attempt at a direct attack was launched on the two main gates of the city (modern Jaffa Gate and Damascus Gate). A six-week siege followed, which ended on Friday 15 July when a battering ram was used to knock down the barbican near the eastern corner of the north wall and the moat was filled to enable the approach of a siege-tower. The Franks broke into the city and headed for the Temple area where they took al-Aqsa Mosque. The slaughter of the citizens then commenced.[3] The Fatimid commander fled to the citadel and subsequently surrendered it to the Franks in return for being allowed to flee to Ascalon.

For the first eighty-eight years of Frankish rule Jerusalem was both the spiritual and political capital of the kingdom. Under the Franks the city took on some of the aspects of a Western city, while retaining others typical of the East. Romanesque churches rose up amongst the twisting alleyways and typically Middle-Eastern souks continued to function under the Franks.

Contemporary maps

Prior to the twelfth century the only important map of the city is also the earliest one known, the sixth-century mosaic map in Madaba in Transjordan. A number of maps of Jerusalem were drawn up in the twelfth century; they are of considerable value as a source of information on the layout of the medieval city (Figure 2.2).[4] Most of these maps were drawn in the form of a circle oriented to the east and usually divided by a cross formed by the two main roads: the *Cardo* (*Vicus ad Porte St Stephani* and *Vicus ad Porte Montis Syon*) and the *Decumanis* (*Vicus ad Templum Domini*, elsewhere called *Via David*). The *Vicus ad Templum Domini* terminates at the Temple Mount entrance known as the *Porta Speciosa*. Beyond this gate are the two principal buildings of the Temple Mount. The seventh-century Dome of the Rock, known by the Franks as *Templum Domini*, is rendered on the maps as a circle with four doors; the rock is illustrated with the word *lapis*. To its right is the eighth-century al-Aqsa Mosque, known as *Templum Salomonis*. An east–west road called *Vicus ad Porta Josaphat* leads from *Vicus ad Porta St Stephani* to *Porta Josaphat*, the modern Lions Gate. To its north is the *Templum Sanctae Annae* and the Sheeps' Pool, usually depicted as a semi-circle and marked as *piscina*. Between the four roads at the heart of the city is the money exchange, *Cambuim Monete*, and opposite it to the right is what may have been an open market square, the *Forum Rarum Venalium*. In the Armenian Quarter in the south-west corner of the city is the cathedral church of the Armenians, *Ecclesia S Iacobi*, south of the *Turris David*. In the north-west corner of the city are the Holy Sepulchre (*Sepulchrum Domini*), rendered as a circle often with three doors and the tomb, and the site of the crucifixion, *Calvarie locus*. Five city gates are generally shown in the walls: *Porta David*, *Porta St Stephani*, *Porta Josaphat*, *Porta Aurea* and *Porta Syon*. *Porta Speciosa* is the western entrance to the Temple Mount. Around the city various important sites are shown: *Mons Gaudi*, *Mons Syon* with the *Coenaculum* (the room of the Last Supper), Bethlehem, Rachel's Tomb, the field of Akeldama, the city's main natural water source – *Fons Syloe*, Bethany, the Kidron rendered as a flowing stream, Jericho, Gethsemane and the Tomb of the Virgin Mary.

Defences

The walls of Fatimid Jerusalem encountered by the Franks when they captured the city ran very close to the position of the walls of the Umayyad period. They had been repaired on a number of occasions over the years, most

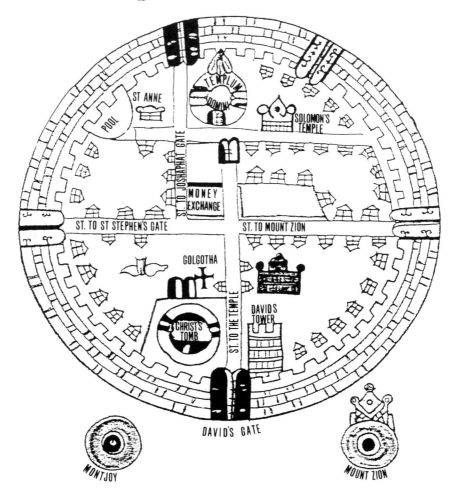

Figure 2.2 Copy of a twelfth-century map of Jerusalem

recently in the middle of the eleventh century. During the siege of Jerusalem of June to July 1099, the damage in the main areas of attack must have been considerable. Although there is no direct evidence for this it is probable that repairs were made to the walls in these areas – near the citadel to the west, in the south-west on Mount Zion, in the north-east and at the point where they breached the wall opposite today's Rockefeller Museum. In addition, they appear to have carried out some work on the various gates of the city. The walls were repaired and strengthened twice in the twelfth century, first in 1116 and again in 1177. In today's walls, sixteenth-century work from the time of Suleiman the Magnificent, it is not easy to distinguish Frankish construction. The Ottoman walls are largely built of reused stones from earlier times, including the Crusader period. Simple observation at almost any point along the walls reveals numerous ashlars with tell-tale Frankish markings such as fine diagonal tooling and masons' marks (see pp. 219–21). However, there are some sections of the walls that demonstrate original Frankish construction. The lower courses in the stretch between Jaffa Gate and modern Zahal Square appear to be medieval and are quite possibly part of the Frankish wall. This section is built of roughly shaped fieldstone and chips; unlike the Ottoman wall, the construction is uniform with no reused stones.[5]

Since Herodian times the principal gate of Jerusalem has been in the west. In that area Herod built three great towers: Mariamme, Hippicus and Phasael. They were destroyed in AD 70 by Hadrian, and by the end of the Byzantine period (seventh century AD) only the massive ashlar podium of the south-eastern tower, usually identified as Phasael's tower, survived (Plate 2.1). This was identified as King David's citadel by the early pilgrims and given the name Tower of David. This name, in its Latin form *Turris David*, was adopted by the Franks (the modern use of this name refers to the small minaret of an Ottoman mosque in the south-western corner of the citadel).

In 1099, when the city fell to the Franks, the citadel consisted solely of this tower. This is how it is represented on medieval maps. Raymond of Toulouse occupied the tower and refused to hand it over to Duke Godfrey. He did, however, agree to leave it in the care of the Bishop of Albara until the matter could be arbitrated, and the bishop promptly handed it over to Godfrey. It was a massive building of solid masonry. The upper part, which was reconstructed in the Middle Ages, consisted of a tower with a cistern and store-rooms and is described as having five iron doors and 200 steps leading to the battlements (Daniel 1888: 17). The tower served as the royal palace until 1104, when the king moved his court to al-Aqsa Mosque (*Templum Salomonis*). The strength of the citadel was tested in 1152, when Queen Melisende fortified herself there against her son, Baldwin III, who wished to remove her from the city. He did not succeed in taking the citadel despite the use of siege engines, and only after negotiations did the queen leave the tower (William of Tyre 1986: 17.14). In the 1160s or early 1170s the citadel was expanded by the construction of additional towers and curtain walls to form a fortified enclosure. In around 1172 it was described by Theoderich as protected by ditches and outworks, and by William of Tyre as having towers, walls and forewalls (William of Tyre 1986: 8.3). When Saladin attacked the coastal plain in 1177 many of the citizens of Jerusalem took refuge in the tower. In 1219 al-Malik al-Mu'azzam 'Isa, who had earlier strengthened the city walls, had them dismantled to make the city less defensible should the Franks retake it, but the citadel appears to have survived this destruction. During their brief renewed occupation of the city between 1229 and 1244 the Franks restored sections of the defences, including the barbican in front of St Stephen's Gate and the citadel. In 1239 it fell to al-Nasir Daud of Kerak,

Plate 2.1 Jerusalem: the Tower of David (photograph by the author)

who destroyed it; it remained in ruins until the early fourteenth century. In the 1930s C.N. Johns, the head of the Palestine Antiquities Department, conducted excavations in the citadel, which were published in 1950 (Johns 1950, republished 1997: 121–90). According to Johns, although little of the Frankish work survives, its present-day form was established in the twelfth century. Johns suggested that the glacis dates from the Crusader period with some Mamluk reconstruction in its upper courses. Crosses carved on some of its stones support the Frankish dating. Johns suggested that the eastern tower of the citadel may also have been Frankish. In the south-west corner the Crusaders built a massive bastion, of which Johns found remains under the mosque. There were two posterns and an undercroft which he suggested were used for stabling and storage. The present north-western tower is Mamluk, but the presence of a Frankish cistern beneath it with a large Latin cross rendered in the plaster suggests that it replaced a Frankish tower on the site.[6] The eastern, western and northern curtain walls are of post-Crusader construction but probably follow the twelfth-century line.

A large tower, built with marginally drafted ashlars, stood in the south-west corner of the city. It consists of walls about 7 m wide pierced by seven arrow slits and entered via a doorway within the city. On the interior four groin-vaulted bays were supported by a massive central pier measuring 4 × 4 m. Tancred's or Goliath's Tower (Burj Jal'ud), measuring 35 × 35 m, was situated in the north-western corner of the city. It was built by the Fatimids and expanded by the Franks (Bahat and Ben-Ari 1976: 109–10). As can be seen from the presence of typically Frankish stonework, some of the smaller towers around the city are of Frankish date, or partly so. Just west of Dung Gate is a small gate with a fortified tower which is easily recognizable as being of Frankish construction. The location of this gate at the southern end of the Valley Cardo points to it as being the Tanners' Postern.[7]

The main gates of Jerusalem were David's Gate to the west, St Stephen's Gate to the north, Jehosaphat Gate and the Golden Gate to the east and Mount Zion Gate to the south. St Stephen's Gate (modern Damascus Gate) and Mount Zion Gate have both been excavated. Excavations in 1965 uncovered the remains of the Crusader St Stephen's Gate consisting of an external gate and a bent-axis passage leading to the main gate, a church and what may have been a customs house (Hennessy 1970: 24ff., Figure 1, Plate XV; Wightman 1979: 45–60) (see Figure 2.3). In an article (1989–90: 62), Dan Bahat argues in favour of a thirteenth-century date for this complex (personal communication). *Porta Montis Syon*, the Frankish Zion Gate, was located at the southern end of the Cardo some 100 m east of the modern Zion Gate (Plate 2.2). Remains of a square tower were uncovered in the 1970s. This tower measures 21 × 21 m with walls about 5 m thick and two doors, the inner door at 90 degrees to the outer one. The vaults were supported by a massive central pier and there were apparently two storeys. From this gate Mount Zion Street and the Street of Judas' Arch headed north in the

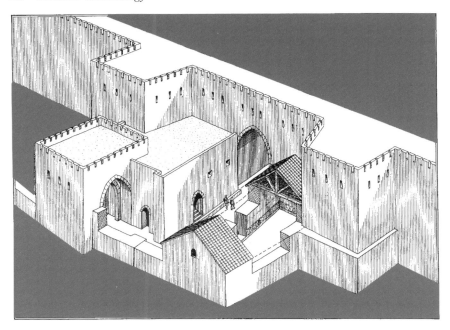

Figure 2.3 Jerusalem: isometric drawing of the Crusader bastion at Damascus Gate
(courtesy of Dan Bahat)

Plate 2.2 Jerusalem: medieval Zion Gate (photograph by the author)

direction of St Stephen's Gate. Archaeologists have dated this structure to the Ayyubid period because of an inscription found in the excavations, albeit not *in situ*.

There were several posterns: St Mary Magdalene's Postern and St Lazarus' Postern in the north, Tanners' Postern in the south, Beaucayre Postern on Mount Zion, the Single Gate on the southern wall of the Temple Mount and a postern in the moat of the citadel. The remains of two of these, Tanners' Postern and Beaucayre Postern, have been discovered in recent excavations. Tanners' Postern was situated just to the west of the modern Dung Gate. The external gate tower was excavated in 1975–7 (Ben-Dov 1987: 115–19). It is a square structure measuring 14 × 14 m, roofed with a groin vault and attached to the exterior of the city wall. The entrance was on the west side, giving indirect access into the city. There are five archer embrasures on the east, south and west. Though the tower is partly reconstructed, the surviving original stonework, including parts of the doorways and archer embrasures, is constructed of typically Frankish diagonally tooled ashlars. Recent excavations within the gate have exposed the Byzantine street paving stones of the Valley Cardo two metres below the level of the Frankish gate.

A small section of a medieval tower on Mount Zion has recently been excavated; its position at the southern end of the Armenian Patriarchate Road supports its identification as the Beaucayre Postern (Seligman forthcoming). Another postern, now blocked, that can be seen today is the gate on the southern Temple Mount wall known as the Single Gate. It apparently gave access to a passage that led into the underground vault known as Solomon's Stables.

Beyond the walls, the moat to the north was already in existence when the Franks took the city in 1099. After the city fell they would certainly have cleared and restored it. They may also have extended and deepened it, though there is no evidence for this. Parts of the rock-cut scarp can be seen in the north-east and excavations have recently exposed another section of it to the west, just north of Jaffa Gate.

The palace

When the Order of the Knights Templar was established in 1119, the king granted them the Templum Salomonis (al-Aqsa Mosque) as their headquarters and he moved to the new palace built on the southern side of *Turris David*. Of the palace we have only an imaginary rendition on one of the twelfth-century maps. However, a barrel vault was excavated in the Armenian Garden in 1971 (Bahat and Broshi 1975: 55–6) and additional remains were uncovered in the courtyard of the Qishle police compound excavated in 1988–9 (Bahat 1991: 69, n. 6). It is possible that these are fragments of the palace.

Quarters and churches of the city

The basic cross shape formed by the principal roads in the Byzantine period divided the city into the four quarters that it retains today, albeit with different populations. The north-west quarter of the city was known as the Patriarch's Quarter. The patriarch, who represented the leadership of the Latin Church in the kingdom of Jerusalem, claimed the whole of the city but eventually settled for the area around the Church of the Holy Sepulchre, which he was granted by Godfrey of Bouillon. The quarter was bounded on two sides by the western and northern walls of the city stretching from David's Gate to St Stephen's Gate. Its southern and eastern boundaries were defined by David's Street and the street running from St Stephen's Gate. At the centre of the quarter was the Church of the Holy Sepulchre, with the patriarch's palace to its north. The quarter was administered by the *curia patriarchae*, a mixed lay and ecclesiastical body which was both a court of law and a record office. The patriarch was responsible for the upkeep of the quarter, its squares and streets, and issued permits for building. Of the buildings in the quarter we have only limited knowledge. The patriarch's palace has not survived, or at least has not been located, nor is it described in written sources. There were several churches including St Basil, St John the Evangelist, St Michael the Archangel, St Euthymius, St Catherine, St Nicholas, St Theodore, St Demetrius, St George, St George in the Market, Little St Mary, St Anne, St Thecla, Great St Mary and St Chariton. Two streets within the quarter are well known: the Street of the Patriarch and the Street of the Holy Sepulchre. There was a major water source, the Pool of the Patriarch (Hezekiah's Pool). As was the case elsewhere in the city, the area adjacent to the walls was not built up and was used for open markets. There was a grain market north of David's Gate and a pig market probably located further north. A small gate, St Lazarus' Postern, gave access to the city from the leper house and the Quarter of St Lazarus outside the forewall.[8]

The major project of church building carried out by the Franks was the Church of the Holy Sepulchre, which was consecrated on the fiftieth anniversary of the capture of Jerusalem on 15 July 1149. The new church combined the functions of the city's cathedral and principal parish church but was also the principal pilgrimage church, enclosing within its walls not only Christ's tomb but also a number of the most important holy sites of Christianity. The Franks added to the existing rotunda a Romanesque choir, various chapels and a large cloister, and constructed a remarkable facade with a five-storey bell tower. These are described below (pp. 125, 127). The conventual buildings extended to the east as far as the triple market streets and to the north at least up to the Street of the Holy Sepulchre. Here were the dormitories, refectory, scriptorium and other buildings connected with the life of the canons.

The quarter belonging to the Order of the Knights of the Hospital of St John (the Hospitallers) was situated to the south of the Church of the Holy Sepulchre (Patrich 1984: 3–16) (Figure 2.4). It was bounded on its west by

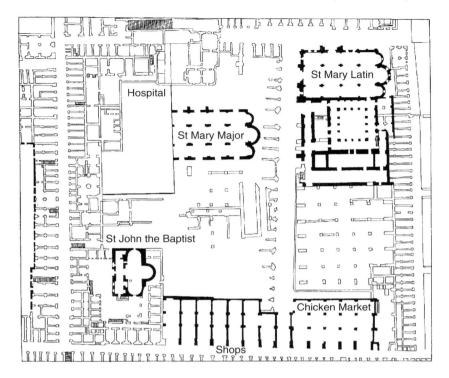

Figure 2.4 Jerusalem: plan of the Hospitallers' Quarter (after Bahat 1991)

the Street of the Patriarch, on its east by the triple market and on its south by David's Street. The ruins of this complex survived until the end of the nineteenth century, when the new market known as the Muristan was built.[9] The quarter included accommodation for pilgrims in a large hospice and infirmary. It is worth quoting a contemporary description of this remarkable building:

> As for this, no one can credibly tell another how beautiful its buildings are, how abundantly it is supplied with rooms and beds and other material for the use of poor and sick people, how rich it is in the means of refreshing the poor, and how devotedly it labours to maintain the needy, unless he has had the opportunity of seeing it with his own eyes. Indeed, we passed through this palace, and were unable by any means to discover the number of sick people lying there; but we saw that the beds numbered more than one thousand.
>
> (Theoderich 1891: 22)[10]

Excavations were carried out in 1867 by Charles Warren and a plan of the quarter was published by Conrad Schick in 1902 on which the remains of this building can be seen in the north-western corner (Schick 1902: 48–49). It consisted of a huge hall of thirty-two groin-vaulted bays with an entrance at the centre of its eastern wall directly into the vestibule of the Church of St Mary Major. The hall measured 28.3 × 57.5 m (each bay 6.5 × 6.5 m) with arches 6 m high. If we assume that it had a second storey, Theoderich's description is not implausible. Some of the underground vaults of this complex are still buried under the modern buildings. There were three churches in the quarter: St Mary Major and St Mary Latin (Minor), the ruins of both of which survived up to the nineteenth century, and St John the Baptist, which still stands to the east (Schick 1901: 50–3, 1902: 42–56; Vincent and Abel 1914–26: 646–68). Surviving fragments of St Mary Latin, which was demolished to make way for the Lutheran Church of the Redeemer, include a large portal decorated with signs of the zodiac, now incorporated into the northern wall of the modern church and a cloister to the south which has been restored.

To the east of the Hospitallers' Quarter and the Patriarch's Quarter was what had prior to 1099 been the Jewish Quarter (*Juverie*); after the conquest and the expulsion of non-Christians from the city the quarter had been repopulated since 1115 with Eastern Christians. It was bounded by the northern wall east of St Stephen's Gate, the eastern wall north of Jehosaphat Gate, the street leading from *Porta Josaphat* in the south and Spanish Street in the west. Churches located here included St Mary Magdalene, situated near the northern wall, St Agnes, St Elias and St Bartholomew, all churches of Eastern Christians. A church named *La Repos* was situated in the south of the quarter under the northern wall of the Temple Mount and to its east, near *Porta Josaphat*, was a large pool. One of the best-preserved Crusader churches in Jerusalem, St Anne, is also located in this quarter. St Anne, built in 1140, was the basilica of a Benedictine convent (see p. 132).

The Temple Mount had two principal buildings, the *Templum Domini* (Dome of the Rock) and the *Templum Salomonis* (al-Aqsa Mosque). In the second decade of the twelfth century the *Templum Domini* was, with minor adjustments, converted into a church. These included the construction of an altar and the replacement of the crescent on the dome with a cross. The walls were decorated with new mosaics and inscriptions were added. The *Templum Salomonis* became in 1119 the headquarters of the Order of the Knights Templar. The Templars extended the mosque to the east and west and partly reconstructed subterranean vaults to the east to serve as stables.

To the west of the Temple Mount the south-eastern quarter was bordered by the southern city wall and the streets built along the line of the Cardo to the west. At its centre was the causeway leading to the Beautiful Gate (*Porta Speciosa*). Along the causeway was an open market street and the Church of St Gilles. Money exchanges were located at the heart of the city, the Latin exchange to the south and the Syrian exchange further north. In the south-eastern quarter there was a church known as St Cosmos. To the south were the hospice and Church of the German Order of St Mary and further south, in an open area, the cattle market and tanneries. A large building, possibly a church, and a bathhouse, were situated here. A covered market and parallel streets bordered the quarter to its west. Other churches known to have been situated in this quarter were St Peter and St Martinus, and some remnants of Frankish houses survive.

The south-western quarter was occupied by Armenians during the Crusader period, as it is today. It was bordered to its west by the city wall south of *Porta David* and by the southern wall up to Zion Gate. Churches in this quarter included St James, St Thomas, St Mark, St Sabas and the most important of the quarter's churches, St James' Cathedral.

Outside the city were a number of important buildings, including the *Coenaculum* (the chapel of the Last Supper) on Mount Zion, the convent and subterranean chapel of the Tomb of St Mary in the Valley of Jehosaphat, and St Stephen's Church to the north of the gate of that name.

Streets and markets

Permanent markets are essential to urban life; their presence is one of the means by which we define a town as opposed to a large village. Each Frankish city had at least one market, and the larger cities had several. We know of numerous markets in Jerusalem, some through the written sources but most of them still surviving and functioning. In the sources we find markets specializing in a single type of goods such as grain, pigs, poultry, palm fronds for pilgrims, herbs, fish, cooked food, cloth, cattle, leather and furs. The markets in Jerusalem were royal possessions, though some were granted to ecclesiastical establishments such as that belonging to the convent of St Anne (the triple market at the centre of the town). The market on David's Street possibly belonged to the adjacent Hospitallers and there seems to have been a market belonging to the Templars near the eastern end of David's Street.

In the centre of the city, on what had once been the Cardo, is the triple market, three parallel vaulted market streets. The central street (Suk al-'Attarin or the Market of the Druggists) was known in the twelfth century as Malquissinat (the Street of Evil Cooking). This unusual name is apparently a reference to the function of this street in the Crusader period as a venue for the purchase of ready-cooked meals. In the twelfth century the large number of pilgrims visiting the city purchased prepared food in this street. In later times the street retained in its name a recollection of its twelfth-century function: the fifteenth-century Jerusalemite author, Mujir al-Din, referred to this street as Suk et-Tabbakhim (Bazaar of the Cooks) (Mujir al-Din 1876: 290). At the end of the nineteenth century a stone which may have originated in this street was found. It was incised with an inscription possibly reading 'COQUUS' (cook), above which appears a group of cooking implements (Clermont-Ganneau 1899: 229; Vincent and Abel 1926: Figure 403) (see Plate 2.3).

Plate 2.3 Inscription of a cook (after Clermont-Ganneau 1899)

Malquissinat and the two adjacent covered markets consists of a groin-vaulted passage 3 m wide and about 6 m high with small groin-vaulted shops with arched entrances on either side. In Malquissinat there are square opening shafts in the vaults to let in light and air and to allow the smoke from cooking to escape. Until the beginning of the twentieth century stone arches or louvres covered each of these openings, allowing only indirect light to enter from the openings and preventing rain from coming in. Almost nothing of these louvres remains but they can be seen on photographs of the market roof taken in 1918–21 and some medieval carving has survived on the roof. This street was built by Queen Melisende in 1152, employing the labour of Muslims from the village of al-Bira (Magna Mahumeria). It must have replaced the vaulted market mentioned by Mujir al-Din as having been built in 878 AD to replace the earlier street which was covered with palm leaves (Peters 1985: 398). Charles Clermont-Ganneau published a number of inscriptions which he discovered on the walls of this market (Clermont-Ganneau 1899: 116–26). These read '*ANNA*' or '*SCA ANNA*'; the letter '*T*' also appears inscribed on the walls (Plate 2.4a,b). These inscriptions identified the market as the possession of the Convent of St Anne. Clermont-Ganneau suggests that the convent had a share in the rents of those shops so inscribed. This apparently continued into the Ayyubid period, when the Convent of St Anne was converted by Saladin into a *madrassa* (school of theological study). Amongst its endowments (*waqf*) is listed the Suk et-Tabbakhim. The incised '*T*'s in Malquissinat suggest that the Templars had shares in some of the shops. There are similar '*T*'s in circles (now almost obliterated as the stone has been redressed) incised on the walls of a Frankish market in Temple Street (the eastern half of David's Street). This marking of properties seems to have been quite a common practice. Clermont-Ganneau notes a deed of 1174 which describes crosses carved on the walls of the Hospital of St John

(a)

(b)

Plate 2.4 Jerusalem: 'SCA ANNA' inscribed on the shops of Malquissinat market
(photographs by the author)

in Jerusalem ('*Signorum S. Crucis, quae in parietibus Hospitalis apparent pro meta*')
(Clermont-Ganneau 1899: 120).

Perhaps the finest and certainly the best-preserved Frankish market street
in Jerusalem is located to the south of Malquissinat and has been excavated
and restored as part of the reopened *Cardo* complex (Plate 2.5). In the
twelfth-century maps a street called *Vicus ad Montis Syon* leads from the
junction with David's Street directly to Zion Gate. On some of the maps
a quadrangular area at the junction is called *Forum Rerum Venalium*. On
others the name refers to the entire length between Mount Zion Street and
the Street of Judas' Arch. Pringle has suggested that the covered market
excavated by Avigad is Mount Zion Street (Pringle 1991a: 110), while Bahat
suggests it may be the *Forum Rerum Venalium* (personal communication). This

Plate 2.5 Jerusalem: covered market street on the *Cardo* (photograph by the
author)

market street was entered through a gate at its northern end of which a small
pilaster with a typical Frankish capital has survived. This is a considerably
finer building than the triple market, with a comparatively broad groin-
vaulted street (6.5 m wide) originally consisting of at least thirteen bays
and possibly more. To the west there are thirteen large barrel-vaulted shops
(two completely blocked at present and three partly blocked) which average
3.5 × 11 m, while on the other side there are eleven groin vaults, two of
which are now used as passages to the street to the east. The shops on the
east measure 4 × 4 m. These are large and high in comparison with the shops
in the triple market. Construction throughout is of very fine ashlars with
diagonal tooling; there are several masons' marks.

Another very fine covered market street is the Cotton Market on the
western side of the Temple Mount (Plate 2.6). It has been suggested by
Burgoyne that the western part of the building may be a Frankish
construction (Burgoyne and Richards 1987: 273). The western entrance has
marginally drafted ashlars, and west of the seventeenth bay the arched doorways to the shops differ from those to the east, with slightly pointed arches
rather than lintels with joggled voussoirs and relieving arches.[11] Burgoyne
raises the possibility that this was part of the system of *fondachi* established by
Frederick II in the thirteenth century whereby merchants were required to
deposit their goods pending the levying of customs dues.

The eastern extension of the southern side of the Hospitaller complex,
today a vegetable market, served in the Crusader period as a chicken market.

Plate 2.6 Jerusalem: the western entrance to the medieval Cotton Market
(photograph by the author)

The building is three bays deep with a gate at the northern side entering the
Hospitaller compound. There is evidence of a second storey. The facade
facing David's Street (the eastern corner of the Hospitaller compound) is
largely built with marginally dressed ashlars. The interior is vaulted, with
groin vaults supported by massive piers. Tether holes on the piers show
that at some stage it was used as a stable; however, they are high above
the present floor level, indicating that in post-Frankish times the floor was
considerably higher than it had originally been or is today.

In the street of Tariq Bab al-Silsila there is a vaulted structure which
may have been a market hall (Burgoyne 1987: 336, n. 18). It consists of six
groin-vaulted bays on the ground-floor level. Piers and at least two limestone

columns carry the transverse arches supporting the vaults. The original facade is largely hidden by later construction, but two of the original arches can be partly seen. The stones are dressed with diagonal dressing and there are masons' marks. If this is indeed a market, it may perhaps be identified with the butchers' market mentioned in the thirteenth-century tract known as 'The City of Jerusalem'. It is almost opposite the street leading to St Mary of the Germans, corresponding to its position in this description: 'Going down this street [Temple Street] you come to Butchers' Place, on the left hand, where they sell the meat of the town. On the right hand there is another street, by which one goes to the German Hospital, which is called Germans' Street' (*City of Jerusalem* 1888: 12). According to Burgoyne the Khan al-Sultan/al-Wakala was originally a Frankish structure, or at least one rebuilt during the Crusader period, containing a market street and hall and a stable (Burgoyne 1987: 480).

In addition to the covered market streets there were also open streets lined with shops. Examples of these are shops on the northern side of David's Street and shops perhaps belonging to the Order of the Templars in Temple Street. Along David's Street are fourteen large shops, each formed by three groin-vaulted bays and with arched openings between them. These shops are still in use, though now much subdivided. In addition, there were open markets in the fields that lined the interior of the city walls, including the large grain market already mentioned north of Jaffa Gate and a cattle market in the south of the city.

Houses

When the Crusaders occupied Jerusalem, it is likely that few buildings in the city were destroyed; the houses that had been in use under Muslim rule were occupied by the new settlers. According to Fulcher of Chartres:

> After this great slaughter they [the Crusaders] entered the houses of the citizens, seizing whatever they found there. This was done in such a way that whoever first entered a house, whether he was rich or poor, was not challenged by any other Frank. He was to occupy or own the house or palace and whatever he found in it as if it were entirely his own.
>
> (Fulcher of Chartres 1969: I, 29)

Since there was no need to build new houses, the Franks have left us with little evidence of their domestic architecture. Those houses they did build have, with apparently few exceptions, either fallen apart or been destroyed. Written sources suggest that these houses were two – and occasionally three or even four – storeys high.[12] As is customary in the East, they had flat roofs.[13] The living quarters were probably on the upper floors, while the ground floor served as shops or for storage and stables. There is little information on the furnishings or other components of the houses, such as fireplaces and latrines. Cisterns of medieval date, however, are not uncommon; water was drained from the roofs and into constructed or excavated cisterns under the houses and in the courtyards (Theoderich 1891: 5). South of the junction with David's Street at the northern end of the Frankish covered market is a house with three barrel-vaulted shops on the ground floor. It was uncovered during excavations carried out in the 1970s under the supervision of N. Avigad (Avigad 1980: 248, Figure 292). The narrow vaults each measure 2 × 7 m. They were uncovered, blocked but intact, with the facade surviving to a height of 4 m (eleven stone courses). The doors are 70 cm wide and 1.9 m high. They have flat lintels comprising five voussoirs each with a carved, stepped profile, forming low arches with pointed ends. Above each arch is a small rectangular opening intended to provide light to the shop when the door was closed. Such a building may have been rented to a poorer class of merchants who occupied the tiny shops and lived in the rooms above them.

Roads leading to the city

The roads to Jerusalem appear on the medieval maps. The *Vicus ad Civitatem* – road to the city, sometimes called *Vicus ad Civitatem Masphat* (road to the city of Mitzpeh, which probably refers to the section between *Porta David* and Nebi Samwil) – was the principal road to Jerusalem.[14] It ran from Jaffa via Ramla, Lydda, Beit Nuba, al-Qubeiba and Bidu to *Mons Gaudi*, and from there probably via the recently discovered village at al-Burj, and close to the farmhouse at Har Hozevim, finally arriving at the main gate of Jerusalem, *Porta David*. A second road shown on the maps is the *Vicus ad Betleem Effrata* (the road to Bethlehem and Ephrata). Most of the maps show no other roads, but there were alternative routes such as that which came from the coast on a more northerly route and reached the northern gate, *Porta St Stephan*, the road from Nablus, and the road from *Porta Josaphat* to the Jordan via Bethany.

Water supply

There were four means by which Jerusalem was supplied with water. Some of the water came from a distance, from the springs and reservoirs at Artas near Bethlehem. From here it was carried on ancient aqueducts to the city. Water was also supplied from the main spring of the city, the Siloam Spring (*Fons Syloe*). In addition to these extra-mural sources, both public and private buildings contained water cisterns which held the rainwater gathered from roofs and courtyards. Water from the heavy winter rains was always the most reliable means of supply; in some years wells dried up or dwindled to a trickle and the quality of the water could become very poor in a drought, whereas water from winter rains was generally quite abundant and of good quality. The fourth means of supplying water was by collecting it in large open reservoirs both within and outside the city walls. One of these was Germain's Pool or the German Pool in the south-west, which may have been donated by a Germain. This is probably the modern Sultan's Pool. The Pool of Mamilla to the west of the city may have been in use at this time. North of the northern city wall in the region of the lepers' colony was a reservoir known as *Lacus St Lazarus*. Inside the city were the Patriarch's Pool at the southern end of the Patriarch's Quarter, the Sheeps' Pool situated to the west of St Anne's Church, and a second pool with the same name adjacent to the northern wall of the Temple Mount.

Burial grounds

The burial places of the nobility differed from those of lesser knights, simple burgesses, pilgrims and the poor. Whereas the nobility were buried in churches or in church grounds, the lower classes were generally assigned to cemeteries outside the town walls. Thus some of the kings of Jerusalem were buried below Golgotha in the Church of the Holy Sepulchre, and the tomb of Melisende is in the Church of St Mary in Jehosaphat but, as William of Tyre and Raymond d'Aguilers mention, in Jerusalem pilgrims were buried beyond the city walls in the field of Akeldama (William of Tyre 1986: 8.2; Raymond d'Aguilers 1846: 354), where a large, barrel-vaulted Frankish charnel house survives (p. 236). This was not a rule, however, and it appears from the presence of elaborate tomb markers that Frankish nobles were also buried in a plot outside the city, beside the pool of Mamilla, which also served as the burial place of the canons of the Church of the Holy Sepulchre (pp. 234–5).

Akko (Acre)

Akko was the most important port city on the Palestinian coast and its capture was no doubt one of the priorities of the Franks after their occupation of Jerusalem (Plate 2.7). Following a failed attempt at taking the city by siege in March 1103, an agreement was reached with the Genoese in the spring of 1104. Aided by the Genoese fleet the Franks renewed their siege in early May and after twenty days the Muslims capitulated.

Sources

Historians and pilgrims have left us with some remarkably graphic descriptions of Frankish Akko. Most of the medieval pilgrims' accounts (*itineraria*) describe Akko, sometimes in considerable detail but not always with complete accuracy. In addition, several useful documents and medieval maps have survived (Figure 2.5). Of particular importance are property lists drawn up in the mid-thirteenth century by the Venetian and Genoese representatives, listing house by house, and even, room by room, their possessions in the city

Plate 2.7 Akko viewed from the Tower of Flies (photograph by Ronnie Ellenblum)

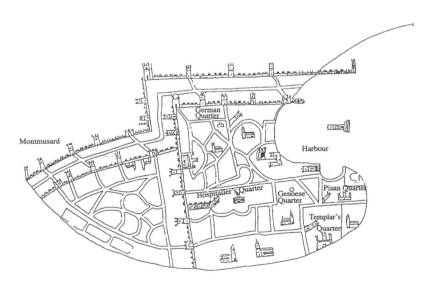

Figure 2.5 Copy of a medieval map of thirteenth-century Akko by Marino Sanudo

(Desimoni 1884: 213–22; Tafel and Thomas 1856–57: 389–98). Equally valuable are the maps of thirteenth-century Akko; several copies of three maps survive. One of these, dating from around 1250, was drawn up by an Englishman, Matthew Paris, for his chronicle of England and the Crusades, another was drawn up by Pietro Vesconte for a fourteenth-century work *Liber Secretorum Fidelium Crucis* written by Marino Sanudo, and a third map was prepared just after 1320 for Paolino Veneto and follows very closely the map of Sanudo. Although the latter two maps, of which several versions are extant, date from the fourteenth-century, they present the city as it appeared in the thirteenth century at the height of its importance as the administrative capital of the kingdom.

Extensive remains of the buildings and streets of Akko have been surveyed and excavated, particularly in the past few years. A detailed survey of Akko's houses and streets was carried out in the early 1960s by A. Kesten (Dichter 1973: 70–98). Excavations in the Hospitallers' Quarter began in the late 1950s and 1960s and since 1990 a full-scale excavation and reconstruction of this remarkable complex has been under way (Avissar and Stern 1995: 22–5; 1996: 20–1) (see Plate 2.8). Excavations have also been carried out in the Templars' Quarter, in the north-west corner of the Old City, in the northern suburb of Montmusard and elsewhere both inside and outside the Ottoman city walls.

Defences

Akko was a walled city when the Franks occupied it in 1104. Until the Third Crusade it had a single city wall, but at some time within the subsequent

Plate 2.8 Akko: excavations in the Hospitallers' Quarter

twenty-three years, probably in the early years of the thirteenth century, double walls were built around the city and its new northern suburb, Montmusard (Jacoby 1982: 213). Between 1251 and 1254 Louis IX of France rebuilt them; these are the walls depicted on fourteenth-century maps of Akko. The maps show the double line of fortifications enclosing the city on its eastern side and including the suburb of Montmusard. Almost nothing of these walls can be seen today, but recent excavations north of the Old City have uncovered part of a tower of the northern outer wall (Hartal 1993: 19–21). There are additional hints at the position of the walls, but these are vague enough to have generated considerable debate and little agreement.[15] Traces of what may be the northernmost part of the outer wall have been discovered to the north of the Ottoman wall; these include the foundations of a round tower, now under water, some 750 m north of the Ottoman wall (Frankel 1987: 256–61). Recently, a convincing case has been presented in support of the view that the walls to the east extended nearly as far as the ancient mound (Kedar 1997: 157–80).[16]

In the thirteenth century there were a number of gates giving access to Akko from the land. These included St Michael's Gate, New Gate (*Porta Nova*), Our Lady's Gate (*Domine Nostre*), St Antony's Gate, Blood Gate (*Sanguinis*), St Nicholas' Gate, Bridge Gate and Patriarch's Gate. In the northern suburb of Montmusard there were two gates: the Evil Step Gate (*Mallopasso*) and St Lazarus' Gate.

The port

The merchants and pilgrims who arrived at Akko by ship entered the city by its port. There are various interpretations of the appearance of this port in the Crusader period. William of Tyre described the port of Akko with the words '*infra moenia et exterius*' (William of Tyre 1986: 10.26). This is usually interpreted as meaning that there were an inner and an outer harbour. The fourteenth-century maps seem to support this view: a small, semi-circular bay is shown just north of the Venetian Quarter. However, recent studies claim that this is the perpetuation on later copies of an accidental ink blot that appeared on the original version of Pietro Vesconte's map. In the eighteenth and nineteenth centuries however, the inner harbour was still to be seen, filled with sand according to M.E.G. Rey (Dichter 1973: 65), and it is shown on maps drawn by Colonel Jaquotin of Napoleon's army in 1799 and by Rey in 1871 (Dichter 1973: 44, 141). Trenches excavated in Khan al-Umdan, widely considered to have been the site of the inner basin, revealed that the Turkish khan was constructed on bedrock (Linder and Raban 1965: 193). In fact the khan is situated just north of the site described in the eighteenth and nineteenth centuries, and the question of the existence of an inner harbour therefore remains open for the moment.

A merchant who entered the city from the port would pass through an iron gate (*Porta Ferrae*) into the Court of the Chain, which was the customs house and seat of the marine court. Along the Street of the Chain, which stretched to the north, were warehouses, palaces and dwellings. This area and the port were under the jurisdiction of the king. From the warehouses along the inner harbour sewage poured into the harbour, possibly giving rise to its medieval name *Lordemer* (Filthy Sea) (Jacoby 1993: 88–91).

Quarters

Following the capture of Akko in 1104 and in accordance with the previously mentioned agreement, the Genoese received a quarter in the city. Somewhat later the Venetians and the merchants of Marseilles also received quarters together with various important privileges, such as judicial rights within their quarters, certain tax exemptions and the right to use weights and measures. In 1168 the Pisans also received a quarter and privileges in the city. The Venetian Quarter was built around the Venetian souk (*Fundus Venetorum*), probably on the site of the modern Khan al-Afranj. It was to the *fundus* that the Venetian merchant would bring his merchandise to sell. The Church of St Mark was to the north-east of the *fundus*. In the Pisan Quarter to the south the *fundus* was in the area now occupied by the Khan a-Shuna. South of it were two churches, St Peter and St Andrew. The impressive ruins of the latter survived until the seventeenth century and are illustrated in two drawings, one dated 1681 and the other 1686. Some medieval houses survive in this quarter (Plate 2.9). The Genoese Quarter contained numerous houses and palaces and a covered street which was recently rediscovered and partly cleared of debris (Kedar and Stern 1995: 105–11). This street extended from the Church of St Lawrence to the border of the Venetian Quarter. Adjoining it were houses, and documents mention amongst them the 'house of the soap makers'. A house in this street was recently surveyed (Boas forthcoming) and a section of the covered street adjacent to it was cleared of debris. The house had direct access to this street via a large arch, possibly the entrance to a shop. Two storeys of this house survive. It consisted of a ground-floor courtyard surrounded by six small rooms with a first-floor hall (Plate 2.10). Part of the groin-vaulted roof of the hall still stands. There are remains of many other medieval houses in this quarter (Plate 2.11).

The Templars' Quarter of Akko was to the south-west. The principal building was the Temple, one of the sturdiest buildings in Akko and the last stronghold remaining in Christian hands when the city fell to al-Ashraf Khalil in 1291.[17] The ruins survived until the mid-eighteenth century, when it was dismantled by the Bedouin governor of Akko, Dahr al-'Umar. Other important buildings in this quarter were the Palace of the Grand Master and the Old Tower, but the only ruin identified at present is the crypt of the Church of St Anne. An important recent chance discovery is an underground street which passed under the Templars' and Pisan Quarters, perhaps extending as far as the port.[18] It consists of a large, vaulted passage extending to the east from near the site of the Temple in the west. It branches into two

Plate 2.9 Akko: ground-floor vaults of a communal house in the Pisan Quarter (photograph by the author)

smaller, vaulted passages that possibly connect the Templars' Quarter with the port, allowing passage under the Pisan Quarter. At one point in the passage, at a slightly higher level above the main vault, there is a room, possibly a guardroom, with the remains of stairs that led down to the passageway.

In the north-east of the city were the quarters of the Teutonic Order, which was established in Akko after the Third Crusade, and the Patriarch. This area, which probably includes the site of the main citadel, has recently been partly excavated (Syon and Tatcher 1998). The architectural finds were of a residential nature and as yet no trace of the citadel has been identified.

The Hospitallers' Quarter

In 1955–64 excavations were conducted in the Hospitallers' compound, concentrating in the refectory, and adjacent complexes popularly known as al-Bosta and the Halls of the Knights (Goldmann 1994). The renewed excavations under way since 1990 have exposed a remarkable complex entirely composed of conventual buildings, mainly dating from the thirteenth century (Figure 2.6). The important buildings which appear on the map of Sanudo include the *hospitale* (hospice), the *ecclesia* (church) and the *domus infirmorum* (hospital). The *ecclesia* has not yet been found, although it has been suggested that it was above the halls of al-Bosta. According to the archaeologist Eliezer

Plate 2.10 Akko: the first-floor hall in a house in the Genoese Quarter (photograph by the author)

Plate 2.11 Akko: a covered street in the Genoese Quarter (photograph by the author)

Stern, the *domus infirmorum* was the large, vaulted hall south of al-Bosta which was recently partly cleared. Al-Bosta itself consists of three halls; the western-most one is largely pre-Frankish, while the central hall, roofed by three groin vaults, is Frankish and in the early twelfth-century Romanesque style. The third large hall to the east has twelve enormous piers supporting groin vaults. The building to the south is similar to the large hall of al-Bosta.

North of al-Bosta is the large refectory, partly buried with the destruction of the city in 1291 and completely so when the Turkish palace was built above it in the eighteenth century, and thus formerly known as the Crypt, although it was originally above ground. It has been identified as a refectory

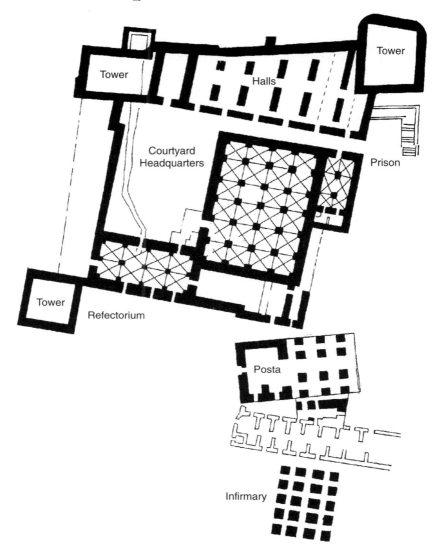

Figure 2.6 Akko: the Hospitallers' Quarter (after Goldmann 1994)

or dining-hall because of its plan, which is typical of refectories in medieval monasteries, and because of the presence of three chimneys in the eastern wall which are probably connected to kitchens in the adjoining, unexcavated halls. The refectory has two aisles measuring 30 × 15 m with groin-vaulted bays supported on three massive round piers, each 3 m in diameter. Goldmann, who cleared the halls in 1954, believes that the hall was originally begun in the Romanesque style and was modified into a Gothic building as it was being constructed (*c.* 1148) (Goldmann 1994: 8–13). North of the refectory is a courtyard and to its east a large, vaulted hall, perhaps the *hospitale*; the latter was partly cleared by Goldmann and completely excavated by Stern and Avissar, and is now undergoing restoration. This building consists of twenty-four large, groin-vaulted connected bays built in the Romanesque style. It is the largest building in the complex, measuring 30 × 45 m. This was the ground floor of the large four-storey palace which appears on seventeenth-century drawings. One of these drawings shows the ruin with a broad staircase leading up from the courtyard to the first floor. This staircase was found during excavations and has also been restored (Avissar and Stern 1995: 22). To the north a covered passage led to what is now known as the Halls of the Knights, a group of eight large, barrel-vaulted halls connected to one another by arched openings in the side walls. They perhaps served as barracks for the knights. There is also a small prison and a small hall, perhaps a reception hall, with elongated windows and fine masonry. The complex has corner towers. Below one of the towers is a remarkable sewage system (Avissar and Stern 1995: 21–2, Figures 24–5); chutes from what is probably an upstairs communal toilet led into an underground vaulted room from which the sewage flowed out into narrow passages and was washed out to sea. Underground passages connect the various buildings of the quarter.

Montmusard

The suburb of Montmusard developed to reach the northern wall of Akko in the later part of the twelfth century and expanded greatly after the Third Crusade with the large influx of new settlers from the inland towns lost after the Battle of Hattin. Our knowledge of this suburb is almost entirely limited to information from the fourteenth-century maps.[19] The area was divided into quarters like the older, walled area to the south. In the north was the quarter of the Knights of St Lazarus. This was the lepers' colony. Unlike in Jerusalem it was within the city walls, but in the most distant part of the city. To its south the Hospitallers had a second quarter. The Templars had a quarter in the south-western corner. According to the maps, the remainder of the area was divided up into other quarters. Virtually no remains appear to have survived in this area. This is partly due to the fact that during the construction of the walls of the Ottoman city the ruins were used to supply building stone, but the quarter may perhaps have never been as densely built up as was the older part of the city. The only apparently Frankish finds to date consist of the round tower in the north-west (Frankel 1987: 256–61, Plates 31a, b, 32a), some walls to its south which may be part of the *auberge* or remains of the leper hospital of St Lazar, a bathhouse recently discovered and partly excavated (Stern forthcoming) and a building situated about 50 m from the sea and 210 m north of the Ottoman wall. The latter building appears on aerial photographs of 1918 and 1923, but is no longer visible because the area has been completely built over (Boas 1997: 181–6). It consists of a street about 30 m wide and at least 140 m long. At its southern end there appears to be a fortified gatehouse, and about thirty shops line the street on either side. The plan recalls that of other medieval market streets such as the Cotton Market in Jerusalem. This may be the *Ruga Betleemitana* (Bethlehem Street) that appears on the medieval maps.

Antioch

Antioch was captured during the First Crusade, after a six-month siege in 1098. It became the capital of the principality of Antioch. It was occupied briefly by Armenians in 1194, 1208 and 1216 and fell to Baybars in 1268.

The city is situated on the River Orontes about eight kilometres inland; from 1200 Port St Symeon (al-Mina) served as its port. The Franks restored and maintained the Byzantine fortifications and traces of possible Frankish work can still be seen (Sinclair 1990 (vol. 4): 243); for example, the rectangular enclosure wall of the citadel on Mount Silpius (Sinclair 1990 (vol. 4): 244). At the centre of the town was the Cathedral of St Peter. This cave-church is identified as being the site of the first Christian meetings after the death of Christ. The three-door facade appears to date from the thirteenth century.

Tripoli

Raymond of St Gilles laid siege to Tripoli in 1099 but after failing to take the town settled on a nearby hill called *Mons Pèlerin*, where he died in 1105. Tripoli fell to the Franks only in 1109 after a protracted siege and with the aid of the Genoese fleet. It became the capital of the county of Tripoli and a bishopric. Despite earthquake damage in the twelfth century, the city prospered. After the loss of Jerusalem in 1187 Tripoli, like Akko, grew in importance and its population increased. It possessed churches, hospitals and convents and was a centre for the trade and manufacture of silk fabric; according to one source, 4,000 weavers lived in the town (p. 186). In 1268 Baybars ravaged the surrounding district but failed to take the town, which remained in Frankish hands until 1289.

Very little remains of the Frankish town. The castle, which stands on a hill beside the river (Nahr Abu Ali) underwent major rebuilding in the Mamluk and Ottoman periods but incorporates parts of the original structure, including sections of the walls and towers to the east. Remains of the Cathedral of St Mary, including the tower and doors, survive in the Grand Mosque, and there are fragments of the large Carmelite Church and of the Church of St John on *Mons Pèlerin*.

Coastal towns

Arsuf (Arsur)

Arsuf was one of the earliest of the coastal towns to fall to the Franks (Figure 2.7). It was taken by Baldwin I with the aid of the Genoese fleet following a three-day siege in 1101. Ladders and a siege tower were used during the siege of the walled town.

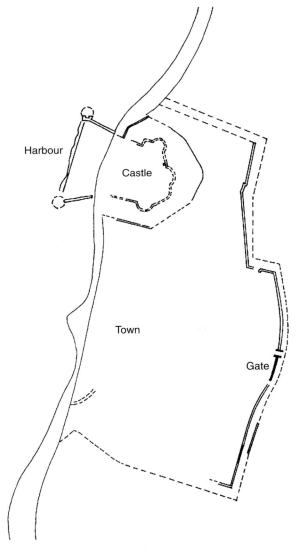

Figure 2.7 Plan of Arsuf (Apollonia) (after Roll and Ayalon 1993)

Under the Franks the defences of this small town were quite impressive. The citadel was constructed high on a cliff with the town to the east and south, and was surrounded by a moat and barbican. A drawbridge crossed the moat from the gate in the south and there was a second gate to the east.

Arsuf fell to Saladin in 1187 but returned to Frankish control after the Battle of Arsuf in 1191. The city was held by the Ibelin family in the 1190s. In 1240 the walls were strengthened and in 1261 Arsuf came into the hands of the Hospitallers, who refortified it, including the undefended suburb to the east. The citadel played an important role in the final defence of the town in 1265. After the town walls fell, the defenders took refuge in the citadel and Baybars mined its southern wall. Though the Hospitallers dug a counter-mine, Baybars dug a second mine and the barbican fell, after which the Franks were forced to surrender and hand over the town.

Ongoing excavations carried out at Arsuf by Tel Aviv University have exposed only a few Frankish buildings inside the walls, including the remains of a small, possibly two-storey courtyard house and a paved lane. The nature of the areas excavated suggests that in the Crusader period the town had lost its urban character and was largely unoccupied inside the walls (Roll and Ayalon 1993: 74). The walls, which were surrounded by a moat, enclosed the city to the north, east and south, while to the west there were steep sandstone cliffs. Within a retaining wall and a moat the citadel had an outer wall with semicircular and square towers which enclosed an area of 65 m × 45 m. The *donjon* was situated to the east. A tunnel led from the citadel to the small, trapezoid-shaped harbour which was enclosed by quays with corner towers and an entrance to the south-east.

Ascalon

Ascalon fell to the Franks only in 1153. Its strong walls and outworks, still visible today, were able to repel the Frankish army long after all the other towns in the Holy Land had fallen. Even in 1153 it took two months of siege and the construction of siege towers and battering-rams, constructed as in the siege of Jerusalem from dismantled ships, before the city fell. The Frankish siege tower used at Ascalon was so impressive that it was known about as far away as Damascus, where it was called the 'cursed tower'. According to William of Tyre, the other trials the citizens had endured were light in comparison to the ills that assailed them from this tower. They tried to set it alight, but the flames spread to the walls which burned all night and finally collapsed. Since the breach of the walls was only partial the siege nearly failed, but the citizens of Ascalon decided to surrender, and fled the city. In 1187, after a two-week siege, the city fell again to the Muslims. However, on the approach of Richard I in 1191, Saladin decided to destroy the city to prevent his regaining it. The walls and towers were filled with wood and burned down. The city burned for twelve days, but the defences were so strong that the principal fortification, the Tower of Blood or Tower of the Hospital, fell only after repeated onslaughts. During a four-month period in 1192 the Crusaders restored the city but, after an agreement with the Muslims the walls were again demolished. In 1240 the Franks built a castle over the ruins, apparently on the north-west hill, but it too was destroyed by Baybars in 1270.

Ascalon is estimated to have had about 10,000 inhabitants. Its walls formed a semicircle surrounding an area of fifty hectares. This was a large area by medieval standards. Jerusalem covered seventy-two hectares and Akko sixty, while Sidon, the next largest town, covered an area of only fourteen hectares. The walls were the continuation of the Roman/Byzantine walls which were rebuilt by the Umayyad Caliph Abd'al Malik in the seventh century and probably restored by the Fatimids in the eleventh. Frankish work consisted largely of repairs and embellishments. The high and very thick walls were built on an artificial mound 7–10 m high, stone-lined to form a glacis, and were constructed of solid sandstone masonry with lateral columns and extremely hard cement. There were also outworks 2 m thick with occasional casemates. There were four gates with indirect access and with high, solid, round and square towers. Sources mention fifty-three towers around the walls, and Benvenisti estimates a distance of about 30 m between them. To the east was the Great Gate (*Porta Major*) or Jerusalem Gate. It was the best defended of the gates and in the barbican before it were three or four smaller gates with indirect entrances. There was a southern gate facing Gaza (Gaza Gate), a northern gate (Jaffa Gate) and a Sea Gate (*Porta Maris*). According to Benvenisti the citadel was by the Gaza Gate, where two large towers, the Tower of the Maidens (*Turris Puellarum*) and the Tower of the Hospital, were located (Benvenisti 1970: 124). This area was called the Hill of Towers and is at the highest point of the defences. As mentioned above, however, it would seem that the castle built in 1240 was in the north-west (Pringle 1984a: 144). Frankish remains inside the walls consist of only two of the town's five churches. The position of the cathedral church of St John is unknown; it was probably located near the centre of the town.

Beirut (Baruth)

The town was captured after a three-month siege on 13 May 1110 and was held by the Franks until 1187, when it fell to Saladin after an eight-day siege. In 1197, after the death of Saladin, the ruined city was regained by the Franks and was held until 1291 when it was destroyed by the Mamluks. Beirut under the Franks was described by travellers as a wealthy city with a fine man-made port. The seigneury of Beirut was held by John of Ibelin, who refortified the city.

Remains of the citadel near the port survived into the nineteenth century and appear on drawings. Little has survived the passage of time and the ravages of recent years. The Cathedral of St John survived as a mosque (Pringle 1993b: 112–15), and recent excavations in the ruined centre of Beirut have uncovered additional Frankish remains; these are yet to be published.

Caesarea (Cesaire)

Caesarea was a walled city before the arrival of the Franks. In Hellenistic, Roman and Byzantine times the area of the city was much greater and the line of fortifications is well known. In the post-Muslim conquest period Caesarea deteriorated in every aspect: the port was destroyed and that which replaced it was small and shallow, the aqueducts went out of use through being filled with sand and the settled area became much smaller, probably the size of the walled city we know today (Figure 2.8). Muqaddasi in 985 describes a well-populated suburb, but Nasir i-Khusrau in 1047 describes gardens as they were at the time of the Frankish conquest (1101), when Baldwin destroyed them. He probably refers to the area south of the Frankish town and this perhaps illustrates the deterioration in the city; the well-populated suburb of the late tenth century may have become an area

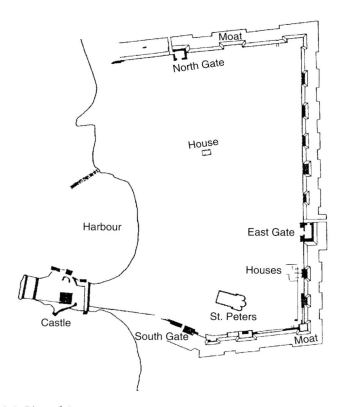

Figure 2.8 Plan of Caesarea

of gardens and orchards sixty years later. Traces of the pre-Frankish walls excavated by Y. Porat are on the same line as the Frankish walls. These walls were described by contemporary chroniclers as impregnable. Descriptions of the attack in 1101 mention two lines of defence. In 1187 Saladin razed part of the defences to prevent the city being reused, but in 1192 he returned it to the Franks as terms of a truce. It appears, however, that the city lay shattered and abandoned until December 1217, when the king (John of Brienne) refortified it. Despite this it remained lightly garrisoned; it was attacked and the new defences razed by the Ayyubid ruler al-Mu'azzam 'Isa. In 1228 work began on repairing the fortifications at the time of the arrival of Frederick II. In 1251 the major work of refortifying the city was carried out by Louis IX. He reconstructed and strengthened the citadel, the walls and gates and sixteen towers. In February 1265 Baybars destroyed parts of the walls and burned down the gates when he took the city from the Franks. The final destruction was carried out by al-Ashraf Khalil in 1291 as part of his policy of destroying all the coastal towns to prevent resettlement by the Franks.

Benvenisti estimated the population of Frankish Caesarea as 4,800. It covered an area of twelve hectares. The fortifications are the finest surviving example from the Crusader period. They were cleared and partly restored by A. Negev in the early 1960s. They extend from the citadel on the shore to the south in a south-easterly direction to the south gate, at which point they turn east. Near the south-east corner is a postern. After this the wall turns north. About one-third of the way along is the eastern gate, the main gate of the town, which originally had a drawbridge supported on a stone vault. This gate has been completely reconstructed. Slightly further north is a second postern. The wall continues north before turning west to the sea. Two-thirds of the way along the north wall is the north gate. The wall continues west to the sea and to the south as far as the Frankish jetty. The entire length of the wall, except on the sea front, has a stone-lined dry moat. Of the citadel we know little, as no serious examination of it has taken place to date. A small moat separated the citadel from the town and was filled by sea water.

There were a number of churches in Caesarea. Pringle lists eight churches, as well as the Houses of the Leper Knights of St Lazarus and of the Teutonic Knights, which would have included chapels (Pringle 1995: 166–81), but the remains of only one can be traced today. This is the cathedral church of St Peter which is situated on the Herodian temple podium. It was built some time in the twelfth century to replace the church which occupied the building of the mosque captured in 1201. We do not know what happened to the church at the time of the Ayyubid conquest or during later attacks on Caesarea, but it would seem on the evidence of texts to have survived through to the fall of the town to the Mamluks in February 1265, when Sultan Baybars adopted it as his campaign post during the siege of the fortress. He probably destroyed the church after the fall of the castle in March.

The church of St Peter was a basilica measuring 45 × 20 m internally with a nave slightly broader than the two aisles. At the eastern end were three sanctuaries with semicircular apses. It was constructed with cut sandstone blocks, diagonally dressed and with a number of masons' marks. A second church stood just inland from the jetty and was still visible at the end of the nineteenth century, when it was noted by the Survey of Western Palestine. Nothing of it can be seen today. Remains of streets and houses have been exposed in excavations along the south-east (Plate 2.12) and on the temple platform, and a large building which Pringle has tentatively identified as a merchant's house is located in the northern half of the town. The harbour in the Crusader period was much smaller than that of Roman/Byzantine Caesarea. It extended from the citadel in the south to a jetty constructed of columns to the north. Cemeteries were located outside the walls of the town to the south and north and probably also inside the town near the cathedral.

Famagusta

The heyday of Frankish Famagusta began in the fourteenth century.[20] It had previously been of little importance, but with the loss of Akko in 1291 it became the major emporium for Eastern trade. In one fourteenth-century source it is described as 'the harbour for the whole sea and the whole kingdom', and 'the richest of all the cities in Cyprus' (Ludolf of Suchem 1895: 41). Famagusta owed its prosperity to its excellent harbour. When the

Plate 2.12 Caesarea: an arched street and house (photograph by the author)

Franks arrived it had only minor fortifications, but it was fortified under Guy of Lusignan and again during the usurpation of Amaury of Lusignan (1306–10). A tower was constructed in 1232 to control the entrance to the harbour. The city had two or three gates: the Limassol Gate to the south, the Sea Gate to the east and possibly a third gate to the north. In the south of the town were the Quarter of the Mint (Zecca), the Greek Quarter and the Arsenal. At the centre of the town stood the royal palace and the splendid French Gothic cathedral of St Nicholas, described below (pp. 134–6). It was built with the support of Bishop Guy of Ibelin, who bequeathed 20,000 bezants towards its construction, and it remains one of the finest Gothic churches in the East. The north-western part of the city around the citadel was the Citadel Quarter.

Other than St Nicholas, several remarkable Gothic structures survive in Famagusta. These include the churches of St George of the Greeks, St George of the Latins, and the two small, well-preserved churches of the Temple and the Hospital. There are also some interesting examples of domestic buildings (Plate 2.13).

Jaffa (Jafis, Japhe)

Despite its poor harbour which was only safe in the summer, Jaffa was the main port of the kingdom south of Akko and served as the port of Jerusalem. The town was destroyed and abandoned by the Muslims in 1099 (Jacques of

Plate 2.13 Famagusta: an arched street and house (photograph by the author)

Vitry 1896 (vol. 11): 22). Rebuilt and refortified by Godfrey, Jaffa was successfully defended six times against attacks by the Egyptians between 1101 and 1123. It became a bishopric under the jurisdiction of the archbishopric of Caesarea, and the centre of the county of Jaffa (after 1153 the county of Jaffa and Ascalon). The Pisans received a quarter of the city and controlled trade through the port. In 1187 it fell but was retaken in 1191 by Richard I. In 1197 it fell again, and though it was recovered by the Franks in 1204 it remained derelict for a long time. In 1228–9 the walls of the citadel were rebuilt and the ditch cleared. At the weakest point of the castle above the sea was the Tower of the Patriarch. A fragmentary inscription discovered in the nineteenth century appears to be evidence of the work carried out at this time. It reads: '[FREDERICUS, ROMANORUM IMPERATOR SEMP]ER AUGUSTUS, I[ERUSALEM REX] . . . . [ANNO DOMIN]ICE INCARNATI[ONIS] . . . . . TI(?) . . . . ' (Clermont-Ganneau 1896: 155–6). In 1252–3 the walls were rebuilt by John of Ibelin and Louis IX with moats and twenty-four towers. On 7 March 1268 Baybars attacked Jaffa, occupied it, expelled the population and razed the town.

In the twelfth century the city comprised two distinct parts: the citadel on the sandstone hill, the site of ancient Jaffa and the lower walled faubourg. Within the castle were the Church of St Peter and the residences of the patriarch of Jerusalem and of the count of Jaffa. There were two quarters in the lower town: that of the Pisans, who occupied a coastal area which had a sea gate in the wall, and to their north the quarter of the Hospitallers. The Templars had a house in the faubourg. There were at least two land gates, Jerusalem Gate and further south Ascalon Gate.

Archaeological remains from the Crusader period were uncovered by J. Kaplan from 1955 onwards and included an oven and some vaults. Ongoing excavations include an area outside the city wall, probably part of the *burgus novus*.[21]

Limassol

Very little is known about medieval Limassol and almost nothing remains. Byzantine Nemesos was a flourishing port when the Franks arrived, but it seems to have been rather poorly fortified (Hill 1948: 15–16). A castle appears to have been in existence by 1228 and the small fort in the centre of the town is part of what must once have been a much larger building which withstood the attacks of the Genoese in the fifteenth century. What remains today is a square vaulted hall with a circular staircase, which comprises the oldest part of the structure, and a large annexe to the north-east containing prison cells and a staircase. A massive wall about 3 m thick was added, probably in the sixteenth century. The square hall apparently originally extended over the area of the annexe. It had embrasure windows and wooden floors on the upper level which have not survived later alterations.

Sidon (Saiete)

As with the other coastal towns, when the Franks marched southward along the coast on their way to Jerusalem in 1099 they passed by Sidon. They returned to lay siege to the town in 1105. The Sidonians agreed to pay a heavy tax and the Frankish army was withdrawn. In 1108 Baldwin renewed the siege, without the support of a fleet and consequently without success. In 1110, aided by the fleets of Genoa and Pisa and King Sigurd of Norway, the Franks renewed their siege. At that time Beirut fell and the citizens were slaughtered. The citizens of Sidon, fearing they would share their fate, surrendered and on 4 December the city fell. The Franks held the city until 29 July 1187, when it fell to the Ayyubid army following the Battle of Hattin. After its fall the city was dismantled, but was recaptured by the Franks in 1197.

It is not entirely clear who held Sidon in the early thirteenth century, but it seems that by 1217 it was again in Frankish hands. In 1227 the armies of Frederick II, who were camped in the city, began to fortify it, concentrating on a small island 40 m from the shore where they built a Sea Castle (Château de Mer) (pp. 103–4).

Between June 1253 and February 1254 Louis IX rebuilt massive city walls with a deep moat. In the south-east a second castle was built on the Murex Hill. It was known as the 'Land Castle' as opposed to the 'Sea Castle'. Directly opposite the Sea Castle was the eastern city wall, about 600 m long with a moat on its eastern side. From the Land Castle in the south the wall turned south-west to the sea at a distance of about 200 m. There were towers along the length of both walls. The Land Castle was built on the remains of a Roman/Byzantine theatre, and as at Beit Govrin, Beit She'an, Caesarea and Banias, the seats of the theatre were used as building stones. The massive piers of the *vomitoria* were incorporated into the lower part of the castle. On the southern wall was a gate with two towers known as Tyre Gate.

In 1260 Sidon was destroyed. A year later it passed into the hands of the Templars and the Hospitallers, and they began to restore its defences. In 1291 the city fell to the Mamluks and, like the other coastal towns, was destroyed.

Tartus (Tortosa)

The town of Tartus was captured during the First Crusade but was subsequently lost and recaptured three years later in 1102 by Raymond of St Gilles. It was a port and the seat of a bishopric. It served, probably from the 1150s, as the headquarters of the Templars in Syria, who built the massive citadel in the north-western corner of the town. The layout is similar to that of Arsuf in the kingdom of Jerusalem, though Tartus is a flat site lacking topographical advantages while Arsuf is built on a steep cliff above the sea (Figure 2.9). Briefly occupied in 1152 by Nur al-Din and, except for a

Figure 2.9 Plan of Tartus (Tortosa) (after Deschamps 1973)

single tower, by Saladin in 1187, it was otherwise continuously in Frankish hands until the Mamluk conquest in 1291. The defences of the town consisted of an inner wall with towers, a moat, an outer *enceinte* with salient towers and an outer moat. Parts of the city and harbour walls survive, as does the citadel on the sea front in the north-western corner of the town. The latter consists of a large and now ruined keep largely obscured by modern buildings. It is surrounded by concentric defences and a ditch. It was probably rebuilt soon after the earthquake of 1202. The entrance to the citadel was to the north and was defended by a large tower. The keep was in the centre of the citadel to the west, and to its north were a large hall and a chapel. In the centre of the town a cathedral, Our Lady of Tortosa, was built in the mid-twelfth century to sanctify the Byzantine pilgrimage site of the

Sanctuary of the Virgin, which is believed to have been dedicated by St Peter. It is a fine example of French Early Gothic.

Tyre (Sur, Tyr)

After abortive sieges in 1102 and 1111, Tyre was finally captured by the Franks with the aid of the Venetian fleet in 1124. Its strength lay in its remarkable fortifications combined with the topographical advantage of being surrounded on three sides by sea. It remained strongly fortified under the Franks, who strengthened the walls and built the citadel in 1210. It was the only city in the kingdom of Jerusalem that did not fall to Saladin after the Battle of Hattin. Subsequently, after the entire kingdom had fallen, Tyre served as the bridgehead for the Frankish reconquest of the coast in the Third Crusade (1189–92). Thanks to its excellent harbour, Tyre soon came to rival Akko in importance. It had a population estimated at 30,000 (Benvenisti 1970: 27), as large as the population of Akko and of Jerusalem. Tyre fell in 1291 after the fall of Akko.

While we are well informed about Tyre in medieval sources, very little remains or has been published of the Frankish city. A large part of the eastern side of the cathedral of Tyre was still standing in 1875 and can be seen in photographs published by Enlart (1927: Atlas, Plate 149). They show the exterior of the southern and central apses of the church and the fallen pillars that had supported the roof. These were later re-erected but little remains of the structure today.

Inland towns

Banias (Belinas)

The city of Banias fell in 1129 to the Franks, who immediately strengthened its fortifications. In 1132 the Muslims attacked; although the fortifications were strong, the Muslims mined them and penetrated the town. The defenders fled to the citadel but soon surrendered. A rare combined effort was then mounted between the Franks and the ruler of Damascus against Zangi, ruler of Mosul, who held the town and threatened both the Franks and Damascus. A month-long siege ended after bombardment of the walls had failed and the Franks built a wooden tower; the besieged, fearing destruction, surrendered. In a new siege in 1157 the Franks took refuge in the citadel, but aid came to the Franks and the siege was lifted. The walls were rebuilt and a second Muslim siege in the same year also failed. However, in 1164 Banias fell to the Muslims.

The fortifications of Banias as seen today probably largely pre-date the Franks. The walls surround a rectangular area measuring about 250 × 200 m. There are eight square towers, moats to the north and east and steep wadis on the west and south. The citadel was in the north-east corner. To the south were the town's two gates, reached by arched bridges built over the Wadi Sa'ar. Frankish remains include a row of Roman vaults which were rebuilt in the twelfth century.

Hebron (St Abraham, Ebron)

In the Crusader period Hebron consisted, as it had in earlier times, of two distinct sites: the Haram al-Khalil (the Herodian structure over the Cave of Machpelah known in the twelfth century as the Castle of St Abraham), and the town itself situated some distance to the east, either at Tel Hebron (Tel Rumeida) or in the valley between the tel and the Haram. The Franks converted the mosque in the Haram al-Khalil into a church. Little is known of the town, but the church has been discussed in length (Pringle 1993b: 224–39).

Hebron was held as a royal domain until 1161 when it was handed over to Philip of Milly and was joined with the Seigneurie of Transjordan. A bishop was appointed to Hebron in 1168 and the new cathedral church of St Abraham was built in the southern part of the Haram. After the fall of Jerusalem in 1187 Hebron was occupied by the Muslims and did not return to Frankish hands.

Lydda

Lydda was destroyed by the Muslims at the approach of the Crusading armies in 1099. The Franks rebuilt the town and fortified it, and built the cathedral church of St George over the traditional site of his tomb. Lydda became a bishopric, together with Ramla forming part of the diocese of Bishop Robert of Rouen which extended over a large area, from Mirabel in the north to Blanchegarde in the south. The church, which is the only Frankish building identified in Lydda, survives, incorporated mainly in the east end of a nineteenth-century Greek Orthodox church (Pringle 1998: 9–27).

Nablus (Neapolis)

Nablus was captured by Tancred and Eustace of Boulogne in July 1099 about ten days after the capture of Jerusalem. Tancred handed it over to Baldwin I, who built a small tower in the centre of the town (*Turris Neopolitano*) which served as the town's only defence. When the town was raided in 1184 the castle held out, but in July 1187 Nablus was occupied by Saladin's nephew, Husam al-Din and did not return to Frankish hands.

Although unfortified the city was important enough to have a royal palace, and the Hospitallers, the canons of the Church of the Holy Sepulchre and other religious orders held possessions there. Remnants of the tower are located near the al-Yasmin Mosque. Regarding the Hospital of the Knights of St John (Jami' al-Masakin), Benvenisti describes it as having been a courtyard building (Benvenisti 1970: 165). A barrel vault measuring 12 m × 6 m and part of a rib vault are all that survive. The Church of the Passion and Resurrection, which was converted into the Great Mosque of Nablus (Jam'a al-Kbir), was unfortunately largely destroyed by the earthquake of 1927. It has recently been described by Pringle along with some other Frankish remains in the city (Pringle 1998: 97–103). Although part of it has survived and been restored, the magnificent Gothic portal which can be seen in photographs (Enlart 1927: Plates 124–5; Pringle 1998: Plates LXV, LXVI, LXVII, Figure 25) was destroyed by the earthquake.

Nazareth

Nazareth, revered since the late Roman period as the site of the Annunciation, was occupied by Tancred in 1099. The Greek churches, including the Church of the Annunciation and the Church of St Joseph, were handed over to the Latins. By 1112 the town was the seat of a bishop and by the mid-twelfth century the Archdiocese of Galilee was transferred there from Beit She'an. At this time the cathedral church of the Annunciation was rebuilt. In 1170 Nazareth was largely destroyed by an earthquake. The town fell to Saladin after the collapse of the Frankish army at Hattin in July 1187. In 1219, al Mu'azzam 'Isa destroyed the town and its churches, but they were partly rebuilt after Nazareth was returned to the Franks under the terms of the treaty of 1229. In 1263 Baybars took the town, destroying the churches and slaughtering most of its inhabitants.

Parts of the Frankish church were uncovered during the construction of the new cathedral in 1955 (Bagatti 1984; Pringle 1998: 123–40) and very important sculptural finds have since come to light (pp. 194–5).

Nicosia

Nicosia is located in a fertile plain almost at the centre of the island of Cyprus on the River Pediéos. It was the capital of the island and the seat of the Latin archbishop. In the twelfth and thirteenth centuries it lacked fortifications but had a strong castle, probably the 'Castellum Nicossie' that appears on the seal of Hugh I (1205–18). A city wall was apparently constructed only in the late fourteenth century. In the sixteenth century the Venetians built an almost circular curtain wall with triangular bastions.

The Lusignan palace in Nicosia has not survived but a fairly detailed description of it was compiled by Enlart on the basis of various descriptions (Enlart 1987: 390–9).[22] It was situated in the lower market place beside the Paphos Gate. It may have been in existence prior to the period of Frankish rule, but it certainly underwent enlargement and embellishment under the new rulers of the island (Enlart 1987: 391). It had a loggia overlooking the square and contained a magnificent Great Hall built by Hugh IV above a vaulted basement.

Over eighty churches are recorded in the city, including the early Gothic cathedral of St Sophia described below (p. 137). There are also remains of the Archbishop's Palace and a number of remarkable medieval houses which were described and illustrated by Enlart (Enlart 1987: 402–14) (see Plate 2.14).

Ramla (Rames)

Prior to the arrival of the Franks, Ramla was an important city, founded in 717 as the capital of Jund Filastin; however, it had been badly damaged by Bedouin attacks in 1025 and by earthquakes in 1033 and 1067. The Seljuks, who had occupied the city in 1071, fled on the arrival of the armies of the First Crusade in June 1099. According to William of Tyre (1986: 10.16), the Franks constructed a fortified and moated stronghold. Once the threat of attack from Fatimid Ascalon subsided in the 1140s the town grew and prospered. In 1177 Saladin approached the town and the inhabitants, together with those of Lydda, fled to Jaffa and Mirabel. The Frankish army won a decisive victory over Saladin at Montgisart (Tel Gezer) but a few years later, following the Battle of Hattin in 1187, the town fell to the Ayyubid army. It served as a Frankish base during the Third Crusade and after 1205 remained in Frankish hands until Baybars took it in 1268. Other than some fragmentary remains discussed by Pringle (1998: 195–7), nothing of Frankish Ramla is known today, except for the very fine basilica church which is now a mosque (Pringle 1998: 187–95).

Plate 2.14 Nicosia: a medieval house near the cathedral of St Sophia (photograph by the author)

Tiberias

Tiberias was captured by Tancred in 1099. Being situated on the border it was subject to several attacks in the first half of the twelfth century and later served as a base for Frankish operations against Saladin. The siege initiated by the Muslims in June 1187 forced the Frankish army away from Saphorie to the Horns of Hattin, where the entire army was destroyed. Tiberias fell the day after the battle. It was recovered by the Franks in 1240 and the citadel was rebuilt, but the town was lost in 1247. A church and parts of the walls and citadel have been uncovered in the centre of the town (Razi and Braun 1992: 216–27; Pringle 1998: 351–66).

Yoqne'am (Caymont, Caimum, Mons Cain)

Caymont was settled in the first half of the twelfth century, when it appears to have been a village possessed by the monastery of Mount Tabor (Kedar 1996: 3). It later became a lordship in its own right, and in the thirteenth century its lord appears in the list of those privileged lords who had the right of *court et coins et justice* (holding seigniorial court and using seals). Caymont was lost in 1187 to Saladin, who camped there in 1191. In 1192 it was restored to the Franks and refortified. The town and citadel were finally lost in the 1260s.

Recent excavations at Tel Yoqne'am have revealed a church and tower, part of the town's double walls, and some streets and courtyard houses (Ben-Tor and Rosenthal 1978: 57–85; Ben-Tor *et al.* 1979: 65–83; Ben-Tor *et al.* 1996). The walls are not particularly impressive: the outer wall is a retaining wall no more than 1.2 m thick and the main inner wall is a mere 1.5 m thick. No towers have been found on the walls. The church of the Crusader period was built over an earlier church of the Byzantine period (fourth to seventh centuries). Houses built of ashlars and fieldstones and with paved courtyards have been found in different parts of the town. One such house had two courtyards, one of which contains a well-built latrine.

Notes

1 One should note, however, that several of the settlements that Pringle lists as towns were extremely small and their qualifications as urban settlements are very slim.

2 Gertwagen however paints a very negative picture of these ports in the Middle Ages (1996: 1511–27).

3 According to one account, in al-Aqsa Mosque alone the Franks slaughtered more than 70,000 people (Gabrieli 1989: 11), an amazing accomplishment considering that there were probably no more than 40,000 people in the entire city. William of Tyre gives the perhaps more reliable figure of 10,000 people killed in the Temple enclosure (William of Tyre 1986: 8.20).

4 As with the travel accounts these maps should be used with caution. They are

often merely copies of other maps and in many cases were probably drawn by travellers after they had returned to Europe. Consequently, not only because of medieval map-drawing conventions but also because of human fallibility, they are never very accurate.

5 A recently discovered parallel wall and rock-cut scarp some metres to the west has been dated to the Ayyubid period.

6 It was a common practice to construct a cistern under a tower which would afford a water supply in times of siege.

7 According to the twelfth-century account the street on the left hand side of St Stephen's Gate (i.e. the Valley Cardo) led directly to a postern called the Tannery (*City of Jerusalem* 1888: 17).

8 This may have been a leper house for men only, with the women being cared for in a separate house by the Tower of David (Clermont-Ganneau 1892: 112). No physical remains have been identified as belonging to the leper house. It has been suggested that Frankish masonry found in the area of the new municipality buildings to the north-west of the Old City may have come from this establishment. While this cannot be ruled out, it would seem more likely that the Quarter of St Lazarus was located further to the east, north of the supposed position of the postern, and close by a field known as Harat el-Birket (Quarter of the Pool), a possible reference to the Lacus Lazarus.

9 The new market indirectly preserves the Frankish name of the quarter. Muristan, which in Arabic (derived from the Persian) means hospital, was the name given by Saladin to the hospital he established there after 1187.

10 According to John of Wurzburg, the hospital had 2,000 in-patients, and as many as fifty might die in a single night (John of Wurzburg 1890: 44). The dead were cast into the great charnel house in Akeldama (p. 236). Additional information on the hospital can be gleaned from one of the statutes of the Order of the Hospitallers of St John in Jerusalem. It suggests that there was a fairly high standard of treatment and care, somewhat surprising in an age when medical care was notoriously poor. The text notes that four doctors were appointed for the sick (King 1934: 35). They were qualified to examine urine and to diagnose different diseases and administer medicine. Beds for the patients were 'as long and broad as is most convenient for repose' (King 1934: 35). Each bed had its own coverlet and sheets, and the patients were provided with cloaks, boots and woollen caps to wear when they went to the latrines.

11 Bahat believes that the masonry is not typical of twelfth-century building in Jerusalem (personal communication).

12 A document in the archives of the Church of the Holy Sepulchre (Bresc-Bautier 1984: no. 68) records a permit granted by the canons of the Church of the Holy Sepulchre to Arnulf, son of Bernald, to build a third and fourth floor on to houses built over arches, belonging to the canons.

13 Theoderich described the houses in Jerusalem as: 'lofty piles of carefully wrought stonework . . . not finished with high-pitched roofs after our fashion but level and flat' (Theoderich 1891: 5).

14 It has been discussed by Ellenblum (1987: 203–18).

15 Kedar gives a good account of the different views on this subject when presenting his own view (Kedar 1997: 157–80).

16 This theory is based on combined evidence from a sixteenth-century drawing of Akko, which shows extensive ruins east of the line of the Ottoman city wall, and

architectural and ceramic finds of Crusader date found well to the east of the Ottoman walls, as well as evidence from aerial photographs.

17 A thirteenth-century chronicler, the so-called Templar of Tyre, described the palace: 'At its entrance it had a high and strong tower, the wall of which was twenty-eight feet thick. On each side of the tower was a smaller tower, and on each of these was a gilded lion passant, as large as an ox' ('Gestes des Chiprois' 1887: 252–3).

18 Excavated by E. Stern (forthcoming).

19 It has been extensively discussed by Jacoby (1982: 205–17).

20 A very good account of the rise of Famagusta in the late thirteenth century is given by Jacoby (1989: 145–79).

21 This is the 'suberbio Joppensi prope portam, qua itur Hierosolyma' (Regesta Regni Hierosolymitani, no. 1085). After a prolonged period of neglect there is renewed interest in the Frankish remains at Jaffa. Excavations by the Israel Antiquities Authority are directed by Martin Peilstocker.

22 It is possible that the Turkish Serai was part of the palace (Enlart 1987: 398–9).

3 The rural landscape

It was long believed that the Franks did not settle outside the towns and fortresses and that agriculture remained almost exclusively in the hands of the local non-Frankish population. The organizational aspects of rural settlement have been described by Prawer (1980: 102–42), Richard (1985: 253–66) and others, and the remains of manor houses scattered throughout the kingdom are clear evidence that Frankish landowners or their representatives were in control in the countryside. However, the view that the Franks played a minor role limited to administration is no longer tenable and has been effectively challenged by Ellenblum (1998).

Land ownership and the rural population in the kingdom of Jerusalem

The Frankish administration replaced the Muslim organization based on the *Iqta'*, fiefs consisting of landed estates, towns, villages or even tax revenues or customs duty held in exchange for rendering service (including military service) to the government in Damascus and Baghdad. The land was divided between crown properties, lands held by the churches, lands held by the military orders and properties held by smaller landowners. Rather than requiring compulsory service in the lord's demesne, as was customary in the West, the Frankish landlords in the East received income from the tenants in the form of monetary payment or a portion of the produce. The rural population was segregated into separate villages of eastern Christians, Muslims or Franks and it would appear that there were no mixed Muslim and Frankish villages.[1] There were an estimated 1,200 villages in the kingdom of Jerusalem, about 900 of which Benvenisti and Prawer placed on their map of Palestine under the Crusaders (Prawer 1972: 356 and n. 3; Prawer and Benvenisti 1970: Part IX, Sheet XII). Ellenblum estimates that about 235 of these were Frankish settlements (Ellenblum 1998: Map I).

Taxes and tithes

Under the Franks there was an annual tax on land that was similar to the Muslim *kharaj* and was sometimes known in a latinized form as *carragium* or *terraticum*. It took the form of a portion of the harvest of arable lands, olive groves and vineyards, sometimes a quarter or a half but generally one-third (Richard 1985: 256). According to Ibn Jubair, the Muslim peasants surrendered half of their crops to the Franks at harvest time and paid a poll-tax of one dinar and five qirat per person (Ibn Jubair 1951: 316). Taxes were levied not only on arable land but also on bees and honey, on livestock, and on certain trees, most notably the olive (usually one-third of the oil). Ibn Jubair mentions a small tax on the fruit of trees (Ibn Jubair 1951: 316). The *portagium* was a tax levied on transporting grain to granaries or on the use of threshing floors (Prawer 1972: 376; Richard 1985: 257). There were payments for pasture rights. Muslim villagers were required to pay a tithe or *dime* to the Church (Runciman 1952 (vol. 2): 298–9); for example, tithes were paid to the bishop of the fief of Margat from villages, mills and olive presses, gardens and demesne lands (Delaville Le Roulx 1894–1906: no. 941). The tithe of *xenia* or *exenia* (a Greek term meaning gifts) was a payment in produce such as eggs, fowl, cheese or wood that was paid to the clergy at festivals (Tafel and Thomas 1856–57: 371). The military orders could also receive tithes: at the expense of the local churches, the Hospitallers were granted possession by Pope Paschal II of the tithes from demesne lands which they cultivated themselves and from produce that they used (Riley-Smith 1967: 43, 376).[2] This grant covered a wide range of produce including animals and fodder, *novales* (noval lands, i.e. previously uncultivated reclaimed land), first fruits, the produce of orchards and gardens, hay, wood, wool, flax, vegetables and fish (Riley-Smith 1967: 381).

Of course, archaeology supplies us with only indirect information on taxes and tithes. The numerous large, vaulted store-rooms found in the manor houses are the local equivalent of the tithe barns in the West, collection points for the taxes and tithes taken from the *villani*.

Monopolies

Peasants were required to use the lord's mills, ovens and other installations. This was through the lord's exercise of a monopolistic right known as the *bannum* (an old Germanic word meaning command or order). Seigniorial monopolies in the East are occasionally documented, as, for example, at ar-Ram (Prawer 1980: 134), Akhziv (Strehlke 1869: no.1) and in the famous *Pactum Warmundi* (William of Tyre 1986: 12.25). In all probability the peasants sometimes tried to circumvent some of the *bans*. In the West, peasants were frequently fined for having furtively used hand-mills (querns) in the privacy of their homes (Bennett 1969: 129–33). We can assume that in the East, where from earliest times hand-mills were present in most houses, the local peasants would try whenever possible to make use of them. Whether this was the case in Frankish villages is less clear, but in excavations at both al-Qubeiba and al-Kurum hand-mills were found in some houses.

The structure of the native *casalia* and the status of the local peasants

There were isolated farms, referred to in the sources as *curtiles*, but in general rural settlement was in the form of villages and hamlets which, together with farmlands, were granted as fiefs.[3] These were known in Frankish sources by the French term *ville* or the Latinized French *casale*. In addition to simple village dwellings, there would be communal installations such as cisterns, threshing floors, dovecots, mills and ovens. The *casalia* differed considerably in size, from about three to thirty-eight families per village in the lordship of Tyre, around forty male inhabitants in the *casalia* around Safed and, in the region of Ascalon, about twenty families per village (Prawer 1980: 160, 167; Tafel and Thomas 1856–57: 398). There were larger villages in the area around Nazareth (Runciman 1954: 297–8). The headman who was chosen from one of the families (*hamula*) to serve as intermediary between the Frankish overlord and the village peasants (*villani* or *rustici*) was the *rais*, known in Latin as *raicius*. There might be more than one *rais* to a village and Prawer mentions that there were sometimes three (Prawer 1972: 367), but this was probably exceptional. The *rais*, aided by a council of elders, represented the lord in the village, an important post in a period when absentee landlords were the rule. He supervised the farming, attended to the collection of taxes and administered justice. His house was larger than those of the other villagers, and he held considerably more land. The *dragoman* was a hereditary administrative office that originated in the post of interpreter. There was sometimes also a *scribanus* or scribe. The court of the *rais* dealt with the business of the estate, including such matters as disputes between the villagers, fines for offences against the regulations and perhaps purchases by the villagers for the upkeep of the property and repairs. Unlike the Frankish villagers, the status of the native peasants was often similar to that of serfs in the West. They were considered the property of the lord, not free but tied to the lands which they could not leave, alienate or otherwise dispose of, and they were obliged to pay part of their produce to the landlord. However, there was in general no demesne.[4] Like the Frankish *villani*, the local peasants were required to use the lord's mills, ovens and other installations.

To date very few twelfth-century villages of the local peasantry have been excavated. A village to the north of Jerusalem called Khirbat Ka'akul was excavated in 1991 (Seligman forthcoming). A section of a second village near the town of Petah Tikva was excavated in 1996 (Vitto and Sion in preparation). These villages show little evidence or organization; in design and construction of the houses and in the street plan they are similar to local Palestinian villages of both earlier and later periods.

The Frankish *villani* and the planned villages

Frankish villages were economically dependent on the towns and depended for security on either towns or castles. Thus we find large concentrations of villages in close proximity to the towns, in the case of the kingdom of Jerusalem particularly around Jerusalem, Akko and Tyre. Rural settlement appears to have taken two forms: settlement in local villages, alongside (but not mixed with) local peasants; and new settlements in planned villages (Figure 3.1).[5] Both documentary and archaeological evidence shed light on new, planned villages, the equivalent of the western European *villesneuves*, which were set up by the Franks in the twelfth century.[6] In these settlements serfdom was completely absent and the settler was *liber homo*. He could alienate his land, although the landlord had pre-emption rights, and was not required to cultivate the lord's demesne. On the contrary, the seigniorial lord did not retain any land and the villages were composed only of peasant holdings, with the settler devoting his entire labour to his own land. Instead of labour requirements the peasant paid an annual tribute known as the *terraticum* or *terragium*, generally one-third of his crops and a tax on fruit trees. The *villani* were required to use the lord's mill and ovens but, as in the West, these and other monopolies did not debase their personal status or exploit them (Pirenne 1936: 73).

What motivated the Franks to set up these organized settlements? It seems likely that they were primarily intended to fill specific needs of the Frankish population and of the Church which were not satisfied by the local peasantry, such as the raising of pigs or the manufacture of wine. It is difficult to estimate the number of Frankish villages. Clearly these were few in comparison to those of the indigenous population and there seems to have been a much greater number of estate centres occupied by overseers and agents maintaining the interests of absentee landowners. We can do no more than speculate as to whether this movement by the Franks into the country-side might have eventually brought about the creation of a substantial Frankish peasantry, but events cut short the process when the majority of the countryside was lost in 1187.

Much of our information regarding Frankish rural activity comes from written sources, including twelfth-century documents describing the terms of agreement between landowners and settlers in the villages established at Beit Govrin and Casal Imbert. Casal Imbert was a royal foundation established in the mid-twelfth century. According to the terms of settlement, the inhabitants received houses rent free together with a plot of land for tilling and for a vineyard and garden. Each peasant gave the king a quarter of his crop. Olive growing was organized on a communal basis: the groves were divided amongst the inhabitants but harvesting was a collective effort. The king received two-thirds of the produce. The king held a monopoly (*bannum*) over certain installations such as the bakery and bathhouse. At Beit Govrin the Hospitallers founded a settlement of freemen around the fortress. Each

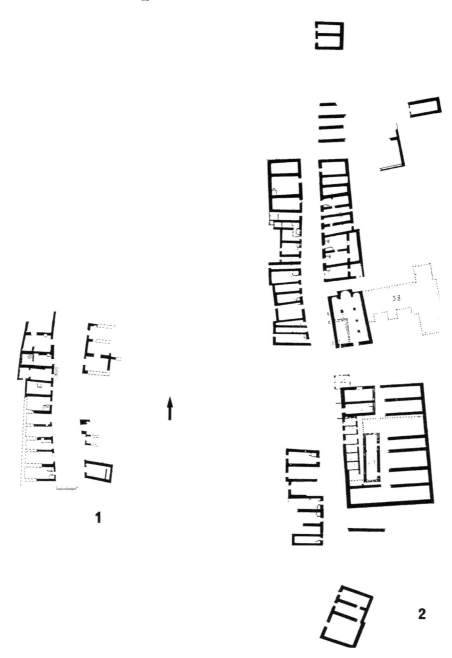

Figure 3.1 Planned Frankish villages. 1. Khirbat al-Kurum; 2. Khirbat al-Qubeiba
(after Bagatti 1993)

settler received two *carrucae* of land for cultivation and on which to build a house. In return he paid the order an annual land tax (*terragium*) and part of his produce. There were also ecclesiastical establishments, with the Church of the Holy Sepulchre being particularly active in this field. This church held numerous properties in the Jerusalem area. One of these, al-Bira (Magna Mahumeria), was established in the third decade of the twelfth century. The settlers received land for farming and on which to build their houses, in return paying the *terragium* to the church. The villages in the area around Jerusalem were primarily involved in grape and olive growing and the production of wine and oil. Wine was intended not only for the church but also for sale in the towns and even for export. Around Akko and Tyre, in the Jordan Valley and elsewhere, sugar-cane and other crops were grown.

The planned villages built by the Franks in the twelfth and thirteenth centuries had little in common with the traditional village in the Near East, which typically had a nucleated form with houses surrounding an open area containing communal buildings and the outer houses abutting one another to provide a type of defensive outer wall. Such villages were a form of natural growth, developing over a long time without intentional planning, whereas the Western-type village introduced by the Franks consisted of a central axial road lined on either side by a row of houses on long, narrow plots.

The use of the linear plan in the layout of Frankish villages is significant. Its advantages are clear – land could be quickly and evenly parcelled out. However, this type of settlement is extremely difficult to defend against attack, and its appearance here points to the success of military and administrative measures taken by the Franks in the first quarter of the twelfth century to improve the internal security of the hinterland. These measures included the occupation of all the large towns and the neutralization of Ascalon, the only city that remained in Fatimid hands, by the construction of a ring of castles around it.

We know of four such villages in the vicinity of Jerusalem: al-Qubeiba (Parva Mahumeria), al-Kurum, al-Bira (Magna Mahumeria) and al-Haramiya (Vallis de Cursu). Akhziv (Casal Imbert) in the north may possibly have had a similar plan (Benvenisti 1970: 221–2). Only limited and unpublished excavations have been carried out at al-Bira. However, al-Qubeiba (Bagatti 1947; 1993) and more recently al-Kurum (Onn and Rapuano 1995: 88–90; Boas 1996: 583–94 and forthcoming) have been extensively excavated, and the newly discovered village at al-Haramiya has also been partly excavated. Combining the evidence from these sites enables us to produce a fairly accurate picture of the typical twelfth-century Frankish village in the Holy Land.

The anatomy of a Frankish village

On the basis of the combined information from the planned villages, each of which adds something to the overall picture, we can describe a typical planned Frankish village of the twelfth century. In the centre of the village (al-Bira, al-Qubeiba) or on a hill above it (al-Kurum, Wadi al-Haramiya) stood the manor house, sometimes incorporating a fortified tower. The church was located at one end of the village (al-Bira) or at its centre (al-Qubeiba), on the street. The houses were small and narrow, averaging about 4 m × 10 m (internal measurements) but varying from site to site and even within a single village (Figure 3.1 (1,2)). They are constructed with thick rubble and ashlar walls. The side walls that supported the vaults are about two metres thick, built with fieldstones and rubble fill. They were plastered on the interior. Door frames and thresholds have the typical Frankish

Plate 3.1 Khirbat al-Kurum, a house with an undercroft (photograph by the author)

Plate 3.2 A house at Wadi al-Harimiya (courtesy of Yehiel Zelinger, Israel
   Antiquities Authority)

diagonal dressing. As the houses share their side walls and the front and back
walls often run the length of several houses, it is obvious that the village was
constructed as a single enterprise and over a short period of time. Many of
the houses probably had two storeys, with a work area and storage on the
ground floor and living quarters above (Figure 3.2). At al-Bira the upper
storey of a house, with internal walls subdividing it into smaller rooms,
survives. The fact that the ground floors of many of the houses are given
over to work areas with installations, and the occasional presence of stairs,
suggests that there must have been upper floors that served as living areas.
In many of the houses there were wine and oil presses and some had fireplaces
(Plate 3.3). Access to the upper storey could have been by a staircase or a
ladder. Some houses also had an undercroft, partly excavated in the bedrock
and partly constructed, reached by stairs from inside the house or directly
from the street. Water was collected on the roofs and fed cisterns via pipes
and channels that ran along the streets. An oven for baking bread was built
into the wall of a house at al-Qubeiba. The fields were measured according
to the standard unit employed to divide land: the ploughland or *carruca*,
reckoned by Prawer at an average of 35 ha (86.45 acres).[7] A more realistic
estimate is given by Ellenblum, who suggests that the *carruca* must have
been close to the European *carruca* which was only three or four ha (7.4–9.9
acres) (Ellenblum 1998: 98–9, n. 15). It is estimated that 36 to 40 bushels
of corn were a minimum requirement for a normal family. A crop of this size
in the West required holdings of between five and ten acres, and probably

Figure 3.2 Khirbat al-Kurum: isometric reconstruction of a house (drawn by the author)

nearer ten (Bennett 1969: 95). In organized settlements Frankish *villani* appear to have generally received one or two *carrucae*. Archaeological evidence for land divisions is limited. In the one instance where the fields of a Frankish village can be identified and measured, at al-Kurum, the average field measures 8 m × 46 m, that is a mere 368 square metres. This is nowhere near Prawer's 'official' *carruca*, but it is exactly half a 'local' *carruca* which appears to be equivalent to the Western toft or garden plot. The villagers must have held additional lands beyond these fields.

Manor houses and farmhouses

Terminology is frequently a clumsy tool, leading us into misunderstanding almost as often as it leads us out of it. The group of buildings popularly known as Frankish manor houses are a case in point. In the kingdom of Jerusalem there are a large number of rural buildings that have been so designated. However, the manorial system with its serfs and demesne land did not actually exist in the Latin East. Nonetheless, this term seems to have stuck and one can perhaps accept its use, considering that even in the West

Plate 3.3 Khirbat al-Kurum: a fireplace (photograph by the author)

where the manorial system originated, the term 'manor' is often used in a very loose fashion.

These buildings are easily dated by their typically Frankish building techniques and features. Their functions are hinted at by the presence of large vaults that could have served as stables, work areas for various industries or storage space for taxes collected in the form of produce such as grain, olives and grapes, or manufactured goods such as oil, wine or sugar. They also served as the residences and administrative centres of the landowner or his caretaker (*locator*).[8] The ground plans always include a hall-house or a tower, sometimes both. The hall-house rarely stood alone. It was probably always built with the intention of enclosing it with walls or incorporating it into a larger complex. Hall-houses were elongated structures with ground-floor storage or stabling and with a large solar or hall on the upper floor reached by stairs built within the walls. A typical example is the hall at Beit 'Itab (Bethaatap), situated 17 km west-south-west of Jerusalem. Pringle identifies the northern, barrel-vaulted undercroft (13.3 m × 29 m) as an earlier phase of this courtyard building (Pringle 1997: 26–7). It has an arched doorway 1.39 m wide in the middle of the south wall with slit machicolation and a single-leaf door. A staircase inside the wall leads up to the living quarters on the first floor.

Another example of a hall-house is Khirbat al-Burj (Khirbat al-Jauz) located at the top of a hill above the village of Khirbat al-Kurum, on the road between Montjoie and Jerusalem. Here there are the remains of an elongated structure measuring internally 15 m × 18 m with the entrance to the east. The fieldstone walls are 1.4–2.35 m thick, with four windows. The interior was divided by an internal wall, there was a cistern, and a staircase was built into the thickness of the eastern wall.

Together with the hall the other features of the manor house were the enclosed courtyard or farmyard and a number of additional vaulted structures which could serve for storage, stabling and shelters for agriculturally related activities. The majority of these buildings fall into one of two categories: (1) courtyard-attached farmhouses (buildings consisting of one or a number of vaults with a walled enclosure attached to them), and (2): courtyard buildings (buildings constructed around a central courtyard) (Figure 3.3).

Courtyard-attached farmhouses

Courtyard-attached farmhouses generally have a large main building and a number of smaller structures around the walled courtyard. In some cases their irregular plan clearly reflects the evolution of a single vaulted building to a larger complex with several vaults and installations and is perhaps evidence of the expansion of Frankish rural activity prior to 1187.

Har Hozevim

A farmhouse in this Jerusalem neighbourhood was completely excavated in 1993–4 and subsequently destroyed (Kletter 1996: 62–3; May 1997: 81–4). The main structure was an elongated two-storey building. The ground floor was a barrel-vaulted room measuring 12 × 19 m. It had two doors, the main one to the east and a smaller one to the west. There were no windows on the ground-floor level, and light would have entered only through the doors. The floor was of bedrock to the west and of stone flags to the east. On the eastern side of the room there were three arched ovens as well as two *tabun*s (clay ovens used for baking) and a stone table. There was also a large, plastered cupboard built into the eastern wall. This ground floor was clearly a work

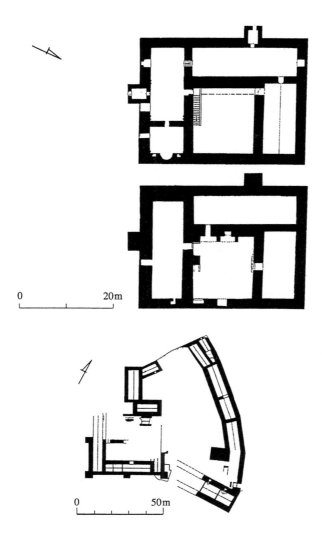

Figure 3.3 Frankish manor houses: 1. Aqua Bella (after Pringle 1992); 2. Burj
   Bardawil (after Pringle 1994).

area, apparently the bakery of the local landowner to whom the neighbouring villagers would have been required to bring their wheat to be milled and
baked.

   In the thickness of the northern wall of the main doorway was a staircase
to the second storey, which would have been the living quarters. When it
was built early in the twelfth century the farmhouse probably consisted of
this structure alone. At a later stage two smaller, barrel-vaulted rooms were

added on either side of the main door, and at about the same time additional vaults and enclosures were built within a walled courtyard.

Khirbat al-Lawza

Khirbat al-Lawza to the north-west of Jerusalem is another complex of this type which has recently been partly excavated (Ellenblum *et al*. 1996: 189–98) (Plate 3.4). Built on three stepped terraces, it consists of a massively constructed barrel-vaulted hall measuring 21 × 5.5 m (internally) which probably represents the first stage of the complex. It has five embrasure windows on the eastern wall, and there was probably a second storey. A group of smaller, barrel-vaulted buildings surrounded a courtyard measuring about 29 × 40 m (Figure 3.4). The main gate to the courtyard was to the east, on the southern side of the hall. To its south-east is a large, trapezoid, plastered reservoir.

Burj Bardawil

One of the best examples of this class is Burj Bardawil (Baldwin's Tower) situated 32 km north of Jerusalem on the modern Ramallah bypass. The complex has two structural phases, the second phase consisting of a courtyard-attached building. At its centre is a fortified courtyard building, apparently of

Plate 3.4 Khirbat al-Lawza: remains of the farm (photograph by Ronnie Ellenblum)

Figure 3.4 Khirbat al-Lawza: reconstruction of the farmhouse (drawn by David
Hully, courtesy of Ronnie Ellenblum)

earlier origin, which originally had two storeys. It measures 22 m square and
has a *castrum*-like plan with projecting turrets (Pringle 1994a: 38).[9]

On the slope to the north-east is the second phase of the complex,
consisting of a sequence of barrel vaults forming a fan-shaped enclosure. The
largest vault, known as *al-Babariyya*, is 41 m long and internally 6.9 m
wide.[10] The side walls are 3 m thick. The vaults below enclosing the courtyard are 6.25 m wide (internally) with walls 2.4 m thick. Just north of the
eastern end of *al-Babariyya* are the remains of a gateway 2.5 m wide. This
may have been the main entrance to the complex in its second phase.

Courtyard buildings

Ar-Ram (Aram, Rama, Ramatha)

At this site just north of Jerusalem there is a rectangular range of barrel
vaults around a central courtyard (Pringle 1983: 160–74). A tower in the
south-west corner probably pre-dates the courtyard building. The tower
measures about 12 × 15 m and its walls are nearly 3 m thick. Four large
vaults and a number of smaller ones make up the courtyard complex. The
vault to the north, the western range of the complex, was the first to be built.
It has now collapsed. The eastern vault range is 30 m long and about 11 m
wide. It has two doors and three windows in its western wall. A small, half-
vaulted range runs north–south between the eastern and southern ranges.
It partly obscures the two southern windows of the eastern vault and is
obviously of later date, as is the vault range to the south which abuts it. The

southern range was apparently about 8.9 m wide internally and possibly about 25 m long or longer, perhaps originally extending further west to the south of the tower. West of the tower is what appears to have been an outer range dating somewhat later to the rest of the complex and at the north-west corner are remains of what may have been another, later tower. The court-yard covers an area of 30 × 25 m.

Jifna (Jafenia?)

This is a large, rectangular courtyard building above the road from Jerusalem to Nablus. On the eastern side there is a monumental gate with a portcullis. There are rooms to either side of the passage from the gate. To the north there is a large, barrel-vaulted hall measuring 23.30 × 7.40 m (internally) and 6 m high. The walls are of fine-quality masonry and are 2.40 m thick. This vault contains an olive press.

Aqua Bella

This is the largest and best preserved courtyard manor house in the kingdom of Jerusalem. It was built on the side of a valley situated opposite Abu Ghosh on the road between Jerusalem and Jaffa (Enlart 1928: 103–6; Benvenisti 1970: 241–5; Pringle 1992: 147–67, 1993b: 239–50). The structure measures 27 × 36 m. The northern side of the ground floor was cut into the limestone of the valley slope, the stone being roughly cut and used in its construction. The stones used for architectural details such as door jambs, lintels, window frames, stairs and quoins were cut from a softer stone which was transported to the site from a distant quarry. These were tooled with a fine diagonal combing and frequently display masons' marks. At the centre of the structure is a square courtyard, measuring 15 × 15 m. It is entered from the east. On three sides of the courtyard are barrel vaults, probably used for stabling and storage. The southern vault contains an olive press. On the south of the courtyard a stone staircase leads to the upper level where there is a groin-vaulted chapel (Plate 3.5). The other vaults on this level were probably used for residential accommodation, kitchens and storage.

Agriculture and rural industry

As noted above, Frankish activity in the countryside took place on two levels: (1) administration of the local peasantry and control of agricultural production and of agriculturally related income (taxes and tithes) maintained through the establishment of numerous estate centres throughout the countryside; and (2) settlement of a Frankish peasantry in the countryside either through the expansion of existing villages or by colonization in new planned settlements. By these means the Franks utilized rural resources and asserted some degree of control over the non-Frankish peasant population.

Plate 3.5   Aqua Bella: courtyard and chapel (photograph by the author)

The extent of this activity is an academic question, as there is no way of knowing what proportion of the hundreds of *casalia* that are mentioned in contemporary sources had a Frankish or partly Frankish population. With increasing archaeological research the picture is constantly changing; whereas until 1992 only one of the planned Frankish villages had been excavated, two additional villages and a farmhouse have since been discovered and excavated and a number of Frankish farmhouses have been surveyed. Nonetheless, the information available today is too limited to permit generalization.

Another possible problem, though one that is perhaps not much easier to solve than the size of the Frankish presence, is whether or not the Frankish peasantry was involved in the same types of agriculture that occupied the local peasantry. What was the impact of the Franks on agriculture in Palestine? Did they introduce new farming techniques, crops, livestock or equipment? If we accept that they never intended to become, or at any rate never did become, an agricultural society but rather relied on a predominantly local peasantry, we can assume that their influence was largely restricted to administrative matters such as collection of taxes and tithes. Where they may have had an effect on the local agriculture was in the increase of viticulture and the raising of pigs, and of sugar-cane production, the former two mainly to fulfil their own needs and the latter to increase their income from export to the West.

The countryside

Throughout most of Palestine the local peasantry practised a simple mixed agriculture which often yielded little more than subsistence. It was mainly in the fertile coastal plain that agriculture was more profitable; here there were fields of grain, orchards, vineyards and sugar-cane plantations. The villagers were not necessarily more prosperous, but the landlords were able to make large profits.

With the approach of the autumn rains the farmers ploughed the fields and the important winter crops, wheat and barley, were sown on some of them. Another part was planted with legumes, and the third part, known in Frankish sources as *garet*, was left fallow until the spring ploughing, after which it was sown with the summer crop or vegetables. In the spring and summer the fields previously planted with corn were left fallow and those which had been planted with legumes were turned over to summer crops or left fallow. The following year the fields were rotated.[11] The principal summer crops were sesame, chickpeas and millet. Olives and grapes were the other main crops, as well as figs and, in certain regions, dates, citrus fruits, cotton and sugar.

Crops and rural industries

Amongst the wide range of produce of Palestine mentioned in medieval sources we find citrus fruits, various types of nuts including almonds from Moab, dates from Zoar, Beit She'an, Darum and Jericho, figs from Ramla (fresh and dried), bananas, apples, cherries, indigo from the region of the Dead Sea, Jericho and Beit She'an, rice from Beit She'an, millet and spelt, sugar-cane grown in the Jordan Valley and on the coast, plums, sycamore fruit, carobs, sesame, balsam, rose hips, shaddock, jujube fruit, mandrake, sumach, lupin and others.[12] Many of these plants were comparatively new to the Near East,[13] but most important were the traditional crops of the Mediterranean region: olives, grapes, wheat and barley. Olives and grapes were grown in the foothills and on mountain terraces. Under the Franks olive plantations and vineyards were usually grouped together (Riley-Smith 1973: 42). In Cyprus olives were grown all over the island and grapes were grown in large vineyards, particularly in the south (Richard 1985: 275–6).

Cereal crops, mills and ovens

The cereal crops on the mainland were concentrated in the area between the coastal plain and the hills, and in the broad valleys, but some grain was grown on the terraced hills of Judea, Samaria, the Lebanon and Jabal Ansariyah to the north. In Cyprus cereals were the main crop and much of the land was appropriate for their cultivation, particularly the Mesaoria plain in the north-east. Carbonized grains have been found at a number of sites but have not been published. Indeed, very little archaeological evidence for agricultural produce has been published and at present one can cite only the material from the excavation of the Red Tower (Burj al-Ahmar) near Tulkarm in the Sharon plain.[14]

A farmer would bring his grain to the lord's mill (*molendinum*) where it was ground, and use the lord's oven (*furnum*) for baking. In return for the use of these facilities he had to pay a stipulated number of loaves to the lord. The presence of a mill together with the bakery was probably typical. Since the lord had a monopoly on both milling and baking, it was natural that for convenience the mill and bakery were combined. The combination of these two institutions at one site is also suggested by the fact that in many documents which include lists of possessions, the oven and mill are mentioned consecutively (*furnum et molendinum*). Bakeries frequently appear in Frankish documents and there is some archaeological evidence for them. Ovens were found at 'Atlit attached to the western side of the bathhouse in the faubourg. They were located in a room which had originally been covered by a light timber roof resting on arches (Johns 1997 II: 126–8). It contained two domed ovens, one constructed of stone, the other of flat bricks. Nearby was a large basalt rotary mill. According to the excavator, this bakery shared the heat source of the bath. He excavated an additional oven attached to the house in the north-east of the town but gives no description of it.[15] Kaplan excavated what he interprets as a thirteenth-century bread(?) oven at Jaffa (Kaplan 1966: 282). He describes it as consisting of a barrel-vaulted outer ceiling, the oven itself measuring 2.5 × 3.5 m. The construction is of sun-dried bricks, some of which were found fused together by the heat of the oven. The vault was supported by two walls, with a row of pillars dividing the underpinnings of the oven into two parts. The oven was heated by hot air flowing from a sink near its entrance into chimneys built along the sides of the structure. Large communal ovens are found at Abu Ghosh (De Vaux and Stéve 1950: 99, Figure 28), at Crac des Chevaliers (Deschamps 1934: 269–74) and at Kerak (Deschamps 1939: Plate 17b). One was recently (1997) discovered at Vadum Jacob (Ellenblum and Boas forthcoming) and another at Nebi Samwil (Magen and Dadon forthcoming). A bread oven was excavated in the south-east corner of House 23 at al-Qubeiba (Bagatti 1993: 94, Plate 20). It was fairly large and probably served the needs of all the village residents. All that survives of this oven is a stone platform just above floor level and a roughly semicircular area partly covered with a vault. It measures 3.36 × 2.5 m. The vault was constructed of rough stones covered with plaster containing sherds. In the main vault of the farmhouse at Har Hozevim, north of Jerusalem, there was an oven with three connected stone arches built directly in front of a low stone wall (May 1997: 82) (Plate 3.6). The space between the arches and wall was originally left open to allow the smoke to escape. It was later blocked up and the installation apparently ceased to function as an oven, becoming instead a raised platform at one end of which was set a small bread oven (*tabun*). Around the installation were an

Plate 3.6 Har Hozevim: ovens in the main building (courtesy of Natalie May, Israel Antiquities Authority)

additional three *tabun*s and a large table formed of a monolithic stone slab raised on stone feet. In the anteroom to the north of the main doorway there were additional arched constructions; these could not have been ovens, as they had no opening at the top to release smoke, but were possibly used for storage of wood. The presence of a substantial baking installation in this rather isolated location suggests that it may have been a communal bakery for farmers from the neighbouring farmlands.

Viticulture and wine manufacture

Wine manufacturing installations were found in a number of houses in the villages of al-Qubeiba and al-Kurum (Plate 3.7). They consist of large treading vats with stone pipes at the base through which the grape juice flowed into collecting basins carved in the bedrock floors. These installations were constructed near the doorways of the houses, leading Bagatti to the unlikely conclusion that these houses were shops and that the installations were vats holding wine for sale.

In the aftermath of the Muslim conquest in the seventh century there was probably a certain decline in viticulture and the manufacture of wine. However, the Islamic laws, while forbidding the drinking of wine, did not prohibit the eating of grapes and grape sugar, nor the drinking of unfermented grape juice. Local Christian communities remained a significant part of the population up to the time of the Crusades; they, together with

Plate 3.7 Khirbat al-Kurum: a grape-treading vat in a house (photograph by the author)

the Jews and Samaritans, required wine for their liturgy and were permitted to produce it. Nonetheless, the great expansion of this industry that took place in the Byzantine period, and that is so vividly evident in the countless wine presses unearthed in archaeological excavations, certainly came to an end. Under the Franks there was a certain revival. We cannot, on the basis of present evidence, estimate how great this was, but the numerous wine presses found in Frankish rural sites, notably in the villages at al-Qubeiba and al-Kurum, hint at this trend.

Olives and oil production

Olives were grown over much of the hill country of the Near East and of Cyprus, as they are today. Olive-oil manufacture probably suffered no decline under Muslim rule, but may have increased during the twelfth century with the opening of new markets in the West and a rising local demand from the churches. Olive presses (*molendinum olivarum*) are found at many sites, including Aqua Bella, Jifna, Lifta, Beituniya, al-Kurum, al-Qubeiba and al-Haramiya (Plate 3.8). As there is no apparent difference between those in use in earlier and later periods and those in use during the twelfth and thirteenth centuries, we cannot normally date them to the Crusader period. However, in some cases, as at Jifna, they are located in Frankish buildings with openings too small to have allowed them to have been placed there at a later date. This does not rule out the possibility that the millstones were

Plate 3.8 Khirbat al-Harimiya: millstones of an oil press (courtesy of Yehiel Zelinger, Israel Antiquities Authority)

of earlier date, but it does clearly establish that they were set up and in use in the Crusader period.

Sugar plantations and refineries

The cultivation of sugar-cane (*canamella*) and the refining of sugar (*zuccarum*) were established in the Near East before the Crusader period. Under Frankish rule the Italian merchant fleets opened up the virtually unlimited Western market to this product, and large tracts of land in well-watered regions were turned over to cane growing.[16] These included parts of the coastal region, particularly around Tyre and Akko, the Beit She'an Valley, the Jordan Valley, the region of Jericho and around Montréal (Shaubak) in Transjordan. In the thirteenth century and particularly after the loss of the Frankish mainland in 1291, the cultivation and manufacture of sugar moved to Cyprus and became one of its most important crops and industries.[17]

Refineries were set up in rural centres and in the neighbourhood of towns as well.[18] A number of sugar mills are known and have been surveyed (Porëe 1995: 377–510). A mill and refinery north-west of Akko at Manueth (Khirbat Manawat) has recently been partly excavated (Stern forthcoming). In Cyprus excavations have been carried out at the mills of Episkopi and at Kolossi (Plate 3.9).

The most complete excavation of a sugar installation is that of the mills at Kouklia (Old Paphos) in Cyprus. A combined Swiss–German team from the German Archaeological Institute and the University of Zurich headed by M.-L. von Wartburg and F.G. Maier have published detailed reports of the excavations of the refinery which was the centre of the royal sugar production of the Lusignan estates in the Paphos region (von Wartburg and Maier 1989: 177–88, Plates lviii–lxiii, 1991: 255–62, Plates lxv–lxx). It consists of a storage area to the north, the grinding hall with two water-powered mills fed by an aqueduct (Plate 3.10), the refinery hall with its eight ovens and the stoke-rooms to the south.

The process of sugar milling and refining involved harvesting the cane which was cut into short lengths (15–20 cm long). These were conveyed to water-powered mills, where they were chopped, crushed and boiled in bronze vats. This process was repeated a number of times depending on the quality of sugar desired. The syrup (molasses) was then placed in ceramic funnels or moulds and allowed to drip into large jars (Figure 6.1(5)).[19] The sugar crystallized in the moulds, and the end product was large conical lumps of crystallized sugar from the moulds and jars of molasses.

Garden produce

In medieval sources the garden is mentioned frequently, as *hortus* or *gardinum* (or *zardinum*). *Hortus* in general probably refers to an orchard, whereas *gardinum* is a place where flowers, vegetables and herbs were grown.

Plate 3.9 Kolossi: the sugar refinery (photograph by the author)

Vegetables included cucumbers, melons, garlic, mustard, fennel, sage, rue and mallow. Onions were an important export crop in Cyprus (Richard 1985: 275). The diet of members of the Templar Order as recorded in the Rule of the Temple included, alongside meat, fish, eggs and cheese, various products of the garden such as lentils, beans and cabbages (de Curzon 1886/1977: 139).

Remains of small broad beans (*Vicia fabia minor*), a type usually grown for animal fodder today, chick-peas (*Cicer arietinum*), lentils (*Lens culinare*), grass peas (*Lathyrus sativus*), barley (*Hordeum distichon*) and bread wheat (*Triticum aestivum*) were found in the medieval levels at the Red Tower (Hubbard and

Plate 3.10 Kouklia: the sugar refinery (photograph by the author)

McKay 1986: 187). Fruit trees included apples, peaches, pistachios, plums, oranges, lemons, bananas (known as apples of paradise), figs, dates, pomegranates, almonds and carobs.

Animal husbandry

Since the earliest times the Near Eastern peasant has been occupied with the raising of sheep, goats, cattle, horses, mules, camels, pigs and fowl. In the period of Frankish rule this continued, though with certain changes in emphasis. In a list of the names of settlers at Magna Mahumeria (al-Bira), surnames appear which denote the occupations of some of the residents. These include three names connected to animal husbandry: *camelarius* (camel raiser or camel driver), *caprellus* (goatherd) and *porcarius* (swineherd). The camel (*camelus dromedarius*) appears as a pack animal on some versions of the thirteenth-century map of Akko drawn by Matthew of Paris, in one instance being led by the *camelarius* (C. Corpus Christi, Cambridge CCC, MS 16). Camels were not only used for transport but also for ploughing or to work a mill or antilliya (wheel mechanism used to raise water from a well). They were also raised for their milk and meat. The donkey was mainly used as a pack animal. It also appears on one version of the map of Matthew of Paris (C. Corpus Christi, Cambridge CCC, MS 26). The horse played a more important role in Frankish life and we are well acquainted with its importance in warfare (Plate 3.11). The chief task of the horse in farm life was to

Plate 3.11 Vadum Jacob: a horse killed on 30 August 1179 in the Ayyubid attack
(photograph by Buki Boaz)

pull the plough. In the West the horse gradually replaced the ox from around
the tenth century, and the effect of this development was enormous. The
horse was some 50 per cent faster and could also work longer hours.[20]
However, at present we lack archaeological evidence for the use of the horse
in agriculture in the East, and in all probability the transfer from ox to horse
did not occur.[21]

In the Near East cattle (*Bos taurus*) maintained their traditional
importance, fulfilling various tasks in agriculture and in transport. Oxen
were used to carry heavy loads and to plough, and cattle were the most
important source of both meat and milk. In addition to supplying wool,
the domestic sheep (*Ovis aries*) and goat, (*Capra hircus*) were important
supplementary sources of meat and milk. As with the manufacture of wine,
the raising of pigs probably underwent a revival in the Crusader period.
Islamic law expressly forbids their consumption, and in most sites during the
period of Muslim rule the ratio of pigs in comparison with cattle, sheep
and goats is low.[22] When Christian rule was restored under the Franks the
raising of pigs must have enjoyed a considerable increase. The pig is valued
because it rapidly reaches the stage where it can be slaughtered and, being
an omnivore, it is easy to feed. Domestic pigs are kept solely for meat.
Because they are a competitive food consumer with humans, it is more
economic for a farmer to keep only a few pigs into adulthood for breeding
purposes and to slaughter most of them while still young (Kolska Horowitz

and Dahan 1996: 252). At Caesarea the majority of pig bones are indeed from young pigs (Cartledge 1986: 178). It is often difficult to distinguish between the bones of wild and domestic pigs, but they were probably not wild boar, as we would have expected to find a number of mature pigs if they were wild animals that had been hunted.

Fowl are a good source of protein and require a relatively low energy investment (Kolska Horowitz and Dahan 1996: 252). They were sold at a special market in Jerusalem (*City of Jerusalem* 1888: 7). Archaeological evidence for the presence of fowl takes two forms: bones found in excavation and columbaria. At the village of al-Kurum there is a small horseshoe-shaped columbarium, possibly for pigeons. As it is completely cut into the bedrock it is impossible to date, but at the nearby farmhouse at Har Hozevim a constructed chicken coop was excavated (Plate 3.12). It was a long, narrow structure (3 × 6 m) with a row of eight coops probably with wooden roofing along one wall (May 1997: 83–4).[23] Chicken bones (*Gallus domesticus*) were found around the keep at Beit She'an. At the Red Tower bones of domestic geese were found (Cartledge 1986: 178) and at Yoqne'am domestic fowl were found (Kolska Horowitz and Dahan 1996: 247).

There is a long-established tradition of beekeeping in Palestine. In the medieval period there was probably a decline in apiculture due to the high increase in sugar production, but there is evidence that honey and wax were exported (Goitein 1967: 125) and honey was sold in the markets of Tyre. One

Plate 3:12 Har Hozevim farmhouse: a chicken coop (courtesy of Natalie May, Israel Antiquities Authority)

source mentions the measure used for honey (Tafel and Thomas 1856–57: 371). In Cyprus, according to the Venetians, wax and honey were amongst the principal products of the island: 70–90 tons of honey a year and about 18 tons of wax (Richard 1985: 280). There is no archaeological evidence at present of honey production and we do not know whether the Franks used beehives made of perishable material such as sunbaked mud, wood, or cow manure, which would leave no trace, or if they employed brick-built hives or hives made of piles of horizontally laid pipes. In Cyprus, according to one account, bees were raised in hollows made in the walls of houses (Richard 1985: 280).

Evidence for the cost of various commodities is given by Joinville. A sheep was valued at 80 livres, an ox at 80 livres, a pig at 30 livres, an egg at 12 deniers, and a measure of wine was worth 10 livres (Joinville 1921: 208). As local production was not always sufficient to fill the needs of the Franks, grain and poultry were imported from Egypt (Mayer 1988: 185). Evidence for the import of pigs, sheep, flour and wine can be found in Joinville's statement that at the time of the feast of St Remigius he found it necessary to stock up on such items, because provisions became dearer in the winter due to the danger of sea transport (Joinville 1921: 261). With the loss of the hinterland in 1187 and the decrease in arable lands in the thirteenth century, the kingdom of Jerusalem came to rely more heavily on imports. This need was particularly acute in the 1270s, when it was necessary to import hens, pigs, wheat, legumes, cheese, salt meat, wine, oil, beans, chick-peas, walnuts and barley from the kingdom of Sicily (Pryor 1988: 134, 137).

Agricultural methods and implements

Ploughing in the Near East traditionally involved the use of a simple stick-plough or hook-plough. In western and northern Europe the use of the heavy, deep-cutting wheeled plough, with a metal colter, flat ploughshare and a mouldboard to turn the soil became widespread in this period, substantially increasing yields (Gimpel 1988: 43). The wheeled plough was a heavy piece of equipment requiring a large team of plough animals, up to eight oxen, and the difficulty in turning the plough at the end of the field resulted in the replacement of broad fields by narrow, elongated strips of land. The deep ploughing with the colter resulted in the distinctive ridges and furrows. In the East, to the amazement of Joinville, the wheel-less wooden plough was retained (Joinville 1921: 182). It was better suited to the climate and soil conditions: if the soil was too deeply ploughed it would dry out, a problem that farmers did not face in most of Europe. A contemporary illustration of ploughing is found on a thirteenth-century map of the Holy Land by Matthew of Paris (Corpus Christi, Cambridge MS 26). It shows a single ox pulling a simple stick-plough. In some places, particularly in the hilly regions, even the lightweight plough could not be used and the soil was

Plate 3.13 Vadum Jacob: a sickle (photograph by Buki Boaz)

broken up using hoes (Prawer 1972: 360). For reaping, the medieval sickle in Europe had a toothed cutting edge which minimalized the loss of grain by decreasing the shaking of the ripe ears. In the Near East in recent times both smooth-bladed and toothed sickles were in use (Avitzur 1976: 23–5), but the few examples of medieval sickles that have been found at Vadum Jacob, Har Hozevim and elsewhere appear to have had smooth blades (Plate 3.13). The iron sickle found at Har Hozevim near Jerusalem is nearly complete, with only the point missing. The maximum width of blade is 2.5 cm and it is only about 30 cm long, including the 10 cm-long handle tang. The more effective harvesting tool, the scythe, has been in use in the West since the twelfth century for cutting hay, but its use as a grain-harvesting instrument began only in the fourteenth century and did not reach the Latin East. Nor did other medieval innovations such as the flail used for threshing, and on the whole the great strides made in farming equipment in western Europe do not appear to have crossed the Mediterranean with the Franks. Some of the new tools, like the wheeled plough, were simply less suitable to conditions in the East, and no doubt the local peasants preferred to stick to their traditional methods.

Notes

1 Who were the peasants? The Frankish chronicler Ernoul and the Granadian pilgrim Ibn Jubayr claim that the majority of peasants were Muslims, while the Andalusian Ibn al-'Arabi claimed that the eastern Christians were in control of the countryside. B.Z. Kedar suggests that these observations reflect the situation in different parts of the kingdom (Kedar 1990: 148–9) and J. Prawer considered the indigenous peasant population to have been predominantly Muslim (Prawer 1969: 1: 570).

2 In cases where crops did not accord with this latter requirement, in order to avoid episcopal taxation they probably induced the villagers, through threat or persuasion, to change their crops.

3 Fiefs could take other forms, such as money fiefs (*fié en besans*).

4 A possible exception is hinted at in the labour services carried out by peasants on the sugar plantations in the village of Casal Imbert (Riley-Smith 1973: 46, n. 79). An even better example concerns a certain lord of Caesarea who borrowed 1,000 bezants from the Hospitallers in 1213. The terms of the agreement for repayment between the two parties included labour services of peasants from three villages held by the borrower (Riley-Smith 1973: 46, n. 78). Peasants from villages held by the Venetian commune in Tyre gave one day's work for each carrucate they possessed, and a charter of 1132 mentions fishermen from two villages held by the canons of the Holy Sepulchre giving the Prince of Galilee labour services of one day each year (Riley-Smith 1973: 46, n. 80).

5 Frankish *villani* may also have settled in abandoned villages.

6 According to Riley-Smith, all the known planned villages were established in the twelfth century and this activity ceased when the Franks lost control of the hinterland in the thirteenth century (Riley-Smith 1987: 62).

7 Prawer calls this the 'official *carruca*' (Prawer 1980: 158). Corresponding to the local *faddan rumi* or the Western *mansus*, it is the area that can be ploughed by a team of oxen in a year. It varies somewhat in different sources, and Richard mentions one assize giving the *carruca* as 75 acres (Richard 1985: 254). Riley-Smith gives it as only 25–6 acres (Riley-Smith 1973: 42). Prawer mentions a second 'local' or 'Saracen' *carruca* as the area of land that can be ploughed by a team of oxen in a single day. This is equivalent to the *faddan arabi*, which varies in size from 734 square metres in hilly regions to almost twice that in the plains (Prawer 1980: 157–9). This measure is always reserved for measuring vineyards or olive groves rather than for arable lands. Wastelands, known as *gastinae*, were used for communal pasture. Since many documents refer to *casalia* as having both pasture and *gastinae*, the latter term was probably used to describe distant pasturelands or, as Riley-Smith suggests, uncultivated lands (Riley-Smith 1967: 434; 1973: 44).

8 Ellenblum considers these buildings to have been the residences of better-off rural settlers rather than of estate officials (Ellenblum 1996: 197).

9 I use the term *castrum* here in its classical sense, i.e. as an enclosure castle with corner towers. In the Middle Ages it took on new meanings and Ellenblum points out that it was used in the Latin East to refer to newly established walled settlements (Ellenblum 1998: 33).

10 The name *babariyya* is a distortion of the Latin *boveria*, meaning ox shed. See Benvenisti 1982: 130–52.

11 The importance of leaving a field fallow for a year or two was not only for the revitalization of the soil but also in decreasing the number of pests that attacked the roots of certain plants, as many of these would die off if the crops they fed on were not planted every year.

12 For mention of these see Muqaddasi, Bakri, Idrisi, Nasir i-Khusraw and various letters from the Cairo Geniza. Processed products of the countryside included dyes, raisins, wine, dried rose petals and rose petal preserves, olive oil, wine and processed sugar.

13 Discussing the introduction of new crops from the East into the early Islamic world and the slow progress of their diffusion from there into Christian Europe in the Middle Ages, Andrew M. Watson expresses the opinion that this was due to the general inability of the Franks to grow specialty crops apart from sugar-cane (Watson 1981: n. 22). He blames not only the Frankish farmer but also the lack of skills of the European peasantry, their lack of incentive to achieve high yields (because of the comparatively low population density in the West), the lack of agricultural manuals available to them, the inability of feudal land-holding arrangements to receive some of the new crops and the limited use of irrigation in the West (Watson 1981: 35–6). Watson sees the period of Frankish rule as detrimental to Near Eastern agriculture, with previously widely grown crops disappearing and being replaced with less specialized land use, notably grazing and the cultivation of wheat, barley and other traditional European grain crops.

14 This site was excavated in 1983 by a team from the British School of Archaeology in Jerusalem headed by Denys Pringle and published in 1986 (Pringle 1986b). Chapter 8 of the report deals with medieval plant remains (Hubbard and McKay 1986: 187–91).

15 The unpublished field diary of the excavations at 'Atlit by C.N. Johns is in the archives of the Israel Antiquities Authority in the Rockefeller Museum, Jerusalem.

16 Evidence for this is mentioned by Marino Sanudo, who notes that the Teutonic Knights had considered turning over to sugar-cane some of their lands in western Galilee which had previously been cultivated with wheat and barley (Sanudo 1972: 93).

17 Sugar-cane cultivation may already have reached the island in the tenth century, but only on a small scale, and in the twelfth century sugar was being imported to Cyprus from Transjordan (Benvenisti 1970: 253).

18 Sugar vessels have been found in storage in the Hospitaller compound in Akko and a sugar refinery is mentioned as having been in that city (Lyons and Jackson 1997: 18), but E.J. Stern suggests that it was most likely located outside the town walls.

19 Sugar moulds and jars are frequently found at sites associated with the industry, even when evidence for the mill itself is absent.

20 Its introduction in the West was slow because of a natural prejudice against change. Jean Gimpel compared it to the tractor which replaced the horse in the twentieth century (Gimpel 1988: 35).

21 An illustration of ploughing on the map of Matthew of Paris shows an ox pulling the plough (Corpus Christi, Cambridge CCC, MS 26).

22 This is not always the case; in Caesarea, for example, the pig remains dating from the Islamic period are very substantial. In Tyre, prior to the Frankish period, a

tax (*tuazo*) was levied on pig-butchers (Prawer 1980: 186). Part of the population must have remained Christian and perhaps the Islamic codes were often not followed by those who did convert. No doubt the eating habits of that part of the population which was forcibly converted resisted change.

23 A latch from one of the coops was found *in situ*.

4 The defence of the Latin East

Even in their most secure period in the mid-twelfth century, the Frankish territories were constantly exposed to the danger of assault. Defensive structures are consequently the type of buildings that most characterize the period, and even non-military buildings including churches, urban houses and farms often display elements of a defensive nature. During the twelfth and thirteenth centuries the Franks built numerous castles in the East. Rather than seeing them as attesting to the strength of the Franks, we should perhaps regard the castles as the most tangible evidence of the instability of their holdings in the East. On a more positive note, they can also be seen as evidence of the resourcefulness of the Franks, and they are a most eloquent testimony to Frankish innovation and inventiveness.

Castles played an important role in defence, though there is some disagreement as to exactly what this role was. R.C. Smail put to rest the old idea that they formed a defensive line along the borders of the kingdom (Smail 1987: 204–20). Rather than the massive castle walls, it was the combined use of castle and field army that allowed the Franks to retain their hold on the East. Their defensive strategy centred around the idea that their safest option was to avoid direct battle whenever possible. When it could not be avoided the castles served to house troops and supplies.

Defence was not the castle's only function; it also played an important role in internal administration. As in the West, a strong castle was a means for a landowner to demonstrate and maintain his overlordship. The Frankish countryside, particularly that of the kingdom of Jerusalem, is dotted with small castles which certainly played no part in frontier defence, were not placed alongside important roads, and were too small to have housed a large garrison. Their main function appears to have been as fortified administrative centres.

Castles also served as places of refuge in troubled times and their very existence gave a sense of security to the surrounding villages. Settlements grew up in the shadow of castles, looking to them for protection. When Fulk built the castle of Blanchegarde in 1142 villages grew up around it and, according to William of Tyre, the whole area became populated and much safer (William of Tyre 1986: 20.19).

The programme of castle building continued throughout the twelfth and thirteenth centuries. There are about a hundred castles in the kingdom of Jerusalem alone. In discussing them we should first define precisely what constitutes a castle. If we include all fortified buildings we must discuss city fortifications, some churches and monasteries and even farms and some urban houses. There are scholars who advocate a broad definition but in a discussion of this nature it is more practical to confine ourselves to independent, fortified structures which were built primarily to fulfil one or a number of military functions.

Amongst the many by-products of Frankish rule in the East, the achievements in the art of castle building rank high. Wherever the sources of their design lay, and this is a subject that has been under debate since the late nineteenth century (Oman 1898; Lawrence 1988), Frankish castles advanced within a very short period from the most basic, one might say primitive, types to highly complex and remarkably inventive buildings displaying the highest understanding of military architecture. The Franks exhibited a proficiency at borrowing and adapting from others, and a genius at inventing entirely new types. The first of these qualities is demonstrated by the employment of two simple designs: the fortified tower, which had its source in the towers of western Europe, and the *castrum* or enclosure castle, a Roman invention which had become common on the eastern borders of the Byzantine Empire and was later adopted by the Muslims. The second quality is best seen in the evolution of a completely new type of castle, the double *castrum*. The Franks also utilized and developed other castle types: hilltop castles and spur castles. These developments took place in the twelfth century, and with each type the Franks were responding to a particular need. Towers were built in order to establish regional administration. The *castra* (at least those around Ascalon) were intended to serve as lookouts against small-scale incursions. Double *castra* and hilltop and spur castles, placed in sensitive border positions, served as outposts for large garrisons and held supplies for an army in the field, but they were probably intended mainly as a show of Frankish strength.

There is a considerable distance between the simple keep-tower and the superior and often complex spur castle, and there is no apparent direct line of development. Although it was often the case, castles of a sophisticated design did not always replace the more basic types. Square or rectangular towers, while mostly dating to the first half of the twelfth century, were still being built in the thirteenth century, for example, at Qal'at Jiddin. *Castra* were built for most of the twelfth century, although none seem to post-date Hattin. The complex spur castles and castles with concentric lines of defence date mainly from the later twelfth and thirteenth centuries, but Kerak was built as early as 1142 (although it is hard to tell at present what form it took at that early stage). While constantly improving their art, the Franks used the type of castle most appropriate in a given situation. The two factors determining castle design were the intended function of the castle and the topography of the site.

Typology of the Crusader castle

Any attempt to categorize Frankish castles cannot be entirely satisfactory because of the complexity of castle design, which T.E. Lawrence aptly described as 'a series of exceptions to some undiscoverable rule' (Lawrence 1988: 37). Although many castles seem to fall easily enough into one or other classification (keeps, enclosure castles (*castra*) and spur castles) some do not, either because they belong to none of these types or because they conform to more than one category. In a general overview of the kind presented here, a basic typology, with all its shortcomings, is indispensable. With the vast amount of discussion that has taken place and in the light of recent fieldwork, it is possible to present a fairly detailed typology. There are four main types: towers, enclosure castles (*castra*), hilltop castles and spur castles. These can be subdivided into seven categories: (1) towers (isolated towers, towers with outworks, castle keeps which form part of a larger castle); (2) *castra* (enclosure castles); (3) '*castrum* and keep' castles (castles combining the *castrum* with the keep); (4) defended *castra* (enclosure castles with outworks); (5) double *castra* (concentric castles); (6) spur castles; (7) hilltop castles (Figure 4.1).

Towers

The Franks built their first towers before they even set foot in the Holy Land. In 1097 and 1098, during the siege of Antioch, the Crusaders constructed three towers with the aim of preventing Turkish sorties. One, outside St Paul's Gate, was named Malregard. A second one, named Mahomerie's Tower, was on a mound at the western end of the bridge across the Orontes, opposite the Bridge Gate. A third stronghold was constructed opposite St George's Gate in the south. Named Tancred's Tower, it made use of an existing fort and monastery. These towers were examples of the most basic type of castle: the Frankish tower keep. In the first half of the twelfth century many such towers were constructed throughout the Frankish-held territories. These were built primarily by landowning nobles as centres of regional administration. This explains why these towers are concentrated not in border areas but rather in the interior, particularly in fertile areas where agricultural activity was intense. In the West at the time of the First Crusade, the Normans built fortified towers in order to establish their rule over the districts they held. These were of the simple 'motte-and-bailey' type, a wooden tower on an artificial hill with a bailey surrounded by a moat and with wooden palisades. In the East the Franks dispensed with the earthen mound or motte and replaced wood with stone.[1] These castles generally appear to have had some sort of outworks enclosing a courtyard with the tower at the centre.[2]

The strength of the tower lay in its massive walls often three or four metres wide, with few and narrow openings. When under attack they could offer only passive defence. The chief disadvantage of these castles lay in the

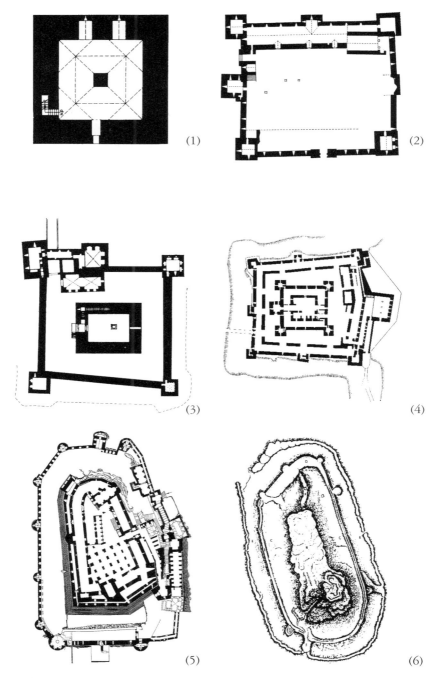

Figure 4.1 Comparative chart of Crusader castles

fact that they could be very easily placed under siege, although Lawrence perhaps exaggerated when he suggested that this only required two men, one each side of the door (Lawrence 1988: 23). They certainly played only a very minor part in offensives as they could not house more than a limited garrison. However, they could accommodate in some comfort an overseer and a few knights. Some of these towers apparently contained a hall where court sessions could be held, and most of them had spacious vaults where agricultural produce, taken as taxes and tithes from the villages in the region, could be stored. In times of danger the local Frankish population would take refuge within their walls.

Towers in the Latin East seem never to have been more than two storeys high, the only exceptions being perhaps the western tower at Qal'at Jiddin and the tower at Jaba' (Gabaa) (Pringle 1994c: 339).[3] Their height was limited because of the weight of the stone vaulting. Some of the towers were quite small: the tower of Maldoim on the road to the Dead Sea measures a mere 9.3 × 8.5 m and that at nearby Beit Jubr at-Tahtani 9.5 × 6.6–8.1 m (Pringle 1994b :159–165). Quite a few towers consisted of a single barrel vault or two parallel barrel vaults on each of the two floors. Pringle has listed some seventy-five towers in the kingdom of Jerusalem, some of which were undefended and some with outworks (Pringle 1994c). Some of the larger examples had four, six or even nine connected groin vaults supported on one or two piers. Occasionally the ground floor was barrel-vaulted and the upper floor had groin vaults. This was the case in the Red Tower. At Qal'at Jiddin there were two barrel vaults on the ground floor and possibly nine groin vaults carried on four piers on the first floor. Stairs in the castles were built either in the thickness of the wall or (as at Beit She'an) against an interior wall, but in some cases there was an external wooden staircase.[4] Lighting was usually via arrow slits which, when they also served defensive functions, were usually on the first-floor level. As at Beit She'an and al-Burj (Qal'at Tantura), there was sometimes a slit machicolation or a portcullis above the door. Floors were of packed lime, flagstones or stone slabs. There was often a cistern under the ground floor (Beit She'an, Montfort, Yoqne'am, Gibelet). Occasionally latrines were built into the walls (Kolossi, Qal'at Jiddin).

The finest towers are in the north: these include Chastel Rouge and Chastel Blanc in the county of Tripoli. Qal'at Yahmur (Chastel Rouge) is a typical twelfth-century Frankish tower situated on a plain south of Tortosa in the county of Tripoli. It was probably built in the first half of the twelfth century but is almost totally ignored in historical sources until 1177–78, when it was given to the Hospitallers by Raymond III of Tripoli. Like other castles in the region, Qal'at Yahmur remained in Frankish hands after the Battle of Hattin and for most of the thirteenth century until it was captured by Qala'un in 1289. The keep measures 16.2 × 14.1 m and the walls are 1.8–2.2 m thick. The ground floor, which was entered from the east, consists of four connected groin vaults supported on a 2 × 2 m central pier. The first floor was originally divided into two levels by a wooden mezzanine floor

3.5 m above the floor level. There is a small door in the east wall of the ground-floor level and a larger one in the west wall of the first floor. A pair of corbels remains from machicolation above the ground-floor door. The first floor was probably reached by an external wooden staircase which has not survived. There were also stairs from the first floor to the second-floor level built in the thickness of the north wall. This unusual arrangement meant that there was no direct communication from inside the ground floor to the first-floor level. The first floor is also roofed by four groin vaults, separated by transverse arches and supported on an octagonal pier. Light reached the first-floor level through several arrow slits in the south wall. There are broader windows in the east and west walls. The outworks consist of walls 1.9 m thick enclosing an area of 37 × 42 m. Small towers in the north-west and south-east corners are perhaps later additions.

Safita (Chastel Blanc), located on the top of a steep hill in the north of the county of Tripoli, is one of the finest Frankish towers (Plate 4.1). Guarding the landward approaches of Tartus, it was built early in the twelfth century, probably before 1112. It was damaged by an earthquake in 1170 and sacked the following year by Nur al-Din. Subsequently Safita was held by the Templars, who carried out a major reconstruction of the castle. It was not attacked by Saladin after the Battle of Hattin but was damaged by earthquake for a second time in the early thirteenth century (Kennedy 1994: 138).

The impressive form of the keep of Safita, towering above the village of Burj Safita dates from its reconstruction, carried out perhaps shortly after the earthquake or by Louis IX, who is mentioned in an Arab source as having strengthened the castle. In 1271 it fell to Baybars. Although this is difficult to see today because of the modern structures surrounding the castle, in the Crusader period Safita was enclosed within two outworks: an outer polygonal ring-wall and an inner wall of uncertain shape. The outer defences included at least two towers and several vaulted chambers, including a large first-floor hall, rib-vaulted in the Gothic style. The tower keep itself was unusual in design, being elongated whereas most towers are square or nearly square.[5] The ground floor contains a high, barrel-vaulted chapel dedicated to St Michael. The chapel is illuminated by arrow slits and has an apse to the east. A staircase constructed in the thickness of the wall leads to the upper floor, which is a rather splendid groin-vaulted hall, perhaps a dormitory, its roof supported by three massive piers. The masonry of the interior is remarkably fine although lacking in ornamentation. Rather than being merely a tower, Safita can be defined as an *eglise-donjon*, a church-keep.

In the kingdom of Cyprus there is a fine keep at Kolossi, about 9.5 km west of Limassol on the Limassol–Paphos road. A castle existed at Frankish le Colos (or Colosso) since at least the reign of Hugh I (1205–18), when it was in the possession of the Hospitallers. After the loss of Akko in 1291 the Hospitallers intended to establish a new centre at Kolossi. Their subsequent move to Rhodes changed this decision but Kolossi served as the seat of the

Plate 4.1 Chastel Blanc from the west (photograph by Jonathan Phillips)

Grand Master of Cyprus and became the centre of a wealthy Hospitaller estate. After damage by the Genoese raids in the fourteenth and early fifteenth centuries, the keep was largely restored by the Grand Commander of Cyprus, Louis de Magnac (*c.* 1450–68) and perhaps by the Venetians, who took possession after 1488.

The tower is three storeys (21 m) high including the basement. It measures 16 × 16 m with walls 2.7 m thick. There are two doors to the south, one leading to the basement and one on the ground-floor level which is now reached by an arched staircase. High above them is a machicoulis carried on six brackets. Above the eastern door is the royal coat of arms of

Cyprus as well as the shields of the two Grand Masters and that of the Grand Commander. On each face of the building are two windows. Inside, beneath the staircase which leads to the upper levels, is a cistern which is fed by a conduit from the roof. The ground floor was probably used for storage while the second storey contained what was probably a kitchen as well as the castle hall. The kitchen has a large open fireplace and a spiral staircase in the southeast corner. This gives access to the upper storey which may have served as the residence of the Grand Master. On this level there are two rooms; both have large hooded fireplaces decorated with shields with a fleur-de-lis. They have windows with window seats and one has a latrine built into the thickness of the wall. The staircase also gives access to the roof. The remains of the surrounding courtyard include various outbuildings and to the east is a sugar mill and refinery.

Excavations have recently been carried out at two keeps in the kingdom of Jerusalem: Tour Rouge (Burj al-Ahmar) and Beit She'an. Tour Rouge is situated in the Sharon plain west of the town of Tulkarm. It was excavated in 1983 by a team of archaeologists from the British School of Archaeology in Jerusalem headed by Pringle (1986b). The tower was built some time during the first half of the twelfth century, possibly by the lord of Caesarea or by the Benedictines of St Mary Latin, to whom one of the lords granted the adjacent village and lands (Pringle 1986b: 127). It was subsequently held by the Templars, probably from around 1191, and from 1248 by the Hospitallers. In 1265 it fell to Baybars. The castle was a two-storey structure measuring 19.7 × 15.5 m, apparently without a moat but with a wall enclosing an area measuring approximately 60 × 60 m. The tower had walls 2.2 m thick. The ground floor consisted of two parallel barrel-vaulted chambers with a flagstone floor. The upper storey had a hall of six connected groin-vaulted bays supported on two piers. Light entered the keep via narrow arrow-slit-like embrasure windows.

In the early Islamic period, probably around the ninth century, most of the population of Beit She'an moved from the area below the ancient mound to a new location on a hilltop to the east of the amphitheatre. There had been a settlement in this area since the Byzantine period but it now became the centre of the medieval town. Beit She'an was captured by Tancred in 1099 and was held by the Franks until 1183 when Saladin sacked it, though it probably remained in Frankish hands until after the Battle of Hattin in 1187. Saladin refortified the town in 1192. During the Fifth Crusade Beit She'an was sacked, and in 1240 it was returned to the Franks. It was lost again, for the last time, in 1260.

Although only a few traces of Frankish construction have been uncovered in the area surrounding the castle, Frankish Beit She'an was probably situated in the immediate vicinity, around the tower. Topographically the castle is situated at the highest point of this area, higher than the ancient mound. The tower is a two-storey square structure measuring 17.3 × 17.3 m with walls over 3 m thick (Plate 4.2). The door is in the northern wall. The

Plate 4.2 Beit She'an: the Frankish keep (courtesy of Jon Seligman, Israel
Antiquities Authority, photograph by Gabi Laron)

ground floor consists of two adjacent barrel vaults. Stairs built against the
western wall led to the upper storey, which has not survived. The keep is
surrounded by a courtyard with barrel-vaulted chambers lining the enclosure
wall. The enclosure wall has corner towers and a gate to the east, in line with
the door of the keep. This outer gate was reached via a drawbridge across the
moat. Archaeological and literary evidence indicates that the moat was filled
with water, an exception in the East, where moats were typically dry. The
only other exceptions to this rule are at Caesarea and 'Atlit, where sea water
filled the moats. When excavations cleared the moat at Beit She'an two
indications of its having been water-filled were noticed: a layer of travertine
(lime) coated the scarp and counterscarp from the base to the top as well
as the pillars supporting the drawbridge; and on the floor of the moat,
under later fill, a silt layer was uncovered which contained large numbers of
shells of freshwater snails (Seligman 1995: 39). In one of those fortunate cases
where the written sources support the archaeological finds, a fourteenth-
century text by the historian Ibn al-Furat describes the fortress at Beit She'an
as 'a small modern citadel built by the Franks, entirely surrounded by water
except where one can reach it by a bridge' (Lyons *et al.* 1971: 46).

Other towers worth noting are Saffuriya (Tsipori), a 15 m square keep
with walls 3.75 m thick, which incorporates antique *spolia* in its construction,
Mirabel (Migdal Afeq), a tower probably built before 1152 which measures
13 × 13.9 m and has walls 3 m thick and outworks including an outer

enclosure wall with a talus and towers, and the Templar road tower of Maldoim (Ma'ale Adumin) on the road between Jerusalem and the Dead Sea. This last is unremarkable in itself, being a small two-storey tower measuring a mere 9.3 × 8.5 m, but it has additional vaults and an impressive rock-cut moat.

Towers were not only built to stand on their own but were often employed as an integral part of a larger castle. I am not referring here to the salient towers built along castle walls but to the main tower of the castle, the keep or *donjon*, a massive building which was intended to serve as a final refuge if the enemy breached the castle walls. Such castle-keeps should be considered as a sub-type. Being merely one feature in a larger castle, their function was somewhat different from that of the isolated keep. Amongst the examples of such towers are the great round tower of Margat, 20 m in diameter and 24 m high, and the keep of Montfort, which is 25 m long and has an apsidal wall to the east suggesting that it was perhaps another *eglise-donjon*.[6] A more regular keep, but one which is remarkable for its size and preservation, is that of the castle of Saone (Sahyun) in the principality of Antioch (Plate 4.3). It forms part of the defences of a great twelfth-century spur castle. Some time before 1132 the Franks expanded and enhanced a Byzantine castle by the addition of towers and curtain walls around the spur and a deep moat to the east. The keep forms part of the eastern defences of the fortress directly over the rock-cut face of the moat. It is a large, two-storey, square tower measuring

Plate 4.3　Saone: keep and fortifications in the south-east (photograph by Jonathan Phillips)

24.5 × 24.5 m, with groin vaults on both levels supported by central piers. It is 22 m high with massive walls 4.4–5.4 m thick. Stairs constructed into the thickness of the wall lead from the ground to the first floor and from there to the crenellated roof, which has survived almost intact.

The castra (enclosure castles)

In answer to specific defensive/offensive needs, the Franks adopted a type of fortress that was in common use in earlier periods: the enclosure castle or *castrum*. This was generally a larger castle than the tower but it too was of a basically simple design: in this case a quadrangular area was enclosed by curtain walls. The *castrum* had corner towers and occasionally interval towers placed at regular distances along the walls. Its advantages were that on the one hand the simple design allowed for easy and quick construction, and on the other that the towers and long stretches of curtain walls with numerous firing positions allowed this type of castle to play an active defensive role. The *castrum* was not new to the region. In Greek *tetrapyrgion* and Latin *quadriburgium*, the four-cornered fort developed out of the Roman fortified camps and in the late Roman and Byzantine periods the design was used for frontier forts, notably those in North Africa. *Castra* built in the late Roman and Byzantine periods in the region include Tamara in the eastern Negev which dates from the third century AD, and a fourth-century *castrum* at Ain Boqek on the west bank of the Dead Sea. The use of this type of fortress continued into the early Islamic period. Under the Umayyads the desert palaces of Khirbat al-Mafjar in Jericho and Khirbat al-Minya by the Sea of Galilee were built in the *castrum* form, as were coastal forts at Ashdod Yam and north of Caesarea at modern Habonim. Both these *castra* were probably used by the Franks from the moment they fell into their hands. Habonim or Frankish Cafarlet (Kafr Lam) is a small castle situated 8 km south of 'Atlit. It was held at times by the Hospitallers and by the Templars. It is a fairly well-preserved trapezoidal structure measuring 57/42.5 E–W × 63 m N–S, and built of sandstone ashlars. It has round towers at the corners and additional towers on either side of the gate to the south. The walls, 1.5–2.3 m thick, were strengthened by external buttresses. This castle has never been properly examined but a plan has recently been published (Pringle 1997: Figure 31). Ashdod Yam, Frankish Castellum Beroart has round corner towers with solid bases and a gate to the east and west, each flanked by two towers.[7]

In the past the use of *castra* by the Franks has been seen by historians like Charles Oman and others as evidence that Frankish fortifications owed little to the West and were mainly influenced by Byzantine military architecture. This idea was challenged first by Lawrence and later by Smail and others. In the case of the *castra* the more direct influence of Muslim architecture has to be considered. There was little direct contact between the Franks and North Africa and the local Umayyad forts are more likely to have served as prototypes (Pringle, introduction in Lawrence 1988: xxxvi).

The Frankish use of the *castrum* plan is known both from surviving examples and from written sources. From 1136 on we hear of the use of the *castrum* design in castles built by the Franks. William of Tyre describes the *castra* which were built around Fatimid Ascalon (William of Tyre 1986: 14.22, 15.24–5, 17.12, 20.19). At Darum the king built a small, square fort with towers at each corner, one of which was more massive and better fortified than the others. Yavne (Ibelin) was a castle with four towers, Blanchegarde (Tell es-Safi) had four towers of equal height and Beit Govrin (Beit Govrin) was more complex, with an outer wall with many towers and a moat. At Gaza there was a similar *castrum*. Of these *castra*, only Beit Govrin has been excavated.[8] It has proved to be of a more complex design than was once believed (see p. 106). Other Frankish *castra* survive at Mi'iliya and possibly at Yalu and Hunin. Smail and Benvenisti include Vadum Jacob (Chastellet) in this category. Benvenisti includes Belvoir (Kochav Hayarden) and calls the *castrum* 'the commonest type among Crusader fortresses in the country' (Benvenisti 1970: 281). However, Vadum Jacob, now under excavation, was not a *castrum* and Belvoir is a more developed type of castle (see pp. 106–8).

The *castrum* of Coliath, south-east of Chastel Rouge in the county of Tripoli, was built after the Franks captured the site in 1118. In 1127 Count Pons of Tripoli gave it to the Hospitallers. They held it, except for a period in the 1140s when it was in the hands of the Assassins (an extremist Shi'ite sect in Jabal Ansariyah, Lebanon) until 1207–8, when it fell to al-Malik al-Adil and was dismantled. Some time later Coliath was recovered by the Franks and was rebuilt, and by 1243 it was in the possession of the Templars. It fell to Baybars in 1266 and was partly dismantled.

Coliath is a classic *castrum*, a rectangular structure measuring 63 × 56 m with corner towers and additional towers at the mid-point of each wall except to the south, where the gate is situated between two small turrets. With its corner towers, one taller than the others, it is reminiscent of William of Tyre's description of Darum. A barrel-vaulted undercroft ran the length of the northern wall and possibly the southern wall as well.

In western Galilee, 22 km north-west of Akko, another *castrum* stands at the centre of the village of Mi'iliya in the royal domain, Frankish Castellum Regis. The castle was first mentioned in 1160. At about that time it came into the possession of a knight named Henri de Milly. In the 1170s it was held by Joscelin de Courtenay and perhaps rebuilt at that time; it was also known as Castellum Novum (Pringle 1997: 71). In 1220 Mi'iliya was sold to the German Teutonic Order, which held it until it fell to Baybars in 1268–71.

At the high point of the town is a rectangular *castrum* with square corner towers. The northern side with its towers survives to its full original height. The corner towers on the south-east and south-west were somewhat larger than the others measuring 9 × 9 m. The tower on the north-west stands on a slightly different alignment. Little is known of the interior of the castle and it has never been excavated. A survey carried out by the British School of Archaeology in Jerusalem produced a plan of this castle, which shows that the interior was divided north to south by a wall that perhaps supported a barrel-vaulted range along the east side, with a doorway near the south.

On the western side of the Hula Valley is Qal'at Hunin (Chastel Neuf). This castle, which overlooks the road from Damascus to the coast, was built in 1105–6. Part of the fortress was sold to the Hospitallers in 1157 and sold back in the same year. Ten years later it was taken by Nur al-Din and he probably razed it. In 1178 the Franks recovered Hunin and Humphrey II of Toron repaired it. After the Battle of Hattin it was lost again and was subsequently dismantled by al-Malik al-Mu'azzam 'Isa, the ruler of Damascus, in 1212. The treaty of 1240 returned the castle to the Franks, who held it until 1266 when it fell to Baybars. He rebuilt the castle in 1267 and much of the surviving medieval work probably dates from his repair. In 1994 limited excavations were carried out by the Israel Antiquities Authority in and adjacent to the eighteenth-century gatehouse (Shaked 1997: 17–18). Traces of two twelfth-century towers were found, placed 20 m apart with a curtain wall between them. They belong to the first phase of the castle destroyed by Nur al-Din. The towers measure 13 × 13 m and have walls 3 m thick. They were built of ashlars with marginal dressing and they may form the eastern side of a *castrum*. At a later stage, after the destruction by Nur al-Din, the complex was enlarged to form a much larger castle (about 86 × 65 m) with a moat (14–16 m wide) but no towers, in the view of the excavator because it was never completed. The existing round, non-projecting towers date from the eighteenth century, when the walls were reconstructed and the present gatehouse built.

The sea castle at Sidon was built on a small offshore island 40 m from the northern shore of the town in 1227, when the armies of Frederick II were camped in the city. It was enlarged by the Templars from 1260 onwards. Various versions of its plan have been drawn up. Ben-Dov has given the castle the form of a *castrum* by adding an enclosure wall to the north and corner towers to the north-east and north-west (Ben-Dov 1986: 113–20). The other versions do not attempt to extend the outer defences to the north. The gateway to the inner part of the castle was situated to the east. Within is a large building with a hall consisting of sixteen connected groin-vaulted bays supported on seven piers. The entrance to this hall was at the centre of its south wall. A few smaller rooms were situated to its south within the outer walls, and on the south-east a massive structure containing a kitchen and various service rooms. A staircase built into the wall of the hall led to the upper floor. Here on the south-east side there was a small chapel with massive walls about 5 m thick and with arrow-slits in its northern and southern walls. It was decorated with alternating courses of light and dark stone (*ablaq*), more typical of Mamluk than Frankish stonework. The outer fortification consists of a thick curtain wall (c. 5 m) which survives to the south and east, with arrow-slits placed about 5 m apart. At the corners were round towers of which two, on the south-east and south-west, survive. As at Ascalon, Caesarea and Beit She'an, pillars were laid laterally in the wall to strengthen it.

The fortress gate was on the south facing the land. It consisted of a broad outer arch and a narrow, slightly lower inner arch with a slit for a portcullis between the two. Directly above the outer arch was a large machicoulis supported on four stone brackets. Beneath each bracket is a carved figure, a lion on the outer brackets and on the inner ones a human figure carrying a stick-like object. The gate has been partly reconstructed from stones recovered from the sea. A bridge leading to the gate was supported on massive piers 4.5 m apart. They were rectangular in shape but triangular on their eastern side to withstand the blows of the waves. Between them were stone arches, with the exception of the last pier before the gate of the castle. To cross the final distance a wooden drawbridge would have been lowered by means of chains which extended down from the machicoulis above the gate. The drawbridge was supported on a smaller stone pier.

There is a thirteenth-century *castrum* in the small harbour town of Kyrenia on the north coast of Cyprus. The castle was originally constructed at the end of the twelfth or early in the thirteenth century.[9] It was captured after a protracted siege by Frederick II in 1232, underwent various improvements and was extensively rebuilt by the Venetians in the sixteenth century.

The castle is rectangular with corner towers. The rampart walk and crenellation in the northern curtain wall have survived remarkably intact and there are some early remains in the east and in the interior, including barrel-vaulted basement galleries. Much of the rest of this castle is later, mainly Venetian, including a large circular bastion in the north-west corner and all of the defences in the south.

The citadel of Famagusta was built in the reign of Henry II (1285–1324) and completed by 1310. It is rectangular with square corner towers. Rib-vaulted halls surround the central courtyard; the six bays in the north are the best preserved. To the west, four bays form a large hall with six arrow-slits and a gate. There was originally tracery in the windows, but on the whole the hall shows little evidence of decorative elements. To the south are five rib-vaults. Three of the towers survive in part, though the tower to the north-east has been destroyed. The largest surviving tower is to the north-west adjoining the hall. Enlart writes that 'although it may have been the keep, it is more likely that the keep was at the other end of the hall in the south-west, commanding the entrance to the port' (Enlart 1987: 451).

'Castrum and keep' castles

It has been suggested that the Franks were limited to building towers at first, since they did not know how to fortify a curtain wall, and that their building of *castra* can be considered a major advance. However, in eleventh-century Europe wooden and occasionally stone castles were built with enclosure walls. What may perhaps be seen as a true advance was what Smail called 'the marriage of *turris* and *castrum*' (Smail 1987: 228), such as the structure which William of Tyre described at Darum. One of the best surviving examples of this combination is at Gibelet (Jubayl), ancient Byblos in the county of Tripoli. It was built shortly after the town was captured by Raymond of St Gilles in 1102. The early twelfth-century date of this castle suggests that the Franks did not take very long to become experts and innovators in the art of castle building. In 1187 Saladin acquired the town as ransom for Hugh III of Gibelet. It was recovered by the Franks in 1197 and held by them until 1298.

The entire enclosure of Gibelet Castle measures 45 × 40 m. It has quadrangular projecting corner towers and an additional tower on the eastern side of the gate to the north. The gate is within the city walls and the fortress extends outside the walls and is surrounded by a moat. In the courtyard stands the keep measuring 22 × 18 m. It was two storeys high with a first-floor entrance, a not uncommon feature which added to the security of the building.

Defended castra (enclosure castles with outworks)

Concentric lines of defences were aimed at making it more difficult for the besieger to gain access to the inner ward. A number of *castra* are contained within outworks that may have been intended to protect a settlement which had developed outside the castle walls, perhaps as the result of some new threat. The castles built around Ascalon, Yavne (Ibelin), Tell es-Safi (Blanchegarde), Beit Govrin (Beit Govrin) and Deir al-Balah (Darum) are examples of this. Darum, which was built as a small *castrum*, had by 1191 become a much larger castle with outworks including seventeen towers. This was probably in response to the attack by Saladin in 1170. Blanchegarde appears to have undergone a similar process, as did Beit Govrin. Blanchegarde, also known as Alba Specula or Alba Custodia, was built by King Fulk in 1142.[10] It was situated on the highest part of Tell es-Safi, 215 m above sea level, overlooking a vast area stretching from Ramla and Latrun in the north, the Hebron hills and Judean foothills in the east, the northern Negev in the south, and across the plain to the coast from Yavne to Gaza. The white chalk cliffs below the castle to the west gave the site its Frankish name.

Blanchegarde fell to Saladin in 1187 after the Battle of Hattin. He dismantled the castle in 1191. The following year it was recovered by Richard I but shortly thereafter it was handed over to the Muslims in fulfilment of the terms of a treaty between Richard and Saladin. It was recovered in 1241 but held only until 1244. William of Tyre's description of Blanchegarde is of a typical *castrum* with a central courtyard and four projecting corner towers. Two of the towers can still be seen on the surface, and the hillocks formed by the remains of the other two are visible. In the mid-nineteenth century Rey drew a plan of the castle on which he showed a central keep. The small size of the enclosed area (less than 16 × 16 m) makes the existence of an internal keep unlikely.[11] However, the existence of the outworks which are also shown on Rey's plan is better founded and is supported by the excavations of Bliss and Macalister in 1899–1900, which revealed the ruins of a gate-tower to the north of the *castrum*.

Beit Govrin was built in 1134 and granted to the Hospitallers in 1136. After the Battle of Hattin it was lost to the Franks but returned to them between 1240 and 1244. Recent excavations (1993–97) have exposed a *castrum* with two outer lines of defence.[12] The *castrum* covers an area of 46 × 48 m. It has towers on three corners, and to the south is a church which shares the southern wall of the fortress and is connected to it by a vaulted passage. The *castrum* has a barrel-vaulted gate 5.5 m high in the west. Two-thirds of the area of the interior (28.5 × 48 m) was covered by groin vaults 13 m high supported on piers; at the centre there was an open courtyard. A single arrow-slit was found in the east wall. Most of the outer fortifications of the castle surrounding the *castrum* have been exposed. They enclose a large area containing within it the Roman amphitheatre and probably the remains of the town of Beit Govrin, which has not yet been found. These defences appear to form a double line, the inner one with vaults supported on piers. Both outer lines of fortification have a number of salient towers.

Double castra (concentric castra)

From the inherited design of the *castrum* and under the influence of Byzantine double-line fortifications, such as the fifth-century Theodosian walls of Constantinople, the Franks derived a more sophisticated type of castle. This was the double or concentric *castrum*, found in its most perfect state at Belvoir overlooking the Jordan Valley and at Saranda Kolones in Cyprus.[13] Indeed as far as we know at present, these are the only examples of this type of castle found in the East. This was a *castrum* within a *castrum*, with the inner building almost identical to the outer one. Belvoir (Kochav Hayarden, Kaukab al-Hawa) is the earliest example of this type. It is situated north of Bet She'an, overlooking to the east the River Jordan and the Damascus–Jerusalem road. To its south is the road from Beit She'an to Akko. In the Second Temple period there had been a Jewish town called Kochava at this site. A castle was probably first built here in 1138–40. It was purchased by the Hospitallers in 1168 and it was they who built this remarkable building. Belvoir represents a landmark in castle design and became the prototype of some of the finest castles built in the West.

Construction throughout the castle was of basalt ashlars and fieldstone excavated from the moat and limestone ashlars possibly brought from nearby Mount Gilboa (Plate 4.4). The two lines of defence consisted of an inner *castrum* – a vaulted structure with corner towers and a large gate-tower enclosing an inner bailey of 20 × 20 m and an outer bailey (50 × 50 m), surrounded by an outer *castrum* with corner and interval towers. The lower part of the tower walls were built with a slight incline to make scaling

Plate 4.4 Belvoir Castle: the inner ward (photograph by the author)

difficult. Some of the towers had internal staircases leading to posterns at their base within the moat through fortified doors. On three sides of the outer ward, to the south, the west and the north, the rock-cut moat (10 m deep and 20 m wide) strengthened the defences. On the east side facing the cliff above the Jordan Valley the Hospitallers built a large barbican and a steep talus.

The inner *castrum* contained a refectory, storerooms and a kitchen. The excavators found ovens in the kitchen. A staircase from the inner bailey led to the upper floor, where there were service rooms, living quarters and a chapel with two rib-vaulted bays which were decorated with sculpture. In the courtyard were cisterns that could hold 100 cubic metres of water. Water was carried through an aqueduct from the spring in the south to a larger vaulted cistern in the eastern outer ward. This cistern had a capacity of approximately 650 cubic metres of water and supplied the adjacent bathhouse. A forge and smithy was located in the north-eastern wing and was identified by the discovery of iron tools, nails and horseshoes.

Shortly after its construction Saladin's troops tried unsuccessfully to destroy Belvoir. The strength of the double fortifications proved extremely effective, as they did later after the Battle of Hattin, when the castle held out against a Muslim siege for a year and a half, falling only on 5 January 1189 when the Ayyubids successfully undermined the barbican. The Franks surrendered although the attackers had not managed to penetrate the inner fortress. Saladin demolished the church and repaired the walls. Between 1217 and 1219 Belvoir was partly dismantled by al-Mu'azzam 'Isa, who apparently destroyed the upper storey of the inner *castrum*. The fortress was thereafter abandoned but in 1241 it was returned to the Hospitallers. They probably did not manage to carry out any restoration before they finally abandoned it around 1263 (Benvenisti 1970: 297). Early in the nineteenth century Bedouin squatters settled in the ruins and a village developed there, named Kaukab al-Hawa. It was abandoned in 1948. In the 1960s trial excavations were carried out and in 1966 Belvoir was cleared and partly restored.[14]

A second double *castrum* known as Saranda Kolones is situated at Paphos in the kingdom of Cyprus (Plate 4.5). It is only about half the size of Belvoir, about 60 square metres (about the size of the inner *castrum* at Belvoir), but it is an equally fine example of this type of castle. It was built in 1200, possibly by the Hospitallers, and was destroyed by earthquake in 1222.

Plate 4.5 Saranda Kolones Castle (photograph by the author)

Saranda Kolones differs from Belvoir in the use of round towers on the outer *castrum* corners and triangular towers at the mid-points, whereas all the towers at Belvoir are rectangular. The inner *castrum* has rectangular corner towers but a semicircular gatehouse. In addition, rather than the outer *castrum* having vaults, it is merely a curtain wall with towers. As at Belvoir, Saranda Kolones has its accommodation in the smaller inner *castrum*. There are stables, a bakery, a forge and a mill-room. The upper floor holds a chapel and several latrines that empty out via piers to the sewers below. There were also latrines on the ground floor constructed in the piers which supported the vaults.

At the end of the thirteenth century the concentric *castrum* design was adopted by Edward I, who employed it in the castles he constructed to secure his conquests in North Wales. Beaumaris Castle in Anglesey, which was built in 1295, is one of the finest examples of this type.

We should perhaps ask why such a remarkable castle design, which proved to be extremely effective in 1187–89, is represented in the kingdom of Jerusalem by only a single example. The answer may lie in the fact that it was built a mere ten years before the Battle of Hattin which resulted in the loss of most of the Frankish territory, and control of the limited area which was regained in the Third Crusade did not require new castles.

Spur castles

Spur castles made use of a particular topographical feature, a high spur cut off from the surrounding countryside by two river valleys. These castles were located in some of the more vulnerable regions under Frankish rule, particularly the hilly regions to the north and east. They exploited the steep cliffs on two sides of the spur as a natural defence which needed only the addition of a curtain wall and an occasional tower. The third and most vulnerable side that faced the ridge was strengthened by the construction of more extensive defences: parallel walls, towers and a moat. The great spur castles often controlled major roads and valley passes. They could house a large garrison and contain supplies necessary for a major campaign. At the same time, like smaller castles, they served as administrative centres.

The castle of Montfort or Starkenberg (Qal'at Qurein) is situated about 19 km north-east of Akko, 300 m above sea level on the southern bank above Wadi Qurein. It is 180 m above the wadi. It was built in 1226–27 after the site came into the hands of the Teutonic Knights, who possessed extensive property in the region including Château du Roi (Mi'iliya) and Judin (Yehi'am). Montfort became the administrative centre, treasury and repository for their archives. It was destroyed by Baybars in 1271.

The keep to the east (see p. 100) was surrounded by a ditch 20 m wide and 11 m deep. A second moat was excavated by the builders about 50 m to the east, isolating the keep from the spur to the east and also from the rest of the castle to the west. It was constructed over a large cistern. To the west was a groin-vaulted hall and a large building with rib-vaults supported on a central octagonal column. Part of an outer line of defensive wall survives to the west and north.

Kerak of Moab was built on the ruins of a Roman fortress by Pagan le Bouteiller, lord of Montréal and Oultrejordain, in 1142 (William of Tyre 1986: 15.21). It was obtained by Reynald of Châtillon through marriage. Kerak withstood Ayyubid sieges in 1183 and 1184. After the Battle of Hattin in 1187 and the death of Reynald at the hands of Saladin, the castle held out for over a year until it fell to Saladin's brother, al-Malik al-Adil in November 1188. He refortified the castle in 1192 and in 1264 Baybars strengthened the site and improved the fosse. Most of the defences visible today date to these post-Frankish phases.

The castle is situated on a spur on the southern side of the town of Kerak. There is a broad rock-cut ditch to its south and a narrower but very deep ditch to the north. The entrance of the castle was in the north. According to Deschamps there are two phases of Frankish construction, an inner wall to which was added an outer wall with five square towers. An impressive stone-lined talus was constructed against the southern and south-eastern walls. Other than the study of Deschamps, no serious work has been done on this important castle.

Beaufort or Belfort (Qal'at al-Shaqif Arnun) is situated in southern Lebanon 300 m above the Litani river commanding the southern approaches to the Beqa' Valley. It was built after the site was captured by King Fulk in 1139, at first with a keep of about twelve square metres and subsequently with more extensive fortifications taking advantage of the spur formation. These included a vaulted hall and the broad *enceinte* with round towers to the south. It was besieged for a year after the Battle of Hattin, only falling when the garrison was starved into submission. The Ayyubids strengthened the fortifications, particularly to the north and south. Beaufort was restored to the Franks following the terms of the treaty of 1240 and was held by the Templars until 1268. Improvements carried out in the thirteenth century included the addition of the chapel and strengthening of the outworks to the south. In 1268 the castle fell to Baybars.

Beaufort is an impressive structure despite the considerable damage it has suffered in recent years. The eastern side of the castle was unapproachable because of the steep cliff. Its main line of defence was concentrated at the most vulnerable approach to the west. Here, as to the south, a moat and curtain wall follow the edge of the rock and the large keep is situated near the central point where the wall bends.

A castle which is not built on a spur but which follows the same principle of utilizing natural defences on all sides but one is 'Atlit Castle (Figure 4.2). Between 1217 and 1218 the Templars dismantled a small twelfth-century fort known as Le Destroit (Districtum, Petra Incisa) situated on the sandstone ridge just east of the small promontory at 'Atlit and replaced it with one of the largest castles of the kingdom of Jerusalem. 'Atlit Castle or

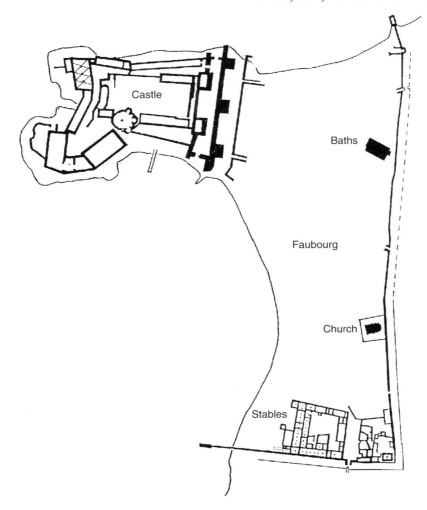

Castle

Baths

Faubourg

Church

Stables

Figure 4.2 Plan of 'Atlit Castle and faubourg (after Johns 1997)

Château Pelerin, so named because it was built largely with the aid of pilgrim manpower, withstood attack by al-Mu'azzam 'Isa in 1220. In the following years a town grew up on its eastern side. In 1265 the town fell to Baybars and was destroyed. The castle, however, stood its ground and remained in Frankish hands until August 1291, after the fall of Akko.

Earthquakes and dismantling of much of the stonework by Ibrahim Pasha in the early nineteenth century have taken their toll on the ruins, but 'Atlit is still an impressive site. Between 1931 and 1936 C.N. Johns excavated the castle and faubourg, exposing the main lines of defence to the east (Johns 1997). It was in this area that the Franks concentrated their efforts. The north, west and south had the natural protection of the sea. A moat was excavated the entire length of the eastern side, 27 metres wide with two gates on the counterscarp. There were two lines of massive walls on this side. The outer bailey wall was 200 m long, 6.5 m thick and 16 m high. It had three towers positioned so that archers on the inner eastern line of defence could fire their arrows between the towers and over the outer wall and moat. The towers had gates that gave indirect access to the outer bailey. There were two firing levels in this wall. At a height of 3 m above the ground was a passageway (*chemin de ronde*) leading to casemates with embrasures, each of which could hold four archers. At the top of the wall was the parapet from which there was an additional line of fire. Beyond the outer bailey was the huge inner bailey wall, over 30 m high and 12 m thick, with two large towers. The northern tower still stands to a height of 34 m. The towers were about 27 m long and contained various chambers. In the northern tower the ground-floor level was barrel-vaulted and above it was a monumental Gothic, rib-vaulted hall. Around the remaining sides of the castle were two concentric rows of vaults including some broad halls in the south-west, a polygonal church and a fine rib-vaulted hall which may have been the refectory.

Crac des Cheveliers was the finest of the Hospitaller castles (Plate 4.6). Lawrence, with understandable enthusiasm, called it 'perhaps the best preserved and most wholly admirable castle in the world' (Lawrence 1988: 77). Crac des Chevaliers guarded the north-eastern flank of Tripoli and

Plate 4.6 Crac des Chevaliers from the south-west (photograph by Jonathan Phillips)

controlled access to the Orontes and the Syrian interior. It originated as a Kurdish military outpost built by the emir of Homs in 1031 and was known as Hosn al-Akrad (Castle of the Kurds). Nothing of the architecture of this stage is known to have survived. It was captured by the Franks in 1110 and acquired by the Hospitallers in 1142 from Raymond II of Tripoli. Earthquakes struck the castle in 1157 and again in 1170, when it was damaged to such an extent that according to one source not a single wall remained standing. The inner part of the castle post-dates the latter earthquake. A third earthquake damaged the castle in 1202, and in the thirteenth century the three great towers to the west, the talus and the outer fortifications were constructed.

Crac remained in Frankish hands after 1187. Because of its strength Saladin did not try to take the castle in 1188. At its peak in the thirteenth century Crac had a garrison of 2,000 knights. It eventually fell to Baybars in 1271 after a siege that lasted just over a month.

Crac was built at the northern end of a spur. Its twelfth-century form and size is similar to that of Vadum Jacob (see pp. 118–20) which was built in 1178–79, probably at the same time that Crac was being built. At this stage it had a few towers and consisted of barrel-vaulted halls running adjacent to the outer wall, a large hall in the courtyard, a chapel to the north-east and a large gate in the centre of the eastern wall. In the thirteenth century the castle took on its present remarkable form. The outer wall with semi-circular towers was built to contain the entire castle and a lower gate was constructed to the east. By this means Crac became an enormous concentric castle.

Another remarkable castle of the Hospitallers is Margat (al-Marqab) situated in the south of the principality of Antioch, north of Tortosa, south of Latakia and west of Assassin country (Plate 4.7). A small castle apparently existed here in the mid-eleventh century. It was captured in 1117 by Robert of Antioch, who made it over as a fiefdom to the Mansoer family. It was damaged by earthquake in 1157, 1170 and 1186, the latter apparently making its possession too great a burden on its owners, who in the same year sold it to the Hospitallers. Like Crac des Chevaliers, it served as an administrative centre. The knights built a tower on the coast, now known as Burj as-Sabi, with a wall connecting it to the castle so that they could exact tariffs from travellers using the coastal road.

As with Crac des Chevaliers, Saladin did not try to take Margat in 1188 because it was too strong. It withstood a siege in 1204–5 by the Sultan of Aleppo, al-Malik al-Zahir, and remained in Frankish hands until 1285, when it was taken by Qala'un. It subsequently became an important Mamluk stronghold in Syria. Margat is somewhat smaller and rather less imposing than Crac des Chevaliers, but it is nonetheless amongst the finest examples of Frankish military architecture. It was constructed using the local basalt stone, which is more difficult to cut and as a consequence the workmanship is not as fine as at Crac, but the contrast between the basalt and the limestone which was used for architectural details is some compensation for

Plate 4.7 Margat Castle (at Marqab) viewed from the south (photograph by Jonathan Phillips)

this.[15] Lawrence described the features of Margat as 'typical of the best period of French architecture'; he seems to have been referring to the remarkable round keep, the finest of its type in the Latin East (Lawrence 1988: 88).

The weak part of this spur castle was to the south and it was on this side that the defences were concentrated, including the citadel, a rock-cut reservoir and the great round *donjon*. To the north below the citadel and *enceinte* is the moat. To the west is a large open area surrounded by the wall with semicircular towers. To the south on the outer *enceinte* below the *donjon* is another large round tower. Entrance to the castle is via stairs over the ditch to a bent-angle gateway in the middle of the west wall. The gate was two storeys high and had a portcullis. The citadel has an outer gate to the west and a long passage giving indirect access through an inner gate to the court-yard. As at Crac, large, barrel-vaulted chambers surround the courtyard. There is also a large, vaulted hall near the keep. The chapel to the north of the keep served as the cathedral for the bishop of a nearby town of Valenia (Banias), who in times of insecurity took refuge in the castle. It is a fine example of French Romanesque architecture.

Lawrence considered Saone Castle (Sahyun) as 'probably the finest example of military architecture in Syria'. It is situated on one of the lesser routes from Latakia to Aleppo. A Byzantine castle, probably built around 975, occupied this narrow spur. It consisted of a citadel at a high point in the centre of the ridge, with a ditch to the west and probably another to the east. Around the citadel were several parallel lines of outworks. The castle was expanded and greatly improved by the Franks in the twelfth century, mainly by the defences to the east. It fell to Saladin in 1188 and was never regained by the Franks. As it was not added to under post-Frankish rule, Saone remains a largely twelfth-century Crusader castle. Saladin arrived in July 1188, surrounded the castle with his army and set up six mangonels to bombard the walls. A breach was made, probably in the north-east corner, and the Muslims climbed the walls and entered the courtyard. The defenders took flight and sought refuge in the keep. An agreement was reached with Saladin and they were allowed to leave after paying a ransom. The walls of Saone were partially repaired and it survived remarkably well until the nineteenth century, when Ibrahim Pasha bombarded it during his campaign in Syria.

The easiest approach to this castle was from the east. In the twelfth century the Franks enlarged the eastern section of the 128 m long moat to a width of 18 m and a depth of 26 m. Since it was too broad to carry a bridge, a stone pinnacle was left to support the drawbridge. The gatehouse was built to the west of the ditch with two slightly projecting rounded towers. South of the gate is the great keep (see pp. 100–1), situated at the half-way point of the moat with its entrance to the west. There is also a large vaulted hall, and further south are three round towers. To the south are three rectangular towers. A second gateway is in the third tower.

Amongst the interesting details of military design is the rampart walk (*chemin de ronde*) around the curtain walls. This is not an uncommon feature in castles, but at Saone there is no access from the towers to the walk. They are cut off from it and the only means of reaching the walk, except from the gatehouse, is via stairs from the courtyard to each section. This would seem to have been an inconvenience to the defenders during attack but, as Smail noted, it was probably an intentional design to enable the isolation of an enemy who had gained a tower or a section of the wall (Smail 1987: 241).[16] This was a feature of Byzantine military architecture adapted by the Franks at Saone but it does not appear to have been adopted in later castles, not even the large castles of the military orders. A second defensive feature, one that is not uncommon in Frankish castles, is the indirect access via the towers into the fortress.

Oman saw the use of interval towers on the curtain wall and of concentric lines of defence at Saone and other twelfth-century castles as an adaptation of Byzantine military principles (Oman 1898: 29). But, as Smail pointed out, the use of salient towers appears in the pre-Crusader west (Smail 1987: 239–40) and the towers at Saone are in any case almost on the wall line extending only a few centimetres. Second, as he notes, there is in fact no evidence here for consecutive defensive lines, as the Byzantine and Frankish lines clearly could not have worked together. The outer Frankish fortification towers overshadow the earlier inner line, whereas in concentric defences the inner line is always higher than the outer one.

Construction at Saone was of large marginally drafted blocks, roughly bossed in typical twelfth-century fashion, some with masons' marks. The lack of arrow-slits in the walls except at the base of the towers necessitated the use of the parapet alone to defend the walls. This is another twelfth-century feature.

Hilltop castles

This is a more problematic group, as there is little similarity between the different examples apart from their location on isolated hilltops. The Hospitaller castle of Belmont (Suba) is situated in Kibbutz Sova west of Jerusalem. It is not known when Belmont was built, but it existed in 1169 (Harper and Pringle 1988: 102) and was possibly constructed twenty or thirty years earlier. The castle fell to Saladin in 1187 and was destroyed in 1191.

A team from the British School of Archaeology in Jerusalem headed by Denys Pringle and Richard Harper carried out excavations at Belmont in 1986–88 (Harper and Pringle 1988, 1989).[17] They exposed parts of this complex, which consists of an inner ward with a rectangular courtyard building contained within an outer octagonal wall, sloping and partly rock-cut, partly constructed. This wall, which apparently had no towers, enclosed an area of 100 × 115 m. The gate was to the south-east. Within the outer wall were a parallel vault and an inner gate, not discovered during the excavation. The inner rectangular building measured 32 × 38.5 m.

Juddin (Qal'at Jiddin) is situated in western Galilee 16 kilometres north-east of Akko. It has never been excavated but between 1990 and 1992 the Crusader and Ottoman structures were studied by members of the British School of Archaeology in Jerusalem (Pringle *et al.* 1994: 135–66). Juddin was probably not built before the thirteenth century when the region came into the hands of the Teutonic Order. It was apparently handed over to the Mamluks under the terms of the treaty between Baybars and King Hugh III of Cyprus in 1272. Juddin may possibly have been destroyed by Baybars.

The castle consists of two massive towers enclosed by a curtain wall high above Wadi Jiddin. The tower to the east, which appears to be the earlier of the two towers (Pringle *et al.* 1994: 139), is more massively constructed. It was about 12.5 m high and measured 16 × 15.5 m with walls 3.5 and 5.3 m thick. The entrance was to the west on the ground-floor level. This gave access to a narrow passage to the right built into the thickness of the wall which may have led to a latrine. There is a second latrine on the first-floor level. A second door in the entrance passage led to a staircase rising to the first floor which, like the ground floor, was barrel-vaulted. A staircase originally led to the second floor or the roof.

The second tower measures 16.1 m square and its walls are between 1.6 and 3.25 m thick. Unlike most Frankish towers, it has three storeys. The ground and first floor each consist of two adjacent barrel vaults, while the second floor apparently had nine groin-vaulted bays. The entrance was at the first-floor level.

Montréal (ash-Shaubak) was built on an isolated hill in southern Transjordan. It was built by Baldwin I in 1115 in order to establish control over the caravan route from Damascus to Egypt and the Hijaz. William of Tyre described the castle thus:

> There, in an elevated spot well suited to his purpose, he built a fortress strongly defended by its natural site and by artificial means. When the work was finished, he placed a garrison of both cavalry and infantry forces there and granted them extensive possessions. The place was fortified with walls, towers, forewalls and a moat, and was well equipped with arms and machines.
>
> (William of Tyre 1986: 11.26)

If this description represents the castle as it was built by Baldwin I it is a remarkably early example of the use of double concentric defensive lines. It is more likely that this is how it appeared in the late twelfth century at the time William wrote his history. One of its most important features is the water system, construction of which involved the excavation of a staircase tunnel with 365 steps which led to cisterns fed by subterranean springs inside the hill. Montreal fell to Saladin in 1189 after a protracted siege and was dismantled by the Ayyubids. It was later restored by the Mamluks, who built a palace there. Although considerable attention has been paid to the Mamluk palace, the Frankish castle has not yet been properly studied.

A castle on the hilltop at Saphet (Safed), north-west of the Sea of Galilee, was built perhaps as early as 1102. It was refortified by King Fulk c. 1138–40, possibly in the form of a *castrum*, and came into Templar hands in 1168. By this time it was an enormous castle measuring 120 m E–W × 280 m N–S. Following the Battle of Hattin the fortress fell in 1188 and was subsequently dismantled in 1219 by al-Mu'azzam 'Isa. The Templars recovered the castle under the terms of the treaty of 1240 and it was refortified by them in 1240–43. Safed fell to Baybars in 1266 after a sixteen-day siege. Baybars carried out repairs to its defences and constructed a large cylindrical keep. The castle was badly damaged over the years and few visible remains survive. It has yet to be systematically studied.

How the Franks built their castles

There are two important sources of information on how the Franks built their castles. One is a thirteenth-century manuscript describing the construction of Safed Castle by the Templars from 1240 on: *Du constructione castri Saphet* (Huygens 1965: 355–87; English translation in Kennedy 1994: 190–8). The other is an archaeological source, the information from the excavation of the twelfth-century castle construction site of Vadum Jacob (Ellenblum and Boas forthcoming). The Safed document is concerned with describing how the castle came to be built, the cost of the project and its value to the defence of the region, and throws little light on the actual methods of construction. The excavation of Vadum Jacob, however, has proved invaluable in this regard. Five seasons of excavation have been carried out at the site located on an ancient mound at the southern end of the Hula valley just south of the modern Bridge of Jacob's Daughters. The castle was recorded in Frankish times as Vadum Jacob (Jacob's Ford). Excavations were begun in 1993 and are continuing at the time of writing (Ellenblum and Hartal forthcoming; Ellenblum and Boas forthcoming).

Construction of the castle began in October 1178. Baldwin IV came to the aid of the Templars, employing the entire Frankish army in its construction. Saladin attempted to end the Frankish effort to fortify the ford by offering them 100,000 dinars to halt the construction. However, building went ahead and in August 1179 Saladin attacked the castle. With the approach of the Ayyubid army the Franks gathered their livestock into the area inside the southern gate and hastily constructed firing positions in the smaller gate to the east. Excavation has revealed that the Muslims attacked from the north, east and south, setting fire to the wooden doors in the gates and firing a hail of arrows at the defenders stationed there. Mines were dug under the northern wall, probably near the north-eastern corner and on 30 August 1179 the castle fell and the Muslims slaughtered the defenders. An outbreak of plague caused the Muslims to abandon the castle. The site remained unoccupied until some time in the mid-thirteenth century when local villagers settled on the eastern side of the castle and made use of the stones from the half-constructed vault in that area.

The excavations of Vadum Jacob have increased our knowledge of the construction techniques employed in Frankish castle construction. At the time when Saladin attacked, construction was at its height and the castle consisted of half-finished walls and incomplete vaults probably with scaffolding in place, temporary walls, iron tools scattered about, piles of mortar and lime, dressed stones and earthen ramps. Around the exterior and interior of the walls were plastered tracks intended for the carts hauled by oxen which carried stones from the quarry. The latter was located on the slope to the west. Stone troughs to feed and water the oxen were placed on these tracks beside the walls. Excavations revealed earthen ramps on either side of the outer wall as well as a large number of tools in and around the gates, including axes and chisels for cutting the stone, spades and hoes, and spatulas for laying mortar and plaster. Inside one of the gates was a pile of lime with tools buried in it and iron hubs, perhaps belonging to one of the carts carrying the stone. The layer in which the tools were found contained hundreds of arrowheads, evidence that construction was underway up to the time of the Ayyubid attack.

On three sides of the castle, to the north, west and east, are small gates just over 1 m wide with a stepped entrance, bolt-holes and beam channels in the side walls to secure the door. The function of these entrances is not certain. They could be entrances to intended towers which there was no time to build, or, as Ellenblum suggests, gates between the inner ward and a proposed outer ward which could have been built had an outer wall been constructed and the area between the two walls levelled. In favour of this hypothesis is the fact that the position of the channels that contained the beams to bolt the doors shows that these doors opened towards the court-yard. If the openings were intended for towers, we would expect them to bolt on the other side, within the tower, so that defenders could take refuge within the towers if the castle fell. However, if these openings were intended as passages into an outer bailey rather than as entrances to towers, the position of the beams would prevent an enemy which had taken the outer bailey from breaking into the inner one. Pringle suggests another possibility, that these gates were to be reached by timber stairs or bridges (Pringle 1997: 85). This arrangement, however, would endanger the castle unnecessarily without providing any benefit.

On the exterior wall of the castle is an artificial slope composed of layers of rubble and soil probably taken from inside the fortress. This fill was levelled out every so often and covered with a layer of lime. Oxen hauled the prepared stones from the quarry along the lime surface thus formed to the base of the wall, where the stones would be lifted into position. Simple manually powered cranes were probably used to raise the ashlars to the height of two or at the most three courses. It may have been the intention of the builders to leave this fill in place in order to form the base of a talus; or perhaps it would be used to raise and level the surface outside the wall at some time in the future when an outer wall had been constructed, forming the suggested outer bailey. On the interior of the walls a soil fill was also used to raise the level as the interior face of the wall was constructed. By this means the Franks saved on the use of wood, which was always in short supply. Wooden scaffolding was employed in wall construction as a higher level was reached and in the construction of vaults. Barrel vaults were constructed on a half-wheel-like wooden framework supported in putlog holes in the upper parts of the walls.

Siege warfare

No remains of siege weapons have been recovered by excavations except for the occasional mangonel stone or Greek fire vessel. Our knowledge of siege techniques and siege weapons depends entirely upon written sources, illustrations in illuminated manuscripts and architectural elements in urban defences and castles that were constructed as preventive measures against these weapons.

In medieval siege warfare the mangonel and trebuchet were used to batter the walls from a distance, and battering-rams were used once the wall had been approached. At that point mines could be dug (sapping) to induce the wall to collapse and siege towers, ladders and ropes were used to scale the walls. A number of measures could be taken by castle builders to oppose these threats. We have already looked at the use of topography, particularly in the case of spur castles. To lessen the damage caused by missiles propelled against the walls the medieval fortifications were extremely thick; most large castles had walls three or four metres thick. At 'Atlit the outer curtain wall on the east side was 6.5 m thick and the inner wall (with its inner passage-way) was 12 m thick.

In order to stave off direct attack by battering-ram and siege tower, walls were protected by a moat and talus. In order to approach a wall protected by a moat it was necessary to fill the moat, no easy task considering that this took place under attack and taking into account the size of these moats (that at Belvoir was 20 m wide and 10 m deep and at Saone the moat was up to 18 m wide and 26 m deep!). The talus made scaling difficult and since it was often constructed from heavy rubble lined with stone facing, its great weight was liable to cause the mine to collapse before it reached the wall. An additional measure against sapping was the construction of walls directly on the bedrock. Curtain walls were enhanced with arrow-slits, salient towers and machicolations. Gates, always a weak point in the defences, were often guarded by towers and were strengthened with iron plates. A portcullis could be lowered in front of the gate and a wooden beam strengthened it from within.

Notes

1 Stone keeps had already begun to gain popularity in the West following the construction of the White Tower in London by William the Conqueror.

2 Lawrence wrote that the keeps never stood alone (Lawrence 1988, Appendix I: 128). This may be true, but sometimes the outworks appear to have been quite insubstantial.

3 One might also include Chastel Rouge, the upper level of which was divided into two by a wooden floor.

4 The construction of stairs within a wall is typical of Frankish building, both domestic and monumental. The advantage of this arrangement was that it did not detract from the internal space but this came at the expense of the strength of the wall; as Pringle notes, this area of the tower was often the first part to collapse (Pringle 1994a: 340).

5 It is also the highest of surviving Frankish towers, 27 m, compared to Saone which is 22 m high, Giblet and Kolossi in Cyprus 21 m, and Chastel Rouge a mere 12 m high. Most of the smaller towers were about 12 or 13 m high.

6 The castle chapel at Montfort was identified by the excavators as a large hall further to the west. However, there is no apse in this hall and the identification seems to be based solely on the stained-glass finds that were recovered here.

7 The use of round towers was not adopted in Frankish *castra* except at Kyrenia (where the towers are late) and the sea castle of Sidon (if it is indeed a *castrum*), and in general, square towers were preferred by the Franks. The round tower has nonetheless a distinct advantage, pointed out by Lawrence (1988: 30, Figure 12). Flanking fire from the curtain walls covers nearly the whole area encompassing a round, or rather half-round tower, whereas there is a fairly large blind area in front of a square tower.

8 A survey was carried out by the author and A. Maeir at Blanchegarde.

9 Wilbrand, Count of Oldenburg, who visited Cyprus in 1211, wrote: 'We first touched at Kyrenia, a small town but fortified, which has a castle with walls and towers' (Wilbrand of Oldenberg 1908: 13).

10 A survey of the castle was carried out in 1996–97 in preparation for excavations by Bar Ilan University and the Hebrew University of Jerusalem (Boas and Maeir forthcoming).

11 Following Rey's plan, subsequent descriptions have given erroneous measurements for this castle (Kennedy 1994: 32; Pringle 1997: Figure 51).

12 These excavations were conducted by the Israel Antiquities Authority, the Government Tourist Corporation, the Jewish National Fund and the National Parks Authority under the direction of A. Kloner and M. Cohen.

13 The more conventional term, concentric castle, does not differentiate between this very distinctive type as represented by Belvoir, Saranda Kolones and in the West by Beaumauris, and the various other types of castles which can also have concentric defences: keeps, castra, hilltop castles and spur castles.

14 The trial excavations were carried out by N. Tzori and from 1966 the site was excavated by Meir Ben-Dov and the National Parks Authority. Unfortunately it has yet to receive a thorough publication.

15 Similar use of a combination of basalt and limestone is found in other fortresses built in predominantly basaltic regions, most notably at Belvoir.

16 One can perhaps draw a parallel with the tower at Castel Rouge, where there is no connection between the ground and first-floor levels. Thus if the ground floor was taken, the defenders were still safe on the first floor (see pp. 95–6).

17 Final publication is now nearing completion (1998).

5 Frankish ecclesiastical architecture

Introduction

The return of Christian rule to the East brought about a revival of pilgrimage and a great increase in the number of pilgrims reaching the Holy Land. Theoderich mentioned having seen eighty pilgrim ships on a single day (Wednesday in Easter week) in the harbour of Akko (Theoderich 1891: 60). Pilgrims who reached Jerusalem and the other holy sites found accommodation in hospices and infirmaries for the sick run by the Knights of St John. Prepared food could be obtained in special markets. Guides and guidebooks helped them find their way and the Knights of the Order of the Templars guarded them on the roads. In order to cater for the pilgrims' religious needs the ecclesiastical organizations constructed, repaired and expanded numerous churches and founded new ones. A great many of the Byzantine churches had been destroyed in the early years of the eleventh century during the rule of the Fatimid Caliph al-Hakim (996–1021), chief amongst them the Church of the Holy Sepulchre. It is hardly surprising therefore that church construction was a major priority under the newly established Christian rule.

The first major study of Frankish churches in the East was published in the mid-nineteenth century by M. de Vogüé, *Les Églises de la Terre Sainte* (de Vogüé 1860). C. Enlart's *Les monuments des croisés dans le royaume de Jérusalem* (1927–28) followed, and a number of important surveys have appeared over recent years (Boase 1977a; Folda 1995; Kühnel 1994). The most comprehensive study of the churches of the kingdom of Jerusalem is the three-volume corpus by Denys Pringle and the British School of Archaeology in Jerusalem. The first volume of *The Churches of the Crusader Kingdom of Jerusalem* (Pringle 1993b) lists 132 churches. The second volume (Pringle 1998) completes the corpus except for the major cities. Pringle estimates that there were possibly over 400 churches built, rebuilt or simply in use during the period of Frankish rule (Pringle 1993b: 1). The survey includes information gathered from charters, chronicles and *itineraria*, and other documents, as well as modern studies. Fieldwork carried out by Pringle and members of the British School since 1979 provided the detailed descriptions and accurate ground plans that form the basis of this important work.

In the East the Franks made certain changes in church design, particularly in roof construction, that were necessitated by the more extensive use of stone. The Frankish basilica had a flat roof covering the stone vaults, rather than a gabled roof as had churches in the West. Frankish churches were frequently of more massive construction than their European counterparts, reflecting the general trend towards defensive construction that naturally developed due to the hostile conditions of the East. The church at Abu Ghosh (Emmaus) has walls over 2.5 m thick and the cathedral at Tortosa has two projecting towers at its north-east and south-east corners.

On the mainland most of the churches are of twelfth-century date and were built in the Romanesque style, whereas in Cyprus the Gothic style was used for Latin churches. The majority have a basilical plan with a central nave and a single aisle on either side. Roofs were barrel-vaulted, groin-vaulted or a combination of the two. Decoration was often simple. Many of the churches appear to have originally been decorated with frescoes, mosaics and sculpture. The loss of these decorations over time has given a deceptively severe appearance to many of the churches.

With the re-establishment of pilgrimage under Frankish rule, a number of new pilgrimage churches were built and some of those destroyed by Caliph al-Hakim early in the eleventh century were reconstructed. The most important of these was the Church of the Holy Sepulchre. Several towns had new cathedral churches, some of which survive almost intact or are partly preserved (Sebaste, Ramla, Lydda). In both towns and villages there are the remains of smaller churches and chapels. Some of these have undergone excavation in recent years (Caymont, Jezreel, Beit Govrin) and most of them have been surveyed.

Typology

In church design one comes across the same problem of diversity that one encounters in military architecture, albeit not to the same extent. Churches fall more easily into certain main categories; the variety of their functions is more limited and Lawrence's phrase describing castles as 'exceptions to some undiscoverable rule' (see p. 93) is less applicable here. The diversity in the churches lies not so much in the overall plan as in the form of particular elements such as the *chevet* (the eastern wall). The principal plans found in Frankish churches are: (1) basilicas with broad transepts and chevets with radial chapels; (2) simple basilica churches; (3) basilicas with transepts; (4) single-nave churches; (5) polygonal churches (Figures 5.1 and 5.2).

Basilicas with broad transepts and chevets with radial chapels

This church plan was taken from the pilgrimage churches on the road to Santiago de Compostela. These were large structures with a long nave and aisles, a broad transept and an ambulatory with radiating chapels around the

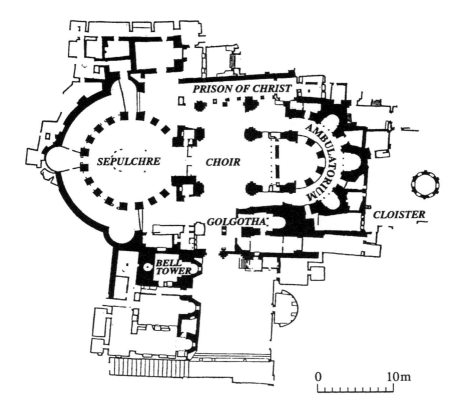

Figure 5.1 Plan of the Church of the Holy Sepulchre (after Harvey 1935)

apse. There are a number of such churches, including St Martin at Tours, Sainte-Foi at Conques, Saint-Martial at Limoges, Saint-Sernin at Toulouse and Santiago de Compostela. In the Latin East this plan was chosen for the most important pilgrimage site – the Holy Sepulchre. The Church of the Holy Sepulchre is a complex building containing numerous *loca sancta* (holy places) and substantial earlier remains. The need to function as a pilgrimage site, together with the desire of its builders to include in the new building the remains of the earlier churches on the site, dictated the choice of this plan but also certain changes to the regular design. In place of the long nave is the Byzantine rotunda around Christ's tomb. The main entrance, instead of being from the west, is from the south into the transept. Otherwise the source of the design adopted by the Franks is, except for the use of ogival rib-vaulting, clearly southern France.

The reconstruction of this church was the major project of church building carried out by the Franks. The Holy Sepulchre, built in the fourth century by Constantine, had been damaged over the years by fires and earthquakes,

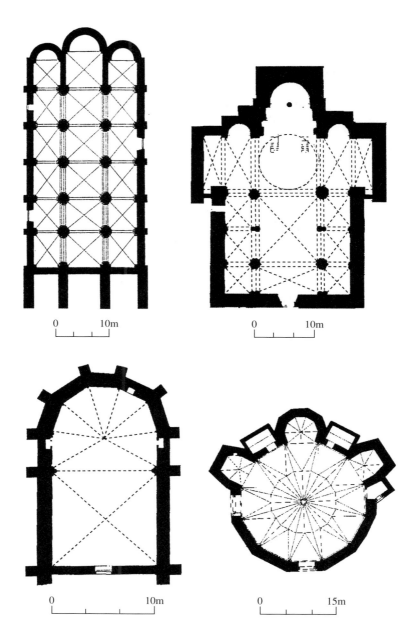

Figure 5.2 Comparative chart of Crusader churches

the Persian invasion in 614 and the Muslim conquest in 634. The most serious damage was done on 28 September 1009 when Caliph al-Hakim had the church completely razed. It was later partly rebuilt between 1042 and 1048 by Emperor Constantine Monomachus. The Franks considered the reconstruction of Christianity's most holy site a priority, and work began early in the twelfth century. The new church was consecrated on 15 July 1149, the fiftieth anniversary of the capture of Jerusalem. Instead of the previous free-standing rotunda with a basilica to its east, the Franks chose to include all the holy sites under one roof. Their main project was a large Romanesque choir to the east of the rotunda. It had two bays with the transept crossing at the domed western bay.[1] The eastern bay contains the High Altar. As in the West, an ambulatory curves around the eastern altar. It has three small apsidal chapels: the chapel of Longinus, the chapel of the Parting of the Raiment and the chapel of the Crown of Thorns. A broad staircase in the east descends to the small domed chapel of St Helena and the crypt-cave where, according to tradition, Constantine's mother found the remains of the True Cross. Above the chapel is the canons' cloister.

Other shrines in the church include the chapel of Christ's Prison, the chapel of the Bonds and the chapel of the Apparition. The Franks constructed a two-storey groin-vaulted structure around Golgotha. The entrance was via an external staircase which is now blocked off. Beneath Golgotha, according to tradition, the skull of Adam was found in what is called the chapel of Adam. In a symbolic gesture the Franks buried their kings here, with the aim of linking them to the holy places and legitimizing their rule in the Holy City. This was always a favourite goal of the pilgrims who visited the church but in 1808 following a fire the Greeks removed all traces of the tombs, which had already been largely destroyed. Recently one of the tombs, that of Baldwin V, was restored and is now on display in the museum of the Greek Orthodox Patriarchate Museum in Jerusalem.

At the main entrance of the church from the south they constructed a remarkable Romanesque facade (Plate 5.1) and later added to it a five-storey bell-tower with a polyhedral cupola. As al-Idrisi mentions a tower in 1154, it may have been added to the facade fairly soon after the church was consecrated. That it was not included in the original plan, or at least not in the form in which the facade was built, is evident from the fact that it partly obscures the western side of the facade. The upper part of the tower and the bells were destroyed by Saladin. The facade is elaborately decorated with sculpture that displays both Western and Eastern influences. Two remarkable marble lintels, amongst the most important Crusader sculpture in the country, stood above the two doorways (see p. 194). The church was not seriously damaged when the city fell to Saladin in 1187, and continued to function with only minor changes.

Plate 5.1 South facade of the Church of the Holy Sepulchre (photograph by the author)

Simple basilical churches

The majority of Crusader churches were of the basilical type, rectangular buildings usually divided into three by two rows of piers. The central nave was usually broader and higher than the aisles. The basilica was the traditional design of the churches of early Christianity in the West and especially in the East. Crusader churches differ in the use of the Romanesque style with its massive piers, generally heavier construction and distinctive proportions. In Crusader churches the eastern end or *chevet* usually had three apses, often constructed in the thickness of the wall but sometimes protruding on the exterior. The roof was usually groin-vaulted although barrel vaults were also used.

A typical basilica was St Mary Latin (Minor) in the Hospitallers' Quarter in Jerusalem. According to legend, this church of a convent of monks was constructed at the place to which Mary was carried after she had fainted during the Crucifixion. The legend relates that she tore out her hair in grief in a grotto here. Theoderich writes that her hair was to be found in a glass vessel in the church (Theoderich 1891: 23). The church was established already in the eleventh century as an Amalfitan foundation. It had a simple rounded *chevet* and a magnificent portal on the north decorated with the signs of the Zodiac, which was restored in the northern wall of the new Lutheran church. In the south-west corner was a belfry, and to the south was a cloister which has also been preserved.

A similar church located just to the west was St Mary Major, which was a convent of nuns. In plan it is almost identical, apparently with a similar northern doorway. There was a broad narthex and apparently a belfry in its south-west corner. From the narthex one could enter the Hospitallers' infirmary. St Mary Major was perhaps more elaborate than St Mary Latin. Some very fine architectural sculpture has survived from this church and is now on display in the Greek Orthodox Patriarchate Museum in Jerusalem

The largest church after the Church of the Holy Sepulchre was built on the ruins of a Byzantine basilica on Mount Zion. This site was identified as the City of Zion or the City of David (the actual site of the ancient city is to its east). The Tomb of David was traditionally located on Mount Zion, and in 1170 Benjamin of Tudela noted its presence there. He mentioned the discovery of a cave containing David's golden crown and sceptre. According to Idrisi, the church located here was beautiful and was fortified (Le Strange 1890: 212). All that survives is the southern gallery, which is traditionally identified as the room of the Last Supper, the *Coenaculum*. Opinion is divided over the dating of this building. According to Pringle it originally overlooked the sanctuary of the church in a similar way to the chapel of Calvary, which overlooks the choir of the Holy Sepulchre (Pringle 1993a: 36). However, the style of the vaults is early Gothic, typical of the early thirteenth century and would have to belong to the second period of Frankish rule in Jerusalem between 1229 and 1244. The problem is that by that time the church on Mount Zion had been destroyed.

West of Jerusalem, Abu Ghosh is one of the sites identified in the twelfth century as Emmaus, where Christ appeared before his disciples after the Crucifixion (Luke 24:13–35). The basilical church here dates from the twelfth century. It was abandoned in 1187 but may have been in use again between 1229 and 1244. The building somehow survived, and by the nineteenth century was being used as a stable though still largely intact. In 1901 restoration was carried out by the Benedictines.

The church measures 27.5 × 20.6 m and has walls over 2.5 m thick. Construction is of coarse fieldstone set in mortar with quoins of marginally drafted stones and door and window frames of finely cut ashlars. On the interior the walls and piers are all of diagonally dressed freestone, many with masons' marks, apparently used here as assembly marks (Ellenblum 1992: 175). The ground floor was divided into a nave and two aisles of almost equal width by two rows of three square piers, which together with pilasters and transverse arches, support twelve groin vaults. The vaults in the higher nave spring from elbow columns. The church is triapsidal, the central apse being slightly larger than the others. The crypt is entered via a broad staircase in the centre of the western facade of the church. Originally, two small staircases which had given access to the Roman cistern at the site were planned to be used, and they were partly vaulted in preparation for this, but for some reason this arrangement was abandoned in favour of the central staircase. Six low groin vaults in the crypt were supported on two massive rectangular piers. In the eastern wall were three apses. The central part of the crypt is lower than the eastern and western ends and here an altar was placed over the open spring.

Of the decoration of this church carving is limited to the thick-leaved capitals on the elbow columns of the nave and decoration on the northern door, but remnants of the rich frescoes are preserved (see p. 206). Depictions included the resurrected Christ in the central apse, the Virgin Mary, Christ and John the Baptist in the northern apse and Abraham, Isaac and Jacob in the southern apse. The vault of the crypt was covered with painted stars.

The church in Ramla is the only surviving relic of the Frankish period known at present in this town. It was constructed over a Byzantine basilica, reusing the columns and capitals of the earlier church. After Ramla fell to the Mamluks in 1268 the church was converted into a mosque, which remains in use to this day. The church is divided into a nave and two aisles, with three apses in the thickness of the flat *chevet*. The nave, which is higher than the aisles, has a pointed barrel vault and each aisle has seven groin-vaulted bays. The clerestory is pierced by narrow, pointed embrasure windows; there are also windows in the apses. In the Frankish period the main portal, constructed of marble with three pointed arches, was to the west. Today the entrance to the mosque is from the north and a secondary entrance from the south has been converted into a *mihrab*. A square bell-tower stood on the north side but was later replaced by a minaret.

The Cathedral of St Peter which stood on the southern side of the Herodian podium at Caesarea was constructed at some time in the twelfth century. It replaced the Friday Mosque which had been converted into a church following the occupation of the town in 1101. According to tradition, the new cathedral stood on the site of the house of Cornelius, who had been baptized by St Peter and consecrated as bishop. We do not know what happened to the cathedral during the Ayyubid conquest or later attacks on Caesarea, but it would appear to have survived until the fall of the town to the Mamluks in February 1265, when Baybars adopted it as the site from which to launch his attack on the citadel. He probably destroyed the church after the fall of the castle in March.

This basilica measured 45 × 20 m internally, with a nave slightly broader than the two aisles. At the eastern end were three sanctuaries with semi-circular apses. It was constructed with cut sandstone blocks, diagonally dressed. There are a number of masons' marks. Negev, who cleared the church in the early 1960s, considered the small, roughly built apse to the west of the central sanctuary to be that of a smaller church which was constructed instead of the larger one when the Herodian vault under the northern aisle collapsed during construction (Negev 1960a: 265). According to Pringle, the Herodian vault collapsed long after the Crusader period and the small apse was merely a temporary apse used during a reconstruction of the main apses (Pringle 1993b: 178–9).

The Church of the Annunciation in Nazareth was rebuilt to replace an earlier Greek church. This probably took place around the middle of the twelfth century, when the Archdiocese of Galilee was transferred from Beit She'an to Nazareth. The new church, which measured 75 × 30 m, was basilical in plan, with a central nave and two aisles terminating to the east in three apses. It had a straight *chevet*. The nave was roofed with a pointed barrel vault and the aisles with groin-vaulted bays. The crypt containing the Grotto of the Annunciation was at the eastern end of the nave and northern aisle. The splendid Romanesque carved capitals found here are amongst the finest examples of Crusader carving (see pp. 194–6). The capitals were not actually put in place, since the construction of the church was never completed. The church was destroyed by al-Mu'azzam 'Isa in 1219, but later rebuilt and subsequently destroyed again. It was restored in 1620 by the Franciscans, who used Frankish building material from the ruins; in recent years a modern church was built on the site.

Although nothing of it has survived, we have some idea of the appearance of the Church of St Andrew in Akko, thanks to two drawings made in the seventeenth century. This church was situated in the Templar Quarter at the southern end of the town. Its position at the high point on the tip of the cape made it useful as a landmark for ships and it is recorded in navigational guides. St Andrew was a Gothic-style building with three doors at the east end opening on to a central nave and two aisles. It is evident from the drawings that by the seventeenth century the doors had been removed. On the ground-floor level there were broad, arched windows and at a higher level a row of high lancet windows. At the west end at the clerestory level were three round portals. The church was razed at the end of the eighteenth century.

There are two surviving Crusader churches in Gaza, the larger one now serving as the central mosque, the other still functioning as a Greek Orthodox church. Nothing is recorded of the larger Latin church in Crusader times, nor is it known when the church was converted into a mosque. The building was damaged in the First World War but was later restored. It is a basilica, each aisle and the nave having four bays. The internal measurements were probably about 32 × 20 m. In the west is a groin-vaulted porch preceding the main door. The apses in the east have been destroyed, probably when it was converted into a mosque. The church is constructed of sandstone, and marble *spolia* were used on the interior for columns and capitals. There are masons' marks on some of the stones, including fish and stars.

At Tortosa on the northern coast of the county of Tripoli is the cathedral, Our Lady of Tortosa (Notre Dame). Construction of this church apparently began in the second quarter of the twelfth century but ended only in the thirteenth. Thus both Romanesque and Gothic elements are present. The plan is a fairly standard basilica. An unusual feature, however, is the two fortified sacristies which were built in towers on the north-east and south-east corners and there are massive projecting buttresses on the southern and northern walls. This is a large church by Eastern standards: the barrel-vaulted nave is 47 m long. The aisles are formed of groin-vaulted bays. The facade has rather unusual proportions. A single door is centrally placed, with large double windows set directly above it and a smaller single window above them resting on their frames. Just below the level of the double windows on either side are single windows of similar proportions. The result is a strange, centrally compressed symmetrical design.

Basilicas with transepts

A number of Crusader churches have transepts. Most often these are inscribed, that is they do not extend beyond the north and south walls of the church, but there are a number of churches with transepts extending out beyond the side walls. In some of these churches there is a dome at the junction of the nave and transept.

The Church of St Anne in the north-east quarter of Jerusalem is the most complete example of Frankish ecclesiastical architecture in Jerusalem (Plate 5.2). From the fourth century the site was commemorated as the birthplace of the Virgin Mary in the home of her parents Anne and Joachim. It was given to the Benedictine nuns after the conquest and the church was built in 1144, probably with the support of Queen Melisende, whose sister Ivette was a nun there. The convent of St Anne acquired considerable properties in Jerusalem, including the central covered market (Malquissinat) built by Melisende in 1252. The church survived the Ayyubid conquest, in part because it was expropriated by Saladin and was turned into a theological school (*madrasah*), as an inscription above the door witnesses. It later suffered hard times and by 1835, during the occupation of Jerusalem by Ibrahim Pasha, had become a stable, with refuse piled around the walls to such a height that, according to one account, one could climb over the mounds directly on to the roof. In 1856 the church was ceded to France by the Turks and in 1862–77 it was restored to its present state.

St Anne was built as a basilica with a non-projecting barrel-vaulted transept. Above the center of the transept is a dome. The decoration in the interior of the church is sparse and consists mainly of the simply carved capitals, but there may originally have been frescoes or wall mosaics. The facade includes a central door of pointed arches with a small window above it, and above this a large window with a pillowed arch similar to the arches framing the doors of the Church of the Holy Sepulchre. Boase suggested that the masons who built the Church of the Holy Sepulchre may have built St Anne as well (Boase 1967: 13). The facade of St Anne is similar in its symmetrical layout and ornamentation, albeit on a much smaller scale, to the facade of the Church of the Holy Sepulchre.

A church with a somewhat similar plan is the Armenian Cathedral of St James in Jerusalem. It was rebuilt between 1142 and 1165 over the remains of an older church. It is an elongated basilica, its aisles and a nave of equal height and at the centre has four piers supporting a pendentive cupola. The

Plate 5.2 The Church of St Anne, Jerusalem (courtesy of the Studium Biblicum Franciscanum)

entrance was originally in the south but is now in the west and the apses have been rebuilt since the Crusader period.

In the twelfth century the Franks built a new church over the ruins of the Byzantine church of Jacob's Well in Nablus. The site is at the foot of Mount Gerizim, about 2 km from the town. The church was probably destroyed in the thirteenth century; an attempt to reconstruct it in 1915 was abandoned. The church was a basilica with a broad nave and two aisles. There is a large apse at the eastern end of the nave and smaller apses at the end of the aisles. The slight transept is domed in its central part. The well that gives the church its name, in the crypt beneath the slightly raised sanctuary, is reached by two staircases leading from the front of the sanctuary.

Construction is of finely dressed limestone ashlars. The interior has granite columns and marble capitals. There are several masons' marks, including names (Ode and Qar).[2] The vaulting was supported by rectangular piers with engaged columns and also by paired columns. The decoration originally included frescoes, fragments of which survive in the southern apse. Part of a marble altar table with carved relief has also survived.

The Cathedral of Sebaste was built on the site identified by the Franks as the tomb of St John the Baptist. The discovery of his remains in a silver casket in 1145 led to donations towards construction of the cathedral, which continued until 1170. In 1187 the church fell to Saladin's nephew Hasam al-Din Muhammad, who turned it into a mosque. The building was later destroyed, probably at some time in the fourteenth century. It is a basilica with a nave and two aisles; there are a triple apse and an internal transept, as at Abu Ghosh and Ramla. The *chevet* is triapsidal with a polygonal wall around the central apse. Alternating piers with engaged and double columns divide the aisles from the nave.

When the Crusaders arrived at Lydda in 1099 they found the town destroyed. They rebuilt the town, adding a monastery. The church of St George, built over the tomb of the patron saint, was the seat of the Bishop of Lydda, whose diocese included the *seigneurie* of Ramla as well as Ibelin, Blanchegarde and Mirabel. The church had a nave and two aisles ending in three apses set in an unusual polygonal *chevet*. The interior was 30 m long and was divided into six bays. The surviving remains of this church, the north-east corner, are now integrated into a Greek Orthodox church; the Tomb of St George is in the crypt. The west end of the Frankish church is now in the courtyard of the Great Mosque of Lydda.

The Cathedral of St Nicholas in Famagusta, now the Lala Mustapha Mosque, is one of the finest Frankish monuments in the East (Plate 5.3). Work on the cathedral had begun by 1300 and an inscription dated August 1311, which is set into the wall by the south aisle door, records that by that time the apsidal chapels were completed and the aisles were partly vaulted but the nave was still open. It was completed during the following decades and served as the place of coronation of the Lusignan kings as kings of Jerusalem. The cathedral suffered some damage from earthquakes and in

Plate 5.3 West face of the cathedral of St Nicholas, Famagusta (photograph by the author)

the siege of 1570 it was bombarded with cannon-balls; it was subsequently converted into a mosque.

Built in elaborate fourteenth-century Gothic style, St Nicholas has a quality of elegance that owes something to its having been constructed far from France by a limited number of skilled masons (Plate 5.4). What would seem a disadvantage worked in the cathedral's favour, for what it lacks in detail and quantity of decoration it makes up for in uniformity and simplicity of design. The nave and aisles of the cathedral are of seven bays each, ending in polygonal apses. As is usual in the East, the roof is flat. Buttresses support the north and south walls as well as the exterior of the apses and they become flying buttresses to support the clerestory walls. The stone masonry is

Plate 5.4 Interior of the cathedral of St Nicholas, Famagusta (photograph by the author)

typically French but the richly moulded doorways appear to owe something to southern Italy or Sicily; they are similar to mouldings in churches at Taranto and Catania. The design of the western facade is paralleled in Lichfield Cathedral in England (Jeffery 1918: 119).

In the west facade of the cathedral are three magnificent doorways, each with four moulded arches and with high gables above filled with elaborate tracery. On either side of the facade is an octagonal staircase turret. Above the central door is a large gabled window, decorated with tracery and containing a rose, and there are large but simple windows on the upper level of the two towers. The east end of the church differs from most comparable churches in the West in that there is no ambulatory.

Construction of the fine Gothic Church of St Sophia in Nicosia appears to have begun in 1193 or 1209, but the main impetus for its construction was during the episcopate of archbishop Eustorge de Montaigu (1217–51). Most of the structure was completed in this period, with the exception of the nave and west end, which were finished in the early fourteenth century. The cathedral was consecrated on 5 November 1326.

There is no evidence in this church of Eastern design or decoration but rather a combination of European styles, particularly French Early Gothic. The west end of St Sophia displays its most imposing feature, a remarkable porch consisting of three vaulted portals, the central one larger and higher than the others. Above it is the great west window with its tracery intact. Above the aisle portals rise the unfinished towers. The apse is surrounded by an ambulatory but lacks chapels, resembling in this the original form of the cathedrals of Sens, Auxerre and Notre Dame. On the exterior are great flying buttresses of fourteenth-century date, which have replaced the original buttresses.

A small number of churches have a cruciform plan; that is, the north–south arm or transept crosses the nave and extends well out on either side, giving the plan of the church a distinct cross shape. The traditional site of the Tomb of the Prophet Samuel, and the place where the army of the First Crusade had their initial view of Jerusalem, is on a hill north-west of Jerusalem named by the Franks *Mons Gaudi* (in French, Montjoie – the Hill of Joy). The Premonstratensian Order received the site from Baldwin II (1118–31) and the church was built over the tomb in 1157. Around the church they constructed a *castellum*-type fortification and a village grew up outside the walls. The church was built on a cruciform plan with a nave 36 m long constructed over a crypt which contained the tomb, and a transept 23 m long. A semicircular apse projected from the *chevet*. North of the nave was a groin-vaulted annexe of three bays, as long as the nave itself. The church, in ruins from the thirteenth century, was restored as a mosque early this century, badly damaged in the First World War and subsequently restored.

Another cruciform plan is that of the crypt church of the Tomb of the Virgin Mary in Jehoshaphat. It is situated at the bottom of the Valley of Jehoshaphat at Gethsemane. A second church, which has not survived, apparently stood above it. The subterranean church is entered via an impressive Romanesque facade and a monumental staircase of forty-eight steps. On the left-hand side of the staircase is a niche containing the Tomb of Queen Melisende, who was buried there in 1161. The Tomb of the Virgin is on the right-hand side in the crypt. The crypt has apses on the east and west and a small chamber to the north. This chamber and the staircase opposite give the church its cruciform plan.

Single-nave churches

Many of the chapels in castles and monasteries have a simple plan with a single nave ending in an apse at the east and lacking aisles. There are also some large churches which have this simple plan. These all date to the thirteenth century and later and are built in the Gothic style.

One such church is St George the Latin in Famagusta, a fortified church with a crenellated parapet and originally two turrets to the west.[3] The single broad nave (10 m wide in the interior) ends in a three-sided apse and is covered with rib vaults. The church contains some fine carved decoration including a lion attacking an ass which is remarkably similar to a pair of lions on the eastern corner of the facade of the Church of the Holy Sepulchre.

The parish church of 'Atlit near the south-east corner of the faubourg is similar in layout, consisting of a single square nave with a seven-sided choir and sanctuary on the east end. It measures 11 × 19 m internally. It was constructed of local sandstone and limestone and had rib vaulting. The decoration of the bases and capitals of the pilasters included carvings of oak leaves. The interior was originally painted and remnants of stained-glass windows were found here. On the exterior a series of buttresses strengthened the walls.

Polygonal churches

Only two Frankish churches in the kingdom of Jerusalem have a polygonal plan. The earlier of the two is the twelfth-century church of the Ascension on the Mount of Olives in Jerusalem. The church was built by the Augustinians in the mid-twelfth century. The design of this church was in part dictated by the remains of a round Byzantine church which had previously occupied the site. It was also certainly influenced by the Dome of the Rock, a seventh-century Islamic shrine identified by the Franks as the Temple (*Templum Domini*) which they adopted and converted into a church around 1114–15.[4] The outer octagonal wall of the church is almost the exact same size as the inner octagon of the Dome of the Rock. The central octagonal aedicule, decorated with finely carved capitals, has survived. The dome on this building is a later addition.

The other polygonal church is the castle chapel at 'Atlit, a twelve-sided church with a seven-sided sanctuary on its east bordered by rectangular barrel-vaulted chambers and, beyond these, five-sided chambers. The vaulting appears to have been supported on a central pier or pillar (Pringle 1993b: 72). Entrances to the church were to the north, south and west. Little survives of this building, which was described in the eighteenth century as a ten-sided church built in light Gothic taste (Pococke 1743: II, 57). It is certainly exceptional in design and has no parallel in the Latin East.

Convents and monasteries

Monastic life continued and underwent some degree of revitalization under the Franks. A number of monastic complexes are located in urban centres, others are in the countryside and some monasteries were located at important pilgrimage sites (Figure 5.3). A rural monastery was set up in the twelfth century at Allar as-Sufla (Horvat Tannur), 19 km south-west of Jerusalem. It has been interpreted by Pringle as a monastic establishment, possibly Cistercian (Pringle 1992: 189–95). It consists of a group of barrel-vaulted buildings and an enclosure wall. To the east, extending out from the enclosure, was a single-aisled chapel of three groin-vaulted bays. At the pilgrimage site of Bethany a monastery of Benedictine nuns was founded in 1138. It included two churches, cloisters, a tower and a number of associated buildings. A Greek monastery stood on Mount Tabor prior to the twelfth century. It was destroyed by a Muslim raid in 1113 and was later re-established. There was also a Latin monastery on the mountain. In 1187 Mount Tabor fell to Saladin and he fortified the entire summit. At Nabi Samwil (St Samuel, Montjoie) the Premonstratensian Order built a fortified monastery.[5] Other monasteries of Frankish date include St John in the Woods (Ain Karem), St George de Lebeyne in the village of al-Baina (Dair al-Asad) in western Galilee (Plate 5.5), a Cluniac monastery at Palmarea near Haifa (Caiphas) and St Brochard or St Mary of Carmel in the valley of Ain as-Siyah on the western side of the Carmel Mountains.

One of the finest Frankish monasteries is Belmont Abbey, situated on an isolated hill south-west of Tripoli (Figure 5.3(1)). It was founded by the Cistercians in 1157, was destroyed in 1169 but later reoccupied and, after the fall of the county, passed into Greek hands. The conventual buildings around the cloisters included a church, chapterhouse, refectory and kitchen, a great groin-vaulted hall with buttressed walls, what may have been an infirmary, and several other buildings.

The Premonstratensian Abbey of Bellapais in Cyprus is situated on a spur with a steep cliff to the north. Bellapais is one of the most imposing remnants of the period of Lusignan rule (Plate 5.6). The oldest surviving part is the church which was begun during the reign of Hugh IV (1324–39). The complex consisted of a large square cloister surrounded by various buildings: a refectory to the north, a common-room and chapter house to the east, the church to the south and the abbot's quarters to the west (now entirely lost). The church has a belfry and a fortified gateway with a machicoulis and draw-bridge. The cloister dates mainly from the fifteenth century, with eighteen pillars supporting the surrounding vaults. The remarkably large refectory measures 30 × 10 m and has six groin-vaulted bays. A kitchen was probably situated to the west. The outer wall of the refectory to the north is buttressed and beneath it is a large cellar with octagonal piers.

There were numerous monastic foundations in urban centres, particularly in Jerusalem and Akko. In Jerusalem these included St Mary Latin and St

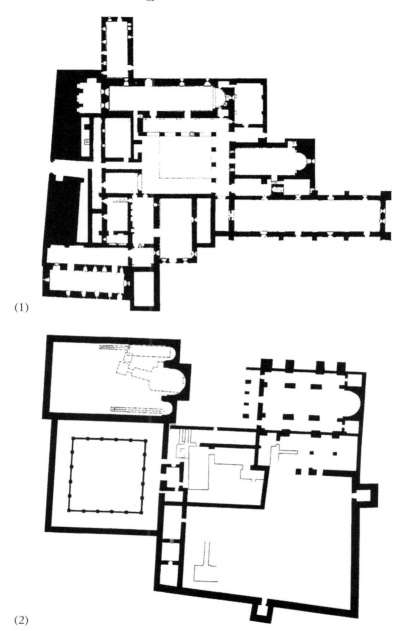

(1)

(2)

Figure 5.3 Monasteries. 1 Belmont (after Enlart 1926–8, album 1, 1926);
2 Bethany (after Saller 1957)

Plate 5.5 Al-Baina (Dair al-Asad) (photograph by the author)

Plate 5.6 Bellapais Abbey in northern Cyprus (photograph by the author)

Mary Major in the Hospitallers' Quarter, the Benedictine convent of St Anne, the Augustinian *Templum Domini*, the Benedictine convent of St Mary in the Valley of Jehoshaphat and the Augustinian monastery of St Mary on Mount Zion. In Akko, monastic houses included those of the Dominicans, the Franciscans, the Carmelites and the canons of the Holy Sepulchre, the Abbey of St Lazarus of Bethany and several others.

Notes

1 This relationship between the nave and the transept is now no longer visible because of unfortunate additions made in recent years, including walls which entirely block off the northern and southern wings of the transept.

2 Names are unusual as masons' marks. There are, however, some other examples: Ogier on the apse at Nazareth and the phrase '*Jordanis me fecit*' in the tower of the Church of the Holy Sepulchre. On masons' marks see pp. 220–1.

3 This was probably due to the fact that it was built at a time, probably towards the end of the thirteenth century, when the city was without walls.

4 Formal conversion of the Dome of the Rock took place around 1142 (Peters 1985: 317). The comparatively minor changes made by the Franks included the replacement of the golden crescent above the dome with a golden cross. In the interior the rock was encased in marble and surrounded by a beautiful iron grille (see p. 156). These were preventive measures against the damage caused by pilgrims, who habitually chipped pieces off holy sites as keepsakes. Christ's sepulchre and the Tomb of the Virgin Mary were similarly encased. An altar was placed above the rock and the Franks decorated the walls with mosaics displaying scenes from the scriptures. Latin inscriptions were placed on the outer walls and an Augustinian cloister was erected to the north.

5 Recent excavations around the church, which dates from 1157, exposed vaulted fortifications and stables. The brothers, having heard of the defeat at Hattin, appear to have unsuccessfully attempted to complete the deep rock-cut moat around their church. Huge cubes of still engaged rock stand in a row along the moat, silent witnesses to the disaster that befell the Franks in 1187.

6 Crafts and minor arts

Evidence of the involvement of the Franks in various crafts is known from contemporary sources and has come to light through the study of finds from excavations. These were mainly crafts which the Franks had developed or brought from the West, while traditional crafts remained largely in the hands of local craftsmen. There is no decisive evidence at present for Frankish involvement in the ceramics industry. With the possible exception of thirteenth-century Cyprus and Port St Symeon near Antioch, ceramic production was carried out by non-Franks.[1] The same is true of metalwork and textiles. The dyeing industry and glass manufacture appear to have been the province of Jews. It would seem that most objects of Western or Christian design were made for the Frankish market by non-Franks.

Ceramics

The ceramics used by the Frankish settlers in the Crusader states came from three sources. The vast majority were manufactured by local, non-Frankish potters. The second source were the neighbouring Islamic states, particularly Syria and Egypt. The third source were countries under Christian rule: Cyprus in the later twelfth and thirteenth centuries, the north-eastern Mediterranean and southern Europe (Figure 6.1).

Fine-quality glazed tableware was prominent amongst the ceramics in use in the Middle Ages (Plate 6.1). The large-scale use of glazes for decorative as well as functional purposes began in the ninth century and by the twelfth century was so well established that glazed vessels are often more numerous in medieval assemblages than are unglazed vessels. Transparent alkaline and lead glazes, and tin-opacified lead glazes are found. Alkaline glaze was used on vessels made of a friable, faience-like material known as frit. Designs were painted on to the surface before the transparent coloured glaze was added. This technique is known as underglaze painting. Lead glaze was usually applied to brown or reddish wares which were first covered with a white slip (diluted clay wash) so that the colour of the transparent glaze would not be affected by the colour of the ware. Decoration was usually carried out by one of two means: (1) incisions (sgraffito) were made in the slip prior to the

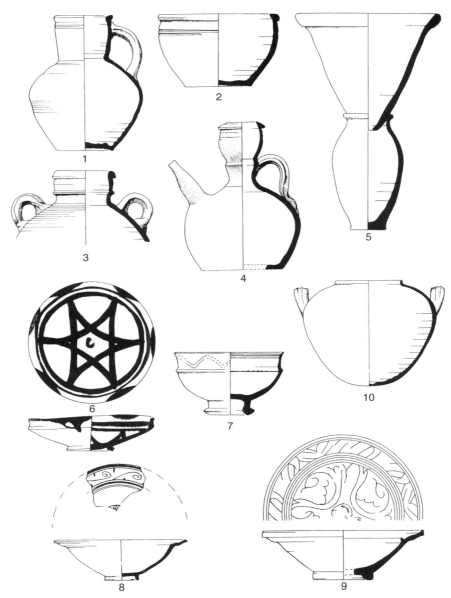

Figure 6.1 Local and imported ceramics of the Crusader period

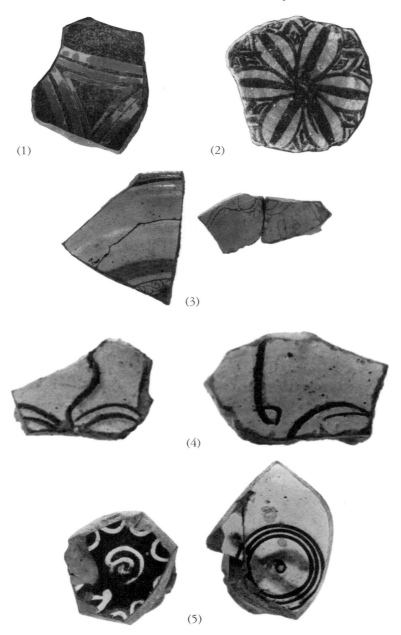

(1) (2)

(3)

(4)

(5)

Plate 6.1 Local and imported glazed ceramics (photographs by the author).

application of the glaze, leaving a dark linear pattern, or (2) rather than covering the entire surface of the vessel with slip a pattern was painted in slip on to the dark surface before the glaze was applied (slip-painting). Because of the transparent nature of the glaze its true colour was apparent only where the glaze covered the white slip. The area on the vessel where slip had not been painted or had been removed by incision appears as dark, usually brown, whatever the true colour of the glaze.

Tin-opacified glazed vessels were decorated with coloured overglaze painting or by a metallic overglaze technique known as lustre. These techniques were already well established before the twelfth century. The innovations of potters in the eastern Mediterranean, particularly in thirteenth-century Cyprus, were in the forms and decorations they introduced rather than in the manner in which the vessels were manufactured. They did however introduce into the region one important technological advance from the Far East, a technique already in use in Iraq and Iran. This was the separation of glazed vessels during firing by the use of small clay tripod stilts which prevented the vessels from adhering to one another. The use of the tripod enabled the potter to pack many more vessels into the kiln in a single firing. This was an important achievement which when introduced into Cyprus turned the island into the major pottery producer in the region.

Local ceramics

The majority of vessels used by the Franks were locally manufactured and included dry-storage vessels and water containers made of a porous, buff-coloured clay. These types continued traditions established long before the arrival of the Franks (Figure 6.1 (1–4)). An industry of simple but decorative handmade wares developed in villages, probably in the twelfth century, and was well established by the thirteenth century (Plate 6.2). These included cooking pots, jars, jugs, basins and bowls. They were often decorated with lively geometric designs painted in red or brown slip on a pale background.

Wheel-made globular cooking vessels used by the Franks continued a form known in the region since the ninth century. They were made of thin red-brown ware and had broad strap handles raised high at the centre, and lead glaze applied to the lower interior in order to prevent food from adhering to the pot during cooking (Figure 6.1 (10)).[2] Also in use were shallow glazed cooking pans and bowls.

Imported ceramics from Egypt and Syria

Considerable quantities of unglazed and glazed ceramics reached the kingdom of Jerusalem from Fatimid Egypt. These included various types of water containers of buff-coloured ware (a type of pottery which was also manufactured locally). A popular vessel in buff ware was the *ibriq*, a spouted jug with a distinctive high neck, one or more handles and often a decorative filter in the neck. In the twelfth century tin-glazed bowls and jugs decorated

Plate 6.2 Handmade geometric painted jug (courtesy of the Israel Antiquities Authority)

with stained, polychrome overglaze patterns, which were manufactured in Fustat and perhaps in Fayyum and were known as 'Fayyumi Ware', appear to have been still reaching the kingdom, particularly the coastal area. In the thirteenth century Mamluk Egypt exported to the region distinctive deep bowls with high trumpet bases decorated with heraldic motifs in sgraffito or slip-painting, and perhaps also mould-made bowls.

Syria also supplied high-quality glazed vessels to the Frankish states. These were alkaline glazed vessels decorated with underglaze designs in blue and black. Some porcelain from the Far East also reached the Frankish states, as did a certain amount of pottery from Iraq and Iran, but these imports were few compared with those of Egypt and Syria.

Imported ceramics from Byzantium and the Christian West

Until the thirteenth century very little pottery was imported from the West by the Franks. The pottery of Syria and Egypt was readily available and greatly superior in quality to European wares. In the thirteenth century tin-glazed bowls and jugs were imported from the kingdom of Sicily and some pottery perhaps reached the Latin East from the Aegean. However, the main source of imported pottery outside Egypt and Syria was Cyprus, which already in the twelfth century was producing for mainland consumption sgraffito-decorated ceramics in the Byzantine tradition. This production, at least in the early stages, was limited to coarse, simple, lead-glazed bowls.[3] They were decorated with white, cream or pale green lead-based slip-glaze. On the interior they had finely incised designs depicting birds or animals, usually an eagle, or floral decorative bands. They are known as 'Mid-Twelfth Century Byzantine Sgraffito' (Morgan 1942: 127). Towards the end of the twelfth century this type appears to have been replaced by a related class which is commonly known as 'Early-Thirteenth Century Aegean Ware' (Megaw 1975). This type differs from the previous class in that the incised decoration is replaced by broad gouging, the designs are simple and usually abstract, and the glaze is generally yellow rather than cream or white. As the name suggests, these vessels were manufactured in the Aegean region. However, Neutron Activation Analysis (NAA) has shown that vessels of both these classes found in sites in the kingdom of Jerusalem were manufactured in Cyprus (Boas 1994).[4] 'Byzantine Sgraffito' is found on many sites in the kingdom of Jerusalem but never in very great quantities. On the other hand the later 'Aegean Ware' is extremely common in the kingdom of Jerusalem, including inland sites which were outside the area of Frankish rule after 1187. This would seem to suggest that in the mid-twelfth century the export of ceramics, and perhaps trade in general, from Byzantine Cyprus to the Frankish kingdom of Jerusalem existed but was limited, but that once Cyprus became a Frankish possession in 1191 the volume of trade (or at least of ceramic exports to the mainland) increased considerably.

Around the beginning of the thirteenth century a new, more advanced type of glazed pottery was imported into the kingdom of Jerusalem. Known as 'Zeuxippus Ware' after a site in Constantinople (Megaw 1968, 1989), these are sgraffito-decorated bowls, distinguished from other lead-glazed wares by the extremely high quality of the fabric and the exceptionally shiny pale green or yellow glaze. They are very thinly potted and fired harder than other medieval ceramics. The decoration on the interior of the bowls combines very fine and broadly incised lines with a variety of new designs including concentric circles, 'S' shapes, mushroom-like patterns, and occasional figurative subjects. The exterior is often decorated with loops or tongues of slip. While many of these vessels found in sites throughout the eastern Mediterranean were probably manufactured in or near Constantinople, NAA shows that they were also manufactured in Cyprus, possibly by potters who emigrated to the island after Constantinople was occupied by the Franks in 1204.

From early in the thirteenth century, potters in Port Saint Symeon (al-Mina), the Frankish port of Antioch, began to produce the distinctive sgraffito-decorated polychrome glazed pottery known as 'Port St Symeon Ware' (Plate 6.3(1)). The frequent use of Christian motifs leaves no doubt that this pottery was intended for the Frankish market. The most typical form is a hemispherical bowl with a ledge rim and a low ring-base. The outer edge of the rim is sometimes decorated with 'pie-crust' impressions. The ware is usually buff-orange or pink but occasionally brick-red or red-brown, and is fairly coarse. The decoration is carried out in a fairly fine sgraffito under a cream-coloured glaze and is highlighted by the application of alternate yellow ochre and green stains. Designs range from floral to geometric and figurative. Port St Symeon Ware was produced from 1200 until the fall of the port to the Mamluks in 1268. Evidence of kiln sites (in the form of wasters – unfinished or kiln-damaged vessels) was found at St Symeon but nowhere else and it is quite possible that the manufacture of this class came to an end with the loss of the port. This was a very popular ware in the kingdom of Jerusalem, as was the somewhat similar pottery that developed in Cyprus in about the third decade of the thirteenth century. What is known simply as 'Thirteenth-Century Cypriot Ware' is a polychrome sgraffito-decorated or slip-painted ware that appears to have incorporated the sophisticated kiln techniques of 'Zeuxippus Ware' as well as the use of colour and design of Port St Symeon Ware. After the Syrian and Egyptian pottery this is by far the most common type of pottery imported into the kingdom of Jerusalem. It makes up over 90 per cent of the non-Islamic imported wares in most coastal sites excepting perhaps only Akko, where a large quantity of Italian pottery is also found. The main innovation in this pottery is the distinctive shape of the bowls with a tall, vertical, outwardly concave rim, a hemispherical body and a high ring-base with an upturned foot (Figure 6.1 (7)). As with the Zeuxippus Ware, tripod stilts were used to separate bowls during the firing. Sgraffito designs include floral and figurative motifs and heraldic signs. Slip-painted designs are formed by loops and spirals (Plate 6.1 (5, 6)).

Only one type of pottery was imported in quantity to the Levant from Europe. This was a tin-glazed ware known as 'Proto-Maiolica' (Plate 6.3(2)). The name indicates that this is the prototype of the well-known Majolica pottery that became popular somewhat later, particularly in Italy and Spain. The use of a tin-opacified glaze and overglaze painting in blue, manganese and yellow made this type of pottery quite distinctive amongst the ceramic repertoire of the Latin East. The clay came from relatively iron-free sources in southern Italy and Sicily and as a result the fabric is generally buff, pale yellow or cream in colour. Bowls once again make up the majority of the vessels, but some jugs were also found. The bowls are hemispherical with a low ring-base and a triangular or ledge rim. The decoration is executed on a white background and includes a wide range of designs such as grid patterns,

Plate 6.3 Port St Symeon Ware and Proto Maiolica from 'Atlit (courtesy of the Israel Antiquities Authority)

floral motifs, fish, birds, human figures, ships and town fortifications. Proto-Maiolica reached the Levant in the thirteenth century. It is found in comparatively large numbers on coastal sites, particularly in Akko, and tails off considerably further east, becoming almost completely absent from assemblages on inland sites. This distribution suggests that it may have been imported specifically for the use of the Italian merchant communities which were located on the coast.

Glass

The manufacture of glass was one of the most important industries in the Latin East. Contemporary sources mention Tyre as a centre of the glass industry (Jaques de Vitry 1896: 92–3). William of Tyre describes beautiful vases famous for their transparency (William of Tyre 1986: 13.3) and the twelfth-century Arab geographer al-Idrisi noted that the Franks made long-necked vases of glass (Le Strange 1890: 344). According to Benjamin of Tudela, Jews in Tyre manufactured the renowned Tyrian glass, and he noted the presence of some ten Jewish glass-makers in Antioch (Benjamin of Tudela 1907: 16, 18). Jaques de Vitry, Bishop of Tyre, wrote in the first half of the thirteenth century: 'In the territory of Tyre and Akko they make the purest glass with cunning workmanship out of the sands of the sea: that is, out of sand and sea gravel' (Jaques de Vitry 1896: 92–3). Red glass was made in Beirut.[5]

Finds

Medieval glass has been found at Montfort Castle (Dean 1927/1982: 40–2, Figures 55–8), at the Frankish village of al-Qubeiba (Bagatti 1993: 161–4, Figure 35, Plates 62, 63), at the Red Tower (Burj al-Ahmar) (Pringle 1986b: 161–2, Figure 53), at the Frankish tower of Beit She'an (Boas forthcoming), at Yoqne'am (Lester 1996: 212–14), and in a tower on the northern Frankish wall of Akko in a thirteenth-century context (Gorin-Rosen 1997: 75–85).

Vessel forms and decoration

Typical forms amongst the free-blown glass manufactured by the Franks are perfume bottles, long-necked vases with mushroom-shaped rims, beakers, hanging lamps and large industrial jars. Window glass, both round panes and plate glass, was also made. Bases and handles on blown vessels were attached by direct fusing. Some vessels had hollow legs formed by placing the leg inside the vessel, reheating it and then pushing it through the vessel wall (Dean 1927/1982: 40). Decoration on the finer vessels includes moulding, trailing, enamelling (painted designs on the exterior or on both the interior and exterior) and prunting (application of marked protuberances to the surface).[6]

Bottles

A common type of bottle has thin walls, a globular body with a high-kicked base, a long neck and a flaring rim. In many examples the neck is decorated with twisted trails, often of a different colour from the vessel. Several examples come from the Frankish tower at Beit She'an. They are present also in finds from Akko (Gorin-Rosen 1997: 76–8, Figure 1:1a–3). There are also broad-necked bottles with a distinctive overhanging rim. Examples come from Beit She'an and from Akko (Gorin-Rosen 1997: 78, 80, Figure 1:4–7). Another form is a bottle with broad bulges in the neck. These have been found at Beit She'an and an example of this type was discovered at the Red Tower (Pringle 1986b: 162, Figure 53:17).

Bowls

Hemispherical bowls with simple folded rims and bases were found at the Red Tower (Pringle 1986b: Figs. 53:8, 53:10, 53:20, 53:21). Similar finds came from the lower levels of the fill in the moat at Beit She'an.

Beakers and goblets

These were drinking vessels used for wine. Undecorated beakers have been recovered at a number of sites. At al-Qubeiba a group of plain beakers made of light blue and green glass was found (Bagatti 1947, 1993: 164, Figure 35, Plate 63). The finest beakers, however, are a variant of the Islamic enamelled glass of the period, known as 'Syro-Frankish Beakers'. The Syrian practice of enamelling glass vessels together with the use of Christian subject matter parallels the combination of Syrian use of colour and incised decoration with Christian subject matter on the pottery manufactured in Port St Symeon (see p. 149). The form of these beakers is simple, with flaring walls and a concave base with a high kick, but the distinctive decoration gives them a unique and remarkable quality.

Finds of Syro-Frankish beakers are fairly numerous, but they are generally found well outside the Levant and very few pieces come from the area under Frankish rule in the East. Other than a complete beaker of unknown provenance, but apparently a local find, which is now in the Israel Museum (inv. 72, 59.194) and two fragments from Akko (Dothan 1976: 37, Figure 41), examples have come from Egypt and Anatolia and as far away as Denmark, Sweden, Austria, Switzerland, Hungary, Italy and the UK. However, it would seem probable that they were manufactured in the Crusader states. In form and decoration they appear to be an offshoot of the Syrian glass beakers. The tone of the glass is similar to that of glass vessels of known Syrian provenance and the technique of applying the paint to both the inner and outer surfaces is also an established Syrian practice (Tait 1968: 151). Additional support not only for the Levantine origin of enamelled glass but more specifically for Akko as its source of manufacture is found in the fourteenth-century inventory of a Bavarian knight, one Erhard Rainer, which includes amongst the list of his property 'acrischew glaz', apparently a reference to glass vessels imported from Akko prior to 1291 (Pfeiffer 1970: 67–9).[7]

These vessels may have been made in one workshop and decorated in another (Engle 1982: 44). Enamelling is a simpler process than glass-making, requiring lower temperatures.[8] The decorations on the vessels vary but are mainly of heraldic shields, animals, birds and mythological beasts. Secondary motifs that are found on most of the beakers are stylized plants or trees with trefoil and heart-shaped leaves. The other major element featured on these vessels is the inscription. Beakers which have representations of the Virgin Mary or other non-related subjects carry the inscription 'AVE MARIA

GRACIA PLENA' (Hail Mary full of grace). A well-known beaker in the British Museum bears the inscription 'MAGISTER ALDREVANDIN ME FECIT' (Master Aldrevandin made me). On other beakers appears the rather apprehensive injunction 'NON. DETUR. PETE+' (do not break it).

Another type of beaker more commonly found in the Latin East is the prunted beaker, a beaker with small protrusions of glass (prunts) attached to its exterior (Plate 6.4). Prunted beakers have been found at Akko (Gorin-Rosen 1997: 82–4, Figure 2:20a–26) and at the glass factory at nearby Somelaria, where some of the finds from Akko may have been manufactured (Gorin-Rosen 1997: 84). A complete example of this type of beaker, now in the Ha'aretz Museum in Tel Aviv, is said to have come from Beit She'an. Fragments of a prunted beaker were found at Montfort Castle (Dean 1927/1982: Figure 56:F). Outside the Latin East finds of thirteenth-century prunted beakers have been made at Corinth (Davidson 1952: 87, 113, Figure 14:742, 744, Plates 57:742, 58:743–4) and in Apulia (Harden 1966: 70–9, Figs. 5, 7, 10, 13).

Another type of drinking vessel, one that appears to have been imported to the East, is known as the 'Biconical Goblet'. A group of these vessels, apparently imported from Europe, was found at Yoqne'am (Lester 1996: 214). The only other example found in the kingdom of Jerusalem is an unpublished find from 'Atlit. Similar examples have been found in southern France and date from the twelfth and thirteenth centuries. Additional drinking vessels are stemmed goblets, a traditional form in earlier periods, of which examples

Plate 6.4 A prunted beaker from Beit She'an (courtesy of the Ha'aretz Museum, Tel Aviv)

have been found at Beit She'an and Yoqne'am (Lester 1996: 213, Figure XVII.14:5,6).

Jars

At Beit She'an a quantity of large industrial glass jars with thin vertical walls and high-kicked bases was found. It is not clear what these jars were used for, and it is possible that they come from the Mamluk sugar factory at this site rather than from a Frankish context.

Lamps

Glass lamps, known of in the Byzantine and Early Arab periods, continued to be used in the twelfth and thirteenth centuries. These generally took the form of an open bowl with a tube in the centre to hold the wick. Some had two or more attached handles by which they could be suspended, the handles often of a different-coloured glass than the lamp itself (Dean 1927/1982: 40, Figure 56B; Pringle 1986b: 162, Figs. 53:15,16). Lamps intended to be placed on a candelabrum had a hollow tube extending below the base (Pringle 1986b: 162, Figure 53:14).

Window glass and stained glass

Window glass is rarely found, although it was probably used in important buildings[9] and perhaps occasionally in minor buildings.[10] At the farmhouse of Har Hozevim near Jerusalem a 4.8 cm wide fragment of green plate glass was found. Stained window glass has been found at Montfort and at 'Atlit. Fragments from a window found in the parish church at 'Atlit were of glass tinted yellow-brown, light green, purple-red, blue and colourless, cut into strips and curves averaging 2.5 cm wide (Johns 1997: 133, Figs. 8, 9). They formed a simple geometric design which has been reconstructed and is on display at the Israel Museum in Jerusalem. The cames (lead pieces which held the glass in place) were comparatively wide (approximately 7 mm) to allow for the varying widths of the quarries (glass panes). At Montfort a large quantity of stained glass was recovered from the chapel and adjacent rooms. Green, blue, horn-coloured and colourless glass was found painted with grisaille bands, interlaced foliation and human figures (Dean 1927/1982: 42, Figs. 55, 57, 58).

A quantity of tinted plate glass painted in grisaille was found in a tomb chamber in the crypt of the Church of Nativity in Bethlehem (Bagatti 1968: 218–20, Figs. 30, 31). The pieces include various floral motifs and one piece is decorated with a fish image. The quarries are 1–3 mm thick and are coloured turquoise and brown. Lead cames 1 cm thick and 5 mm wide were found with the glass (Bagatti 1968: Figure 31: 13). These finds clearly pre-date the fifteenth century when the tomb was blocked, and the style points to the twelfth century.

Some fragments of stained glass were found in the south aisle of the Cathedral of St Nicholas in Famagusta (Enlart 1987: 243). These are the only published examples from Cyprus. They consist of light purple and emerald green glass and plain lozenge-shaped quarries. They date from the end of Frankish rule in the town and are evidently Italian work.

Glass manufacture

In 1969 a glass furnace was excavated at es-Samariya (Frankish Somelaria) about one kilometre inland from the coast and some six kilometres north of Akko (Davidson Weinberg 1985: 305–16). The brick furnace, now on display in the Ha'aretz Museum, Tel Aviv, consisted of two firing chambers, one on the north side of the structure and one on the south, both with vents for air circulation to the west. A flue extended through the furnace from north to south. Above the southern firing chamber was a glass-covered melting tank which had originally been under the roof of the firing chamber to the north. To the east was a work area, where there was a brick stand adjacent to the furnace. It has been interpreted as the 'yoke' or 'pig', a stand on which tools could be laid when not in use (Davidson Weinberg 1985: 309).

This furnace appears to have been used to reprocess blue or greenish-blue glass lumps. The refining process involved the melting of these lumps in ceramic bowls and jars, after which the glass was poured into the tank from which it could be taken for blowing. Fragments of blown flasks and prunted vessels were found on the site, as well as a large quantity of glass waste.

Metalwork

There is no direct archaeological evidence for the mining of metals in the Latin East. Some metals were perhaps mined in the region, but most were imported from the West and from Africa. One recent archaeological find relates to the importation of metals during this period. About fifty loaf-shaped lead ingots were recovered by underwater archaeologists offshore from Ascalon. Their weight varied between 80 and 100 kg each. Carbon 14 analysis carried out on organic components in the ingots dates them to the twelfth century (Sharvit and Galili forthcoming).[11]

Frankish metalwork ranges from important and minor works of art to souvenirs for pilgrims. These were the products of goldsmiths and other metalworkers in Jerusalem, Akko and elsewhere. In addition, utilitarian objects such as tools and various items for household use were the products of smithies found in every settlement or castle. Some of the finest metal artwork was manufactured in the kingdom of Jerusalem, mainly for liturgical use. Other important works of art were imported from Europe and from the East.

Grille from the Templum Domini

One of the alterations made by the Franks when they converted the Dome of the Rock into a church was the placing, probably in about 1140, of an iron grille around the rock (Plate 6.5). The grille was possibly donated to the church by Queen Melisende (Folda 1995: 136). It was a measure intended to protect the rock from pilgrims in search of souvenirs. The grille remained in place until the 1960s; part of it is now on display in the Islamic Museum on the Temple Mount in Jerusalem. It is of French Romanesque style, formed of eight parts consisting of panels of spirals held together by rings and supported by spikes crowned with fleurs-de-lys on which candles could be placed. It is an outstanding piece of metalwork which outshines comparable examples in France and England.[12]

Iron candelabra from the Cathedral of St Nicholas, Famagusta

(See Plate 6.6(1).) Two candelabra from the Cathedral of St Nicholas in Famagusta date from the fourteenth century. They measure 165 × 53 cm. They have three feet, hold five candles each and are formed of cylindrical rods with angular annulets, fig-leaves and fruit, and arms ending in spikes. They are similar to the twelfth-century examples from Jerusalem, if not quite as fine (Enlart 1987: 245, n. 35, Figure 188).

Plate 6.5 The iron grille from the *Templum Domini* in the Islamic Museum, Jerusalem (photograph by the author, courtesy of the Department of the Awqaf in Jerusalem)

1

2

Plate 6.6 Medieval candelabra from Famagusta (Enlart 1928) and Jerusalem (photograph by the author, courtesy of the Department of the Awqaf in Jerusalem)

Iron candelabra from the Templum Domini

Two iron candelabra were placed by the Franks in the *Templum Domini* and stood there above the rock until they were removed, apparently during the British Mandate, to the nearby Islamic Museum (Plate 6.6(2)). They are over 2 m high and consist of cylindrical rods with flowers and pomegranates at the top. They have three feet and hold four candles each (three at their base just above the feet and another at the top) (Enlart 1928: 211, Atlas I, 1926: Figure 139, Plate 40). They are similar to candelabra of thirteenth- to fifteenth-century date in Spain and France and appear to be of Catalan origin.

Pricket candlesticks from Bethlehem

Two silver pricket candlesticks were discovered in Bethlehem in 1869 (Plate 6.7). They were probably intended for use on an altar. They are 27 cm high

Plate 6.7 Pricket candlesticks (courtesy of the Studium Biblicum Franciscanum)

with three gilded projecting feet in the form of a lion's forepaws. The central globes are also gilded. Despite the inscription they bear, 'Maladicatur qui me aufert de loco Sce. Nativitatis Bethleem' (cursed be he who removes me from the place of the Nativity in Bethlehem), they are now housed in the Museum of the Flagellation in Jerusalem.

Three additional pricket candlesticks of Limoges work were found in the Bethlehem hoard. Two of them are 17.2 cm high and are decorated with blue enamel floral motifs and birds. They have three projecting feet with a lion's head at the upper part of each foot and a forepaw at the base. The third candlestick is 47 cm high and is decorated with mainly green enamel. It has three projecting feet, only one of which still has the lion's forepaw. The enamel is decorated with floral motifs.

Brass bowls from Bethlehem

Two engraved brass bowls decorated with scenes from the life of St Thomas were discovered in the same hoard in Bethlehem in 1869 and are also now in the Museum of the Flagellation. They date from the twelfth century. They are 8 cm high and have a diameter of 32 cm. The engraving is very fine. Similar bowls of thirteenth-century date, also illustrated with the life of St Thomas, are in the Louvre and the British Museum (Dalton 1922: 133–60).

Brass bowl of Hugh IV of Cyprus

This fine, if badly deteriorated, brass basin (originally silver plated) was acquired in Cyprus in the nineteenth century. It was apparently a product of a Muslim craftsman. It displays six medallions with sacred figures surrounded by twelve medallions with signs of the zodiac. The basin has a Kufic inscription and around its rim an inscription in Gothic characters stating that it was made for King Hugh of Cyprus and Jerusalem (Hugh IV, 1324–61) (H-R. d'Allemagne, quoted in Enlart 1987: 511–19).

Brass plates from Bellapais Abbey

Two brass plates preserved in the Bellapais Abbey church date to the fifteenth century (Enlart 1987: 186, Figure 132). Enlart suggests that they were probably made in Flanders. One has a running stag in the centre surrounded by a ring of bosses and floral scrolls.[13] The other shows a woman with a hawk on her wrist in the centre surrounded by an illegible Gothic inscription.

Organ pipes and bells from Bethlehem

The bells from the bell-tower of the Church of Nativity in Bethlehem are known to have been removed on the order of Mohammed II in 1452 or perhaps earlier and were buried nearby. Three bronze bells were unearthed in 1863 near the kitchen of the Franciscan convent, and 221 copper *fistulae* (organ pipes of reduced diameter – 3 cm), thirteen small bells and a larger bell with a dragon-shaped mount were found nearby in 1906 (Plate 6.8). The bells are of different sizes. On the smallest is inscribed 'Vox Domini' (the voice of the Lord). The varying size of the bells suggests that they belonged to a carillon. The organ pipes may have come from a water organ (a hydraulic organ using water power).

Ampullae

One of the offshoots of the pilgrimage phenomenon, both in Europe and in the East, was the manufacture of objects which the pilgrims could obtain at holy sites as keepsakes. Amongst these items were ampullae – mould-made ceramic or lead bottles which held oil or holy water (Plate 6.9 (1, 2)). In the Middle Ages lead ampullae were manufactured in the kingdom of Jerusalem, probably wherever there was intensive pilgrimage activity, for example, in Jerusalem and Akko.[14] Evidence of Akko as a source of their manufacture has recently come to light in excavations in the north-east corner of the city (Syon in preparation). Archaeologists discovered, together with an unfinished ampulla, six stone moulds, a quantity of lead raw material and some liquid mercury probably used to silver-plate the finished pieces. The moulds are made from a type of stone that does not appear to be local, and it would seem

Plate 6.8 Bells of a carillon from Bethlehem (courtesy of the Studium Biblicum Franciscanum)

that the workshop was originally located elsewhere but that at some stage the craftsman arrived with his equipment and settled in Akko. The ampullae (a second one was discovered nearby) were small, measuring only about 6 cm in height and 4 cm wide, and were decorated in low relief with geometric motifs. Other examples of medieval ampullae have designs including crosses and sacred scenes such as the Holy Sepulchre, Holy Women at the Sepulchre, the Crucifixion and the Anastasis. Ampullae of unknown provenance are in the collections of the Ha'aretz Museum in Tel Aviv, and in the Convent of St Anne and the Museum of the Flagellation in Jerusalem. Folda has discussed two similar ampullae from the Holy Sepulchre, now in Berlin, which he dates to no later than 1160 (Folda 1995: 294–7, Plates 8B.8, 8B.9). Such ampullae have also been found in the excavations at Corinth in Frankish contexts (Davidson 1952: 75, Plate 53: 573–5) and in Tripoli (Coupel 1941: 51, Figure 13a, b), and two very similar vessels were found in western Sicily (D'Angelo 1972: 58).[15]

Reliquaries

Under the Franks the kingdom of Jerusalem became the most important source of holy relics, and as a natural consequence artisans in Jerusalem were involved in the manufacture of reliquaries. Albert of Aix, Fulcher of Chartres and William of Tyre all describe the relic of the True Cross found after the

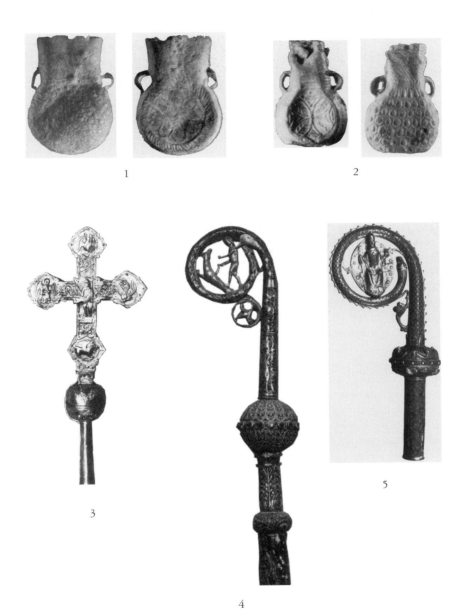

Plate 6.9 Lead ampullae. (1 courtesy of Ha'aretz Museum, Tel Aviv, 2 courtesy of the Studium Biblicum Franciscanum). Processional cross (3 Enlart 1926–8, album 1, 1926) and croisiers (4 Enlart 1926–8, album 1, 1926 and 5 courtesy of the Studium Biblicum Franciscanum)

capture of Jerusalem in 1099 as being encased in a reliquary. According to Albert of Aix this was a long golden cross, Fulcher of Chartres described it as a gold and silver cross and William of Tyre as a silver casket (Kühnel 1994: 127). Both these forms of reliquaries – the cross-shaped container and the casket – were types manufactured by the goldsmiths and silversmiths of Jerusalem, and several examples are known in the West. In various museums and churches there are reliquaries in the form of a double-armed cross (*crux gemina*).[16] They are made of wood with jewelled silver-gilt coverings and contain fragments believed to have come from the True Cross. Many such crosses reached the West in the thirteenth century, suggesting that they may have also been manufactured outside Jerusalem, perhaps in Akko.[17]

Pendant crosses

A number of small bronze pendant crosses have been excavated in medieval contexts. At al-Qubeiba several small pendant crosses were found; some have a glass disc or a semi-precious stone at the centre and the top arm has a loop to connect it to the chain. A bronze cross found at Caesarea, 3 cm high and 2.3 cm wide, is an inverted (St Peter's) clover leaf-type cross (Holum *et al.* 1988: 224). At al-Kurum a heel-shaped slate mould for pendant crosses was found in one of the village houses. It has three hollows for very small (2 × 2 cm) pendants, each one slightly different from the others.

Pendant reliquary crosses

Cross pendants were occasionally used as reliquaries. A fine bronze reliquary cross was found in the sea near the southern gate of the town of Caesarea (Holum *et al.* 1988: 218, Figure 160). It is 9 cm high (including its hinged attachment) and 5.2 cm wide. The cross was made from two pieces and a clasp at the base (which is broken) allowed it to be opened. Inside it contained a relic. The relief design on the front of the cross has the crucified figure of Christ at the centre and four medallions containing busts of the Virgin Mary, St John and two angels. The back of the cross has at its centre the figure of Mary with an abbreviated Greek inscription 'Mother of the Most High'; the medallions contain the four Evangelists, each holding a book. Although it could be earlier (this type begins in the seventh century), the iconography suggests a date in the twelfth to thirteenth century for this cross.

Processional crosses

Two badly corroded bronze processional crosses were found in Gethsemane and are now on display in the Museum of the Flagellation in Jerusalem. One is 14 cm high and 7 cm wide and has a metal staff of 20 cm giving a total height of 34 cm. The second cross is larger, 21 cm long and 13 cm wide, but lacks a staff.

Crosiers

A Limoges work crosier in the Museum of the Flagellation in Jerusalem is 32 cm long (Plate 6.9 (5). It has the form of a snake enclosing a boat-shaped medallion with the figures in relief: the seated figures of Christ on one side, a bishop on the other and a small angel below. The enamel design is of dragons. A second crosier of Limoges work with a figure of St George slaying the dragon (Plate 6.9 (4)) was recorded by Enlart as belonging to the Armenian Patriarchate (Enlart 1926–8, album 1, 1926: Plate 49.159). Similar crosiers in the collection of the Metropolitan Museum of Art, New York, have been dated to c. 1250 (Pijoan 1940: 235).

Varia

Most of the metalwork manufactured in the Latin East was of a utilitarian nature. Blacksmiths spent most of their time manufacturing spikes, nails, tools and other items, above all horseshoes (Figure 6.2 (10)). A remarkable collection of iron tools has been recovered from the excavations at Vadum Jacob. These include spades, axes, picks, hoes, chisels and spatulas. Iron bowls, knives and sickles were also found here as well as numerous large and small nails (Raphael forthcoming). Three iron chisels, varying between 3.9 and 5.2 cm in length, were found at Har Hozevim (Boas forthcoming). Weapons are amongst the more common metal finds (see pp. 176–9). Items of clothing are largely limited to buckles and buttons (Dean 1927/1982: Figure 53.F–J; Johns 1997: 147, 149, Figs. 1, 2, 16; Pringle 1986b: 164, Figs. 55.11, 56.15–17). In Arsuf (Apollonia) a small metal head, perhaps part of a pendant, was found in the southern part of the town (Roll and Ayalon 1989: Figure 58). An incised bronze fish pendant measuring 2.5 cm was found at 'Atlit. A small bronze drill-head, originally on a wooden handle, was found at al-Kurum together with two tiny gilded bronze tweezers and a bronze archer's thimble (Boas forthcoming). The latter was probably used for leatherwork. Small bronze keys were found at 'Atlit. Keys are occasionally found, but locks in the Middle Ages were often made of wood. Knifes and razors were found at Belvoir (Ben-Dov 1975: 104) and a razor was found at Montfort (Dean 1927/1982: Figure 54A).[18]

Iron horseshoes were found in the stables at 'Atlit (Johns 1997: 42–3, Figs. 8, 15.13), at Yoqne'am (Khamis 1996: 220, Figure 18.2: 2, Plate 18.5: 2) and at Vadum Jacob (Raphael forthcoming). At Belvoir unfinished horseshoes were found in the smithy together with a stirrup (Ben-Dov 1975: 106). Two shipments of 3,000 horseshoes each from Sicily in 1280 and 1281 are evidence of the huge numbers of these items needed in difficult times, a need which the blacksmiths in the kingdom were apparently incapable of meeting at the time (Pryor 1988: 140). Spurs used by the Franks were generally of goad form with a single sharp point. A good example was recovered in excavations at Yoqne'am (Khamis 1996: 219, Figure 18.2:1, Plate 18.5:1).

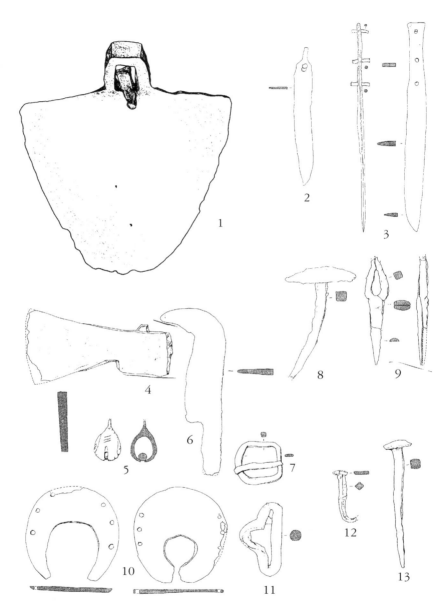

Figure 6.2 Tools and metal objects from Vadum Jacob.

Stone vessels and objects

Stone objects are often found in excavations but, unless they are distinctly Frankish in design or come from well-defined contexts, they are difficult to date. Amongst stone objects found are a brazier or stove, mortars and troughs from Montfort Castle (Dean 1927/1982: Figure 43). Also from Montfort are some very fine stone matrices. One of these displays a Germanic heraldic shield with an eagle on a diaper background as well as a fleur-de-lis (Dean 1927/1982: 32, Figure 38). Another matrix has a finely detailed design of two fish (Dean 1927/1982: 34, Figure 39). These were probably intended for stamping designs in leather. A limestone mould for jewellery pendants was recently found in Akko (Stern 1997: 15, Figure 18).

In 1997 a stone sundial was found in the debris from the collapsed northern wall of Vadum Jacob (Ellenblum and Boas forthcoming) (Plate 6.10). Carved from a large slab of limestone, it is hemicyclic and concave in form and is divided into twelve-hour segments. It is similar to sundials from Bethany (Saller 1957: Plate 77.9) and from the Ophel in Jerusalem (Macalister and Duncan 1926: Figs. 144–5), but lacks the centre with the *gnomon* (the bar which casts a shadow).[19]

Whet stones are found in many Crusader-period sites but are not always recorded. At Arsuf four such stones from Frankish contexts in the citadel and in the southern part of the town were published (Roll and Ayalon 1989: Figure 60). There are two forms: flat, fairly rectangular thin stones and rods

Plate 6.10 A twelfth-century sundial from Vadum Jacob (photograph by Buki Boaz)

with a square profile. They all have a hole drilled near one end for hanging. At Har Hozevim two whet stones were found, one of marble and one of schist. Both are about 5.5 cm long and rod-shaped with a square profile.

A large stone cross from near the tell of Akko found in 1976 may have come from the roof of a church, perhaps from St Nicholas, which seems to have been located in this area (Kedar 1997: Figure 22). A water spout or gargoyle from the Crusader period can be seen on the northern wall of the Franciscan church in Jerusalem and one was found in Ascalon (Plate 6.11).

Inscriptions and heraldry

Whereas placing inscriptions on public buildings was a common practice in earlier periods and under Muslim rule, it is less common in Frankish building and most Frankish epigraphy is from tombstones (see pp. 230–33). The subject of Crusader inscriptions has been dealt with by de Sandoli (1974). One example of a dedicatory inscription from a building is that of 1311 on the Cathedral of St Nicholas, Famagusta (Plate 6.12).

Heraldic signs are occasionally found engraved or carved on Frankish buildings. In Jerusalem the Templars carved their shield on buildings in their possession. Fine heraldic carvings are found on some Frankish buildings in the kingdom of Jerusalem and the northern states and there are numerous examples in the kingdom of Cyprus. A reused chancel post from Ramla is engraved with heraldic blazons and the names of pilgrims. In 1993 a slab of whitish-grey marble with an Arabic inscription dating from the Fatimid period was found near the northern (Jaffa) gate of Ascalon. It had been reused by the Franks, who superimposed on it heraldic emblems – three large shields, each decorated with two bars and three roundels above the upper bar, which were the arms of a knight named Sir Hugh Wake, and smaller shields decorated with ten billets belonging to an unidentified knight (Sharon 1995: 61–86). This stone was apparently placed on the wall of a tower in the northern defences of the town which was built by Sir Hugh Wake during the Crusade of Richard of Cornwall in 1241. As Sharon notes, this is the only material evidence for this crusade.

Wood

Because it is an organic substance, wood rarely survives over long periods unless it is in an extremely dry location or is an object of some importance – a work of art or a basic part of a structure such as a roof beam. Occasionally, however, other wooden objects have somehow survived. One of the few examples of wood carving from the Crusader period is located in the Church of Nativity in Bethlehem. In the central doorway of the narthex are parts of an intricately carved wooden door, a gift from the King of Little Armenia, Constantine, in 1227. The sumptuously carved panels display floral arabesques, crosses and inscriptions in Armenian and Arabic. The Armenian

Plate 6.11 A gargoyle found in Ascalon (courtesy of Israel Antiquities Authority)

Plate 6.12   Inscription of Bishop Baldwin Lambert from the south wall of St
Nicholas, Famagusta (photograph by the author)

inscription reads: 'The door of the Blessed Mother of God was made in the
year 676 by the hands of Father Abraham and Father Arakel in the time of
Hethum son of Constantine, King of Armenia. God have mercy on their
souls.' The Arabic inscription reads: 'This door was finished with the help of
God be He exalted, in the days of our Lord the Sultan Malik al-Mu'azzam in
the month of Muharram in the year 624.'[20]

Amongst the finds from Montfort Castle are minor wooden objects. They
include spoons with 'rat-tail' handles, a wooden tent peg nearly a metre in
length, a wooden panel with canvas painted in tempera, and painted arrow
shafts of cypress wood (Dean 1927/1982: 38–9, Figs. 52, 53:V, 54D).[21] The
only other recorded finds are some fragments of wooden handles found
attached to tools and to a mace head from Vadum Jacob (see pp. 176–7).
Both of these sites are in areas of fairly high rainfall and it is surprising and
certainly fortunate that they have survived.

Games

The Rule of the Templars expressly forbade the knights of the order to play
chess, backgammon and *eschaçons* (apparently a board game using counters)
(Upton-Ward 1992: 90). However, other board games could be played: *forbot*
if the wooden counters belonged to the brother, and *marelles* (Nine Men's
Morris) if played without a wager. Game boards for *marelles* have been found

in the Templar castles of 'Atlit and Vadum Jacob. At 'Atlit one was carved on a stone and one scratched on the plaster surface of a roof (Johns 1997: 32f., Plate 25:1,2) (Plate 6.13). Two were found at Vadum Jacob (Ellenblum and Boas forthcoming). Two were found in the kitchen at Belvoir, one carved on the underside of a stone mortar (Ben-Dov 1975: 106). They were also found at Nazareth (unpublished), Montjoie (Magen and Dadon forthcoming) and even in the Abbey of Bethany (Saller 1957: Plate 84:9,16).[22] Clearly, prohibition of games of chance did not overcome the desire for this form of

Plate 6.13 Game boards of *marelles* (Nine Men's Morris) from 'Atlit Castle (courtesy of Israel Antiquities Authority)

entertainment. The Rule of the Order of the Hospitallers includes a statute expressly forbidding the playing of dice 'on Christmas Eve or any other time' (King 1934: 78). The Templars, on the other hand, did not impose a complete ban on such betting games, but rather only on some of them and on the betting of objects of value. Thus they permitted the wagering of arrows without iron, wooden tent pegs, open lanterns and wooden mallets (Upton-Ward 1992: 89). Gambling was apparently commonplace amongst lay knights and the general Frankish population, and William of Tyre, Joineville and other contemporary writers mention dicing and checkers as being favourite pastimes of the Franks (Holmes 1977: 18). Six bone dice were found at the Templar castle of 'Atlit (Johns 1997: Plate 60, Figure 2).[23] These measure on average 0.5 × 0.5 cm and have tiny drilled holes each within a single circle.

Arms and armour

Archaeological excavations at sites including Montfort, Vadum Jacob, 'Atlit, Akko and recently excavated rural sites have produced finds of arms and limited finds of armour. The principal elements in the knight's armour were his helmet, body armour (hauberk) (Plates 6.14, 6.16) and shield. Few examples of armour have come to light. At Montfort a few small pieces of a round helmet and a pothelm were uncovered, together with scale armour (*jazeran*) and chain-mail. Though scale armour was rarely used in this period, some pieces were also found in the excavation of the twelfth-century Frankish farmhouse at Har Hozevim in Jerusalem. One is rectangular in shape, measuring 2.3 × 2.8 cm, and has five small holes for attaching it to the armour. The second piece is oval and has a diameter of 8 cm and two holes. Fragments of scale armour were also found at al-Kurum. Most of the armour used by Frankish knights consisted of chain-mail, which was especially effective against arrows. Contemporary accounts describe knights who were so densely struck by arrows that they looked like porcupines, but remained largely unhurt. Chain-mail was manufactured in a time-consuming process in which wire was wound around a rod in a helical coil and then cut entirely down one side of the rod, producing a number of open rings. The two ends of each ring were annealed (strengthened by heating) and hammered flat; they were then fashioned by linking the rings with a plier, overlapping the flattened ends and riveting them. At the time of the conquest of England the hauberk had wide sleeves and was long, reaching to the knees, divided at the front and back for riding. It originally opened in front but by the time of the Crusades had no opening but was slipped on over the head. A suit of chain-mail probably weighed about 11 kg. When not worn it was carried in a bag of wire mesh or leather (Upton-Ward 1992: 91). A hauberk in the Museum of the Armenian Patriarchate in Jerusalem (no. 319), said to be of Crusader date, is knee-length with short sleeves. It has rings with single rivets. In the front below the chest are nine metal plates about 16 cm long and 4.5 cm wide and on either side of them smaller plates measuring about 6 cm long

Plate 6.14　Hauberk in St Anne's Convent (photograph by the author, courtesy of the Convent of St Anne, Jerusalem)

and 4.5 cm wide. There are two similar plates near the neck. If authentic, this would seem to be an early twelfth-century example. Two other well-preserved hauberks are known from the kingdom of Jerusalem. One was dug up in the grounds of the convent of St Étienne north of Damascus Gate. The other is in the possession of the Convent of St Anne (Plate 6.14). The latter which is of uncertain provenance is unusual in that rather than having riveted rings each ring is a very finely fashioned spiral (Plate 6.15).

As the art of chain-mail improved and finer rings were manufactured, coverings could be made for the hands and feet. By the late twelfth and

Plate 6.15 Detail of the hauberk in St Anne's Convent (photograph by the author, courtesy of the Convent of St Anne, Jerusalem)

thirteenth centuries hands were covered with gauntlets in the form of mittens with a covering for the thumb and a single covering for the other fingers. Only at the end of the thirteenth century did the technology permit the making of separate coverings for each finger. An opening in the palm allowed the wearer to slip his hand out, leaving the glove hanging from his wrist.

Legs were covered with separate mail hose from the eleventh century on. These were worn fastened under the hauberk. The throat was laced and a mail head-covering or coif was worn under the helmet. The coif covered the forehead, neck and chin but left the nose and eyes exposed. The nasal of the helmet protected the nose. A cloth cap was worn under the coif (Upton-Ward 1992: 91).

Plate armour, which later became popular, was at first not worn except perhaps in limited use on chain-mail hauberks, but it is recorded in the later twelfth century. For example, it was worn by Richard I, not as an outer covering but rather under the hauberk in the form of a thin plate of iron worn over the chest.

Under his armour the knight wore a gambeson, a padded waistcoat which consisted of vertical layers of cloth sewn on to a leather foundation and lined with linen or silk. The gambeson protected him from bruising and was also worn by foot soldiers. Over the hauberk the knight wore a cloth covering called a surcoat, mainly intended to shield the armour from the sun's rays which would otherwise heat it and make it uncomfortable for the wearer. The surcoat also became a means of identifying the heavily armoured knight through the use of heraldic devices. The knight's horse also wore a chain-mail covering and over it a cloth cover called a caparison, which served a similar function to the knight's surcoat.

At the time of the First Crusade the helmet or helm was, as it had been thirty-three years earlier when William the Conqueror invaded England, conical or round in form and made of solid iron. From the eleventh and twelfth centuries it had a nasal (nose-guard). In the twelfth century three types of helmets were worn: conical, round-topped and cylindrical flat-topped (pothelm). The helmet protected the wearer's head but could cause him difficulty because of its weight, particularly in the heat. Even with ventilation holes some of the closed types must have made breathing difficult. If in the heat of battle the helmet was knocked askew the eyes of its wearer would be covered, leaving him completely blind. Hence some knights preferred to wear only a mail coif and no helmet at all. This handicap was eventually overcome by the addition of a visor which could be raised. It was partly because the pothelm completely hid the knight's face that the art of heraldry developed to enable him to be identified in the field.

The knight's shield, which was held in the left hand, was triangular in shape with a rounded top, vertically concave towards the body. It was made of wood covered with leather. It was hung on a strap which the knight wore around his neck and had another short strap by which he gripped it. Shield makers are recorded in Jerusalem in the twelfth century.

On his right side the knight wore a sword, contained in a scabbard or sheath of wood covered with leather and belted to his waist. The sword was generally a cutting weapon but was sometimes used for thrusting. It usually had a two-edged blade about 75 cm long that narrowed to a point; it weighed about 1.5 kg. Its parts were the blade, hilt, tang (a wrought iron piece welded to the shoulder and inserted into the grip), quillon (a guard between hilt and blade), grip or handle and pommel. Some Frankish swords have been found in excavations. Two were discovered in an underwater survey off 'Atlit (Ronen and Olami 1978: 37–8). Daggers were also used by the knight and dagger blades are occasionally found, usually badly corroded. A pommel from a Frankish dagger was seen by Clermont-Ganneau in a goldsmith's shop in Jerusalem (Clermont-Ganneau 1896: 321–2). It was a small bronze disc with red and blue enamel about 1 cm thick. On one side it was decorated with a three-turreted fort with a gate, and on the other was a heraldic shield. The edge had twelve rounded notches. Clermont-Ganneau mentions three other such pommels, one from Jerusalem which had eight notches and a floral design and another, apparently from Sidon, with ten notches and decorated with a turreted fort on one side, similar to the first of the pommels from Jerusalem, and a griffon on the other. He mentions but does not describe another pommel from Aleppo. There is one example on display in the Rockefeller Museum in Jerusalem; it is similar to the above-mentioned examples. It measures 4 cm in diameter and is engraved with a shield with seven diagonal lines. A similar piece with a shield displaying a lion is in the Metropolitan Museum in New York (Met. Mus., no. 29.152.685).

The spear was the basic defensive weapon of the infantry, used in close combat and thus thrust rather than thrown. It had a leaf or lozenge-shaped head. Several spearheads have been found at Vadum Jacob (Raphael forthcoming). In the Middle Ages the lance was another important thrusting weapon. The Crusader lance was about 2–3 m long and light in weight. It too had a leaf-shaped head. It was used to unseat the enemy and the butt often had a spike for stabbing. Axes and picks, tools used in building and agriculture, also served as weapons; both frequently appear in medieval illustrations of battle scenes. The axe was commonly used in warfare in continental Europe and in the East in the Middle Ages. The Western axe had a fan-shaped blade. The pick had a point that could pierce armour and a hammer head resembling a mace. Both axes and picks have been found at Vadum Jacob, but cannot be identified as weapons rather than building tools. The mace is one of the most ancient of weapons and ceremonial maces from the Chalcolithic period (fourth millennium BC) have been found at Nahal Hever by the Dead Sea. In the medieval period the mace was still a popular weapon, used by knights in close combat against mounted warriors. The twelfth century mace usually had a metal head, grooved lengthwise or covered with bosses mounted on a wooded staff. The excavation at Vadum Jacob revealed the only example of a Crusader period mace head found in excavations to date (Plate 6.16). It could have belonged to either the

Plate 6.16 Mace from Vadum Jacob (photograph by Buki Boaz)

Frankish or the Ayyubid soldiers. It is round, 7.5 cm in diameter, with pointed spikes and weighs 432 grams (Raphael forthcoming). Fragments of the wooden handle remained inside the hollow head. The long-hafted mace used by the Fatimids was later adopted by the Franks and eventually introduced into the West.

Unlike the Seljuk horseman, the Frankish knight did not generally use a bow. The bow was a long-distance weapon, whereas the knight was most effective at hand-to-hand combat. The bow required the use of both hands, which was impossible for the heavily armed knight. Archery, which appears to have been held somewhat in contempt by knights, was relegated to the

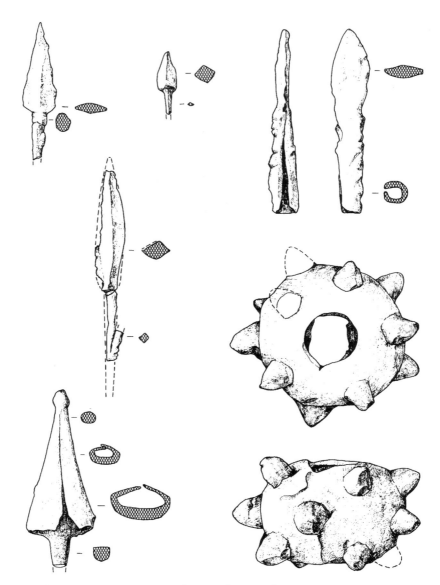

Figure 6.3 Arrowheads and mace from Vadum Jacob

Plate 6.17 Horseshoe, spur and arrowheads from Yoqne'am (courtesy of Amnon Ben-Tor) and painted arrow shafts from Montfort Castle (courtesy of the Israel Antiquities Authority)

foot soldier who, like the Muslims, used three types of bows. The first type was a simple bow, less powerful than other types but light and relatively easy to use and consequently much more rapid in discharge, an important asset in battle. The second type of bow employed by both sides was the crossbow or arbalest. This was a heavy bow with a wooden or whalebone stave mounted on a stock called a tiller. It had a groove in the top for an arrow with a mechanical trigger to release the string. It was too difficult for manual loading and was loaded by the archer, who placed his foot in a metal stirrup to hold it on the ground, and pulled back the bowstring using both arms and a hook attached to his belt. The arrow used with the crossbow had a heavier head called a 'bolt' or 'quarrel'. The crossbow was not a Frankish introduction to the East and was used by the Fatimids and Abbasids before the First Crusade. In the West it was considered a cruel weapon and was used mainly for hunting and by infantry. In the Second Lateran Council in 1139 the church banned its use in warfare except against the infidel.

The third type was the composite bow; that is, one made from more than one type of wood and consequently much stronger than a simple bow. Composite bows were used by the Turks and also developed in the West. A fourth type of bow, well known in medieval warfare in Europe, was the long-bow. It probably originated in Wales and, as it only came into common use in the fourteenth and fifteenth centuries, it was not widely used in the East. It did however make a limited appearance in the Third Crusade, probably mainly amongst followers of Richard I of England. The advantage of the longbow was its power and also the fact that it was easier to use than the crossbow. Because they were made of organic material, no remnants of Crusader bows have been found in excavations. The only published evidence is a number of bone cross-bow nuts (for holding and releasing the spanned cord) which were found at Montfort Castle (Dean 1927/1982: 38, Figure 53M).

Arrows were composed of four parts: the head or pile, the body or shaft, the notch for the bowstring and the feathers glued or tied to the shaft to steady the arrow's flight. Arrows were generally half the length of the bow (which according to English rule should be the same height as the user) (Broughton 1986: 32). Painted wooden arrow shafts were found at Montfort (Dean 1982: 38, Figure 53V). They were made of cypress wood and were painted with alternating blue and red bands and 'eye' forms. On one example the head end is pointed in order to take a Western socket-type arrowhead.[24] (Plate 6.17 (4)).

Arrowheads fall into a number of categories. In common use by the Muslim army and by the Franks as well were small triangular arrowheads, square in section with an elongated tang. These measure on average 4–5 cm in length and weigh about 15 grams. The tang when preserved is usually no longer than 1–1.5 cm. They have been found at 'Atlit (Johns 1997: Figure 15: 2–4), at the Red Tower (Pringle 1986b: 116–19, Figs. 56: 21–2, 57:23) and at Vadum Jacub, where over seven hundred have so far been recovered (Raphael forthcoming) (Figure 6.3). Another type, widespread in the West and probably in common use by the Franks at the time of the First Crusade, are arrowheads with a socket. They measure about 8 cm long and weigh on average 25 grams. They are not usually found in the East but there are a few examples at 'Atlit (Johns 1997: Figure 15: 2–4) and Vadum Jacob (Raphael forthcoming). Even less common in this period are flat arrowheads with a medial rib. At al-Kurum a single, well-preserved example of this type was found. It is 10 cm long and 1.8 cm wide at its base; the tang is preserved to 1 cm. A number of arrowheads were found at Safed Castle (Hanauer 1902: 392–3), including examples attached to long metal shafts. Larger, heavier arrowheads were used with the crossbow. At Vadum Jacob several of these squat and bulbous bolts were found.

Greek fire

Greek fire was an inflammable compound also known as wildfire, wet fire and fire rain. It consisted of sulphur, pitch, nitre and petroleum boiled together. It was poured from walls, hurled in earthenware vessels by siege engines or painted on darts that were shot from crossbows. Joinville wrote of the Muslims in Egypt shooting a great quantity of darts with Greek fire, so that 'it seemed as if the stars of heaven were falling' (Joinville 1921: 213). It burned so fiercely that water intensified the fire and it could be extinguished only by a mixture of sand, vinegar and wine. According to Joinville (1921: 186):

> The fashion of the Greek fire was such that it came front-wise as large as a barrel of verjuice, and the tail of fire that issued from it was as large as a large lance. The noise it made in coming was like heaven's thunder. It had the seeming of a dragon flying through the air. It gave so great a light, because of the great foison of fire making the light, that one saw as clearly throughout the camp as if it had been day.

This account illustrates the fact that medieval warfare could at times be not unlike modern artillery bombardment. There is no direct evidence for the Franks themselves having used Greek fire but 'oleum incendiarium, quod vulgo Ignem Graecum nominant' was used against them by the Muslims in the siege of Akko in 1190 (*Itinerarium Regis Ricardi*, i, 8I), and the presence of ceramic grenades at many Frankish sites suggests that this was not unusual.

Ceramic Greek fire vessels are found throughout the Middle East. They are small, measuring on average 10–15 cm with a maximum diameter of 8–12 cm. They are extremely hard-fired and very thick, often have moulded decoration and on some occasions are glazed. Although they are reasonably common finds, there is so far no conclusive evidence that they were in fact containers for Greek fire and the alternative name, sphero-conical vessels, is usually preferred by students of medieval ceramics. It has been suggested that they were used to contain ink, mercury or scented oils in bathhouses, and even that they were used as water pipes for smoking. However, their frequent appearance at known battle sites, in the debris around fortifications, would seem to support the theory that they were indeed containers of Greek fire.

Textiles

Written sources frequently mention trade in textiles, textile manufacture, dyeing and the cultivation of plants used for dyes (Plate 6.18). Amongst the items that passed through the Crusader ports were cotton and woollen cloth, carpets, silk and luxury textiles from Damascus, Baghdad (including *siqlatin* – silk interwoven with gold), Mosul and Gaza. Egypt produced fine linen and woollen cloths. Raw silk from Syria was manufactured in Damascus, Tripoli, Tyre, Gaza and Ascalon. According to Burchard of Mount Zion, in Tripoli alone there were 4,000 weavers of silk (Burchard of Mount Sion 1864: 28). Tyre produced famous white silk. Al-Idrisi mentions the white *tafeth* of Tyre (Le Strange 1890: 344). Beirut also produced and exported silk and cotton fabrics. Cotton was grown in the plains of Akko and Tiberias and wool came from the region of Ramla.

Because of the perishable nature of textiles there are few finds of medieval date, and at present it is difficult to determine whether any of the fragmentary remains of textiles found in the region of the Latin East were manufactured there or imported. Bearing this in mind, some important finds have recently been studied and, at the very least, throw light on the types of textiles in use. In excavations carried out between 1975 and 1981 on the Red Sea island of Jesiret Fara'un (Frankish Ile de Greye) about 1,500 fragments of textiles were discovered together with fragments of basketry and cordage (Baginski and Shamir 1994a: 4–6; Baginski and Shamir 1994b: 32–3). The finds were dated on the basis of ceramics and Carbon 14 to between the last quarter of the twelfth century and the beginning of the fourteenth century. It is therefore possible that these finds date from the latter part of the period of Frankish rule prior to the Battle of Hattin or to the Abbasid or Mamluk periods, but they certainly give us an idea of the types of fabrics passing through the Latin kingdom and reaching its ports. They include cotton fabric, linen, felt, woollen fabric, cloth woven from goat hair and a few fragments of silk. There is also a quantity of fabric combining silk warp with wool, linen or cotton weft. Decoration of the fabrics was carried out by dyeing, woodblock printing on undyed cotton, embroidery and brocading with coloured silk threads. Some of the finds come from rugs and many of them appear to be items of clothing: cuffs, neck-openings, a complete coif and sleeves.

A second important find was made in 1993 in Cave 38 in the Qarantal cliff to the east of Jericho (Baginski and Shamir forthcoming). Here, 768 textile fragments were found together with thirty-four basketry fragments and ninety-three pieces of cordage. According to Baginski and Shamir, ceramics,

Plate 6.18 Medieval textiles from the Coral Island and Cave 38 at Qarantal
(courtesy of Orit Shamir and Alisa Baginski, photographs by Tzila
Segev and Clara Amit, Israel Antiquities Authority)

coins and Carbon 14 date these finds to between the ninth and thirteenth centuries. Once again, while we cannot date the finds with certainty to the Crusader period, this discovery gives us a good idea of the types of fabrics in use at the time. As at Jesiret Fara'un, most of the cloth appears to have come from articles of clothing – trousers, tunics and coifs. Most of the fabrics are cotton (289 pieces) and linen (265). There are 133 fragments of mixed textiles (linen warp and cotton weft) and thirty-eight fragments of luxury silk coloured cream, ivory, red, gold and various shades of blue. Wool is represented by only twenty-five pieces.[25] Decoration was by dyeing, brocading and silk tapestry (in bands designed with birds, scrolls and other motifs). A small and unimpressive quantity of textiles was found in the excavations at Montfort (Dean 1927/1982: 42). These include poorly made linen, cotton and woollen fabrics but no silk.

Another minor textile find, but one of certain Crusader period date, was recently made when a tomb was uncovered under the Cathedral of St Peter in Caesarea. A fragment of silk brocade with interwoven gold threads was found (Baginski 1996). This appears to have been an imported cloth, perhaps from England or Germany. In addition to the archaeological finds, a piece of embroidered silk forms the spine of the Psalter of Queen Melisende (British Library, London, Ms. Egerton 1139). The silk is heavily embroidered with silver thread and decorated with small red, blue and green crosses.

Leather working

Tanning was carried out in urban sites, usually in areas reserved for it on the outskirts of the town, downwind and near a good water supply. Recent excavations by the Tanner's Gate in Jerusalem have uncovered a medieval industrial complex with a number of plastered pools. A large amount of animal bones was found in this location. This complex awaits publication but a twelfth-century date is certainly possible.

Products made from leather included varied items: gloves, boots, shoes, saddles, book covers, parchment, various containers and leather bags. Examples of medieval leather work rarely survive and much of our information comes from written sources. The Frankish knights kept their hauberks in leather bags (Upton-Ward 1992: 91). Leather gloves were a luxury item not available to the Templar knights except for the chaplain brothers. Masons, however, were permitted to wear leather gloves to protect their hands (Upton-Ward 1992: 91). Pouches made for containing enamel-decorated glass beakers are mentioned in medieval sources and some examples survive in European collections (Pfeiffer 1970: 69, Figure 2).

Ivory carvings

Altar-pieces, book covers and other works in this medium were probably manufactured in Jerusalem, but there is only one example of fine ivory carving that has survived from the kingdom of Jerusalem. The pair of book covers of the psalter belonging to Queen Melisende have received considerable attention over the years (Dalton 1909: Plates 28–9 and accompanying text; Prawer 1972: 462–6; Folda 1995: 157–8). An extensive discussion was recently published by Kühnel (1994: 67–125). The dating of the covers is based on the date of the psalter, in which two people from the period are mentioned: King Baldwin II and his wife Emorfia. It is considered to have belonged to their daughter, Queen Melisende, and apparently dates from 1131–43. The covers are now in the British Museum, as is the psalter itself, both kept as separate items. The front cover has a foliated frame decorated with fish and birds surrounding a central field which contains figures representing the Virtues and Vices. There are six medallions showing scenes from the life of David. On the back cover a foliated frame surrounds the central field, which contains a hare, birds and fighting animals and six medallions with scenes representing the six Deeds of Mercy (Matthew 25: 31–46).

The fine workmanship was enhanced with inlaid precious stones, mainly turquoise, a few amethysts, carbuncles, rubies and green stones which may be plasma (Dalton 1909: 24). The covers were originally gilded and painted. This is the only major work in ivory that has been identified as having been made in the Latin East.

Objects of bone and mother-of-pearl

There are limited numbers of objects made of bone and mother-of-pearl, mainly utilitarian items which were fairly common in the Crusader period. In the Rockefeller Museum in Jerusalem there are several small mother-of-pearl crosses that were found at 'Atlit. They are less than 2 cm high and have a simple incised decoration. Mother-of-pearl was used in Crusader wall mosaics. A bone buckle was also found at 'Atlit Castle (Johns 1997: Plate 60, Figure 2) and in the Rockefeller Museum collection there is a bone comb. A small bone inlay found in Arsuf is decorated with a band of leaves and has two holes at either end for attaching it to a box or a piece of furniture (Roll and Ayalon 1989: Figure 56).

Crusader coins

The study of the coinage of the Latin East has advanced considerably in recent years (Plate 6.19). Following the major work of Gustave Schlumberger, *Numismatique de l'Orient latin* (Schlumberger 1878/1954) there was a lapse of nearly a century before another comprehensive study was made. In 1983 Michael Metcalf published his *Coinage of the Crusades and the Latin East in the Ashmolean Museum, Oxford* (Metcalf 1983) which was followed by an expanded and revised edition in 1995.[26]

Obv.   Rev.
Imitative Dinar ('Bezant')

Obv.   Rev.
Bezant with Christian legend

Billion Denier Baldwin III (1143–63)

Obv.   Rev.
Billion Denier Aimery I (1163–74)

Obv.   Rev.
Baronial Denier of Beirut
John of Beirut (1200–36)

Obv.   Rev.
Billion 'Helmet' Denier
Antioch (late 12th – early 13th century)

Fleur-de-lis Pougeoise of Akko 13th century

Rev.   Obv.
Lead token from 'Atlit

Obv.
Bulla of Aimery, Patriarch of Antioch
(1142–94). Found south of the Temple
Mount, Jerusalem

Plate 6.19 Crusader coins (courtesy of Robert Kool, Israel Antiquities Authority)

Minting

Although minting was a royal prerogative, the princes of Antioch and the counts of Tripoli minted coins, as did a number of Frankish barons in the kingdom of Jerusalem. The gold for Frankish coins was prepared according to the method in use in the East, which was apparently adopted by the Franks when they occupied the Fatimid mints in Tyre and Akko. The process involved boiling the gold with sulphur, salt and pulverized brick. The impurities in the gold would separate and adhere to the sulphur and salt. The thin gold plate thus produced was cut into square pieces of one-dinar size which were then struck to form the coin.

The technique used for the preparation of dies for making bezants was the same as that used in Fatimid mints: they were etched with the design by engravers (incisones) who cut or punched the design into an iron die in intaglio. A coin blank was then positioned between the upper and lower dies. A strong blow with a heavy hammer thereupon impressed simultaneously both designs on the blank. The bezants may have been made in the mints occupied at the time of conquest in Jerusalem, Akko and Tyre,[27] while the other coins were probably made in newly founded minting establishments.

As to the site of the royal mints, we have no direct information, archaeological or historical, but it is a reasonable assumption that as minting was a royal prerogative these establishments were located in or near the royal palaces: in Jerusalem in the citadel or the adjacent royal palace and in Akko in the royal quarter or in the citadel situated by the old northern wall.

Gold coins

The economy of the Islamic states and of the Byzantine Empire was based on gold and the use of gold in the Latin East preceded its reappearance in the West by about a century. In order to integrate their economy with that of their Muslim neighbours, the Franks began to mint gold coins immediately after the conquest. At first these were probably indistinguishable from the Muslim dinars.[28] By the 1130s or 1140s they began to mint a new gold coin known locally as the bezant and in Western documents as the 'bisancios saracenatos de moneta regis Hierusalem'.[29] Its use became widespread within the Latin East in the second half of the twelfth century. In the kingdom of Jerusalem these issues imitated the Islamic gold dinar of the Fatimid Caliph al-Amir (AH 495–524/AD 1101–30). The bezant minted by the counts of Tripoli imitated the dinars of Caliph al-Mustansir (AH 417–87/AD 1036–94). The minting of bezants appears to have been limited to these two states and there is no evidence for imitative bezants being issued in Antioch (Metcalf 1995: 43). These bezants were easily distinguished from the dinars because of their lighter weight, up to 10 per cent less than the true dinar, and because of the faulty Arabic script. In 1250 the papal legate Eudes of Châteauroux, who came to the East with Louis IX, condemned the minting of coins with Arabic script and text, and a ban was placed by Pope Innocent IV on the minting of these coins. This resulted in the appearance of a new design in 1251. On the reverse of the new bezant a cross was inscribed at the centre, but the Arabic script was retained. The epigraphy was improved and the legends were now of Christian subject matter and with Christian dates. The change in design was not, however, accompanied by an improvement in the quality of the alloy or of the weight. The bezant averaged about 80 per cent purity, compared to about 95 per cent for the dinar.

In Cyprus a 'white' bezant of scyphate electrum was minted from the reign of Guy de Lusignan (1192–94) until that of John I (1284–85) by which time it had become extremely rare (Metcalf 1995: 180–9; Malloy *et al*. 1994: 251–4). Its design, in the Byzantine tradition, is based on the nomisma of Alexius I Comnenus, with the figure of the ruler on the obverse, standing and holding a staff with a cross in one hand and an orb in the other. On the reverse Christ is portrayed seated on a throne.

Cut gold

Cut pieces of gold coins with Latin inscriptions have been found in a number of excavations, including Emmaus (al-Qubeiba), Beit She'an and Caesarea. Others of uncertain provenance have reached the market including examples found near Marash and Sidon, and several were purchased in London and Beirut (Metcalf 1995: 107–10). The pieces were cut from coins decorated with hexagram or octafoil devices and bearing the names 'AMALRICVS REX' or 'BALDVINVS REX' or the inscription 'HIERVSALEM CIVITAS'. No complete coins of this type have been found and Metcalf suggests that these may have been minted to serve as gift offerings at holy shrines (Metcalf 1995: 107–16). Alternatively, it was a widespread practise in the East and in the kingdom of Sicily to cut Muslim coins for use as smaller denominations.

Silver coins

After the establishment of the Crusader states and up to the 1140s the coins in use in the Latin East were largely low silver content (billon) deniers from southern France and Italy. With the increase in the commercial activity of the Italian merchants and the growth of trade between the East and the West, the need arose for the Franks to mint their own billon denier; this commenced in the 1140s during the reign of Baldwin III (1143–63). It continued under Aimery (1163–74), whose denier became a *type immobilisé*; that is, it continued to be minted with Amalric's name under his successors for at least another sixty years (Metcalf 1995: 53). On the obverse of these coins were Latin scripts and a cross, and on the reverse the Tower of David or the aedicule of the Holy Sepulchre. Billon deniers were also minted by the barons of Jaffa, Beirut and Sidon.

In the thirteenth century the kingdom of Jerusalem commenced minting high silver content coins, which were imitations of Ayyubid dirhams. These were based on the dirhams of al-Zahir Ghazi, Saladin's son who held Aleppo, and on those of al-Salih Isma'il of Damascus. As with the imitation dinar, the minting of these coins apparently ended with the papal ban that followed the visit of Eudes de Châteauroux. In a similar fashion to the imitative bezants, the post-1250 dirhams continued to resemble the earlier issues, in this case the Damascus dirhams, but with a cross prominently displayed at the centre of the obverse.

Billon deniers, as well as large silver 'gros' struck in the last decades of Latin rule, were minted in the county of Tripoli and billon coins were minted in Antioch from the reign of Raymond of Poitier (1136–49). In Cyprus the Frankish rulers minted large quantities of billon deniers of about 20 per cent silver. At the end of the thirteenth century they replaced the white gold bezant with the gros grand – a good silver coin weighing about 4.50 grams, intended to be valued at half a white bezant. They were minted at Nicosia and from 1310 also at Famagusta (Metcalf 1995: 200). On the obverse the king was shown seated on a throne and on the reverse a crowned lion. In later versions the image of the king was replaced by a large cross and four smaller crosses or a lion with a shield on the reverse. On the gros grand minted from the reign of Henry II and later, the seated king was shown on the obverse and the cross on the reverse; various other combinations occurred until the end of Lusignan rule in Cyprus (1489). A half gros known as the 'gros petit' was also minted.

Copper coins

Possibly as early as 1100 a copper folis or medallion was minted by Baldwin I. Small copper coins were minted from the reign of Baldwin III. The oboles were similar in design to the billon deniers. Copper issues were struck in Tripoli, where they at first imitated tenth- to eleventh-century coins of Angoulême and are known as 'Moneta Coppers' (Malloy *et al.* 1994: 160). Later issues display a star and crescent or a castle on the obverse and a cross on the reverse (Malloy *et al.* 1994: 161, 168, 170).

In Antioch copper coins were at first minted in a quasi-Byzantine style showing Christ, St Peter, Tancred with a sword, the Virgin Mary or St George. They had Greek and Latin legends. Later issues display a gate, a fleur-de-lis, a star and crescent, a helmeted head, a mounted knight or other simple designs. In Edessa too the copper issues were of a quasi-Byzantine style, with a bust of Christ or the armoured figure of the count on the obverse and a cross on the reverse. In Cyprus copper coins were struck from the beginning of Frankish rule. Under Guy de Lusignan they had an eight-pointed star, a cross with pellets and the legend 'REX GVIDO DE CIPRO'. Under Henry I (1218–53) the issues showed on the obverse either the king's head or a gateway. Later base billon and copper issues displayed a lion.

The barons of Beirut, Jaffa, Tyre and Sidon minted small copper issues displaying a variety of designs: a gateway (Beirut, Jaffa, Sidon), the Tower of David (Beirut), an interlaced pattern (Beirut), an eight-pointed star (Beirut), a temple (Tyre), a tower on a wall (Tyre), an arrow (Sidon), the Holy Sepulchre (Sidon) and a six-pointed star (Sidon).

Lead tokens

Crudely cast lead (or lead-tin alloy) tokens have been found in excavations at Akko, 'Atlit Castle, Belmont and Vadum Jacob (Metcalf 1995: 306–7; Akko – Syon 1997: 87–9, Figure 1:4; Vadum Jacob – Kool forthcoming). Two moulds for casting tokens have been found at Akko; one published by Rahmani and Spaer (1965–66: title page and caption overleaf) and a second mould which recently came to light during an excavation in the north-east of the city (Syon and Tatcher 1998). The designs which appear on one or both faces include a cross with four pellets, a gateway, a lion, a mounted knight, a key, a pair of pincers, a hammer, a bridge with a fish below, a fleur-de-lis, an eagle, various heraldic shields, numbers and monograms. Tokens as opposed to coins are almost without exception anagraphic. Only in very rare cases do inscriptions appear, like those from Vadum Jacob which are inscribed with the castle's name. The use of these tokens is not entirely clear. Metcalf suggests that they had some purchasing power and points to the tools of trade which occasionally appear on them as evidence that they may have been issued by craftsmen (Metcalf 1995: 306). Their presence in castles and adjoining faubourgs like 'Atlit suggests two possibilities: that they were used as an unofficial currency, for example, as payment to the blacksmith (Metcalf *et al.* forthcoming); or that they were used in gambling as can be seen in an illustration of the game of dice published by Gimpel (1992: 93). The tokens with Templar emblems found at 'Atlit Castle, and those with the title 'Vadum Jacob' from the castle of that name, may have been used for purchases by the Templar knights within the castle during the period of construction.

European coins in the Latin East

Throughout the twelfth and thirteenth centuries there was a continuous flow of European coins into the Latin East, particularly from southern and central France and some from Italy and other countries. While in the first decades of the twelfth century this constituted most of the petty coinage in use, once the Franks began to mint their own billon following the reform of Baldwin III in the 1140s, the use of foreign coinage in the kingdom of Jerusalem appears to have declined. Metcalf notes that the hoards from the later years of the kingdom prior to 1187 contain few European strays (Metcalf 1995: 169). After the Third Crusade, however, the situation changed once again and considerable quantities of foreign coins found their way into the kingdom of Jerusalem and the county of Tripoli (but few to the principality of Antioch). It is possible that the large number of European coins found in the later hoards represent coins brought by Crusaders to finance the expeditions of the Third or Fifth Crusades. Another possibility is that they were brought to the East by pilgrims (Metcalf 1995: 170–1).

Crusader seals

The Assises de Jérusalem, the code of laws of the kingdom of Jerusalem, contains a list of baronies in the kingdom of Jerusalem which had *droit de coins*; that is, the right to seal documents. Other than the king himself, more than twenty lordships enjoyed this privilege, as did royal officials and patriarchs, archbishops and bishops, as well as the military orders. The use of seals extended to the Frankish states in Syria and to Frankish Cyprus. Seals were used both for administrative and private purposes (Glücksmann and Kool 1995: 90). They were made of lead or wax, either round or boat-shaped, and were a means of authenticating the legal documents to which they were affixed, often suspended on a strip of cloth. Frankish lead and wax seals have been studied extensively by Schlumberger (1943) and recently by Mayer (1978) and briefly by Folda (1995: 90–1, 172, 414). Jacoby published a bulla of the Master of the Hospital of St John of Jerusalem and some matrices found in Akko (Jacoby 1981: 83–8, Plate 17). Glücksmann and Kool have discussed a papal bulla of Alexander III (c. 1159–81) and one of the Patriarch Aimery of Antioch that were found adjacent to the Temple Mount in Jerusalem (Glüksmann and Kool 1995: 87–104). Those of Cyprus have been discussed by Metcalf (1995: 365–75).

The standard of lettering on seals was usually high compared to that of coins, and the designs were carefully carried out. As Metcalf points out, whereas coins were mass-produced objects the seals were 'high quality miniature sculptures' (Metcalf 1995: 367). The precision with which they were made was intended to make forgery difficult. No examples have survived from the short reign of Godfrey of Bouillon. The seal of Baldwin I displayed on the obverse a portrait of the king seated on a throne, holding in his right hand the sceptre and in his left the orb. On the reverse is the *Turris David* with the city gate (*Porta David*) below it and on either side the *Templum Domini* and the Church of the Holy Sepulchre. Later royal seals follow this scheme with variations: the three monuments were replaced on occasion by a city's patron saint or by various heraldic devices. Church leaders were depicted standing or seated, wearing a pallium and a mitre, and holding a crosier.

Notes

1 Port St Symeon and Cyprus both produced ceramics decorated in a decidedly Western style. The artisans may, however, have been local non-Franks who were now producing for the Frankish market. In the case of Cyprus, major alterations

that occurred around 1200, both in the technology of ceramic production and in design, suggest that there may have been a change in the craftsmen involved. As these are similar to changes in the ceramic production of Byzantium rather than of the West, these may have been Byzantine craftsmen who settled in Cyprus after 1204 when Constantinople came under Frankish rule. See Boas 1994.

2 The Franks were apparently blissfully unaware of the toxic properties of lead.

3 Only in the thirteenth century did Cyprus manufacture glazed jugs, and these rarely appear to have been exported to the mainland. The fact that bowls were the dominant type of tableware is perhaps not surprising. The bowl is a multi-purpose form that can serve as a vessel for eating or drinking.

4 Neutron Activation Analysis is a means of tracing the provenance of a vessel by exposing a sample to atomic bombardment in a nuclear reactor. After exposure each element in the sample begins to emit characteristic gamma rays. Since no two clay sources contain the elements in the same proportions, the resultant count is considered to be a chemical fingerprint. It can be compared to samples from various known sources or vessels known to have originated at a particular site. If the fingerprint matches that of a known site, the sample may be considered to have originated at that site.

5 In excavations at Beit She'an red glass has been found in medieval deposits. It appears to be laminated, with a thin layer of red glass on a different coloured background. This may be an example of the process known as 'flashing', in which a thin layer of red glass was applied to a different coloured glass background and re-fired to anneal the layers. This was done because red glass tends to be too dark when used on its own. Flashing was used for red glass in the preparation of stained glass for windows.

6 For examples of these techniques see Dean 1927/1982: Figure 56D (moulding); Prawer 1972: 462, Figure facing p. 436 – British Museum; and Dothan 1976: 37, Figure 41 (painted designs); Dean 1927/1982: 56F; Gorin-Rosen 1997: 82–4, Figure 2:20a–26 (for prunting).

7 That this refers to enamel-painted beakers is suggested by the mention in the inventory of leather cases to hold glass vessels. Such cases are known as containers for enamel-painted beakers and an example is illustrated in Pfeiffer (1970: 68, Plate 2).

8 The technique of enamelling involves the application of finely powdered glass suspended in a liquid medium on to the surface of the vessel. It is then fired, causing the painted design to fuse with the glass of the vessel.

9 Mujir al-Din described Frankish glass (*zujuj al-ifranji*) in the Madrasa of Sultan Qaybay in Jerusalem as being 'of the utmost splendour and perfection' (Burgoyne and Richards 1987: 589–90).

10 At the keep in Beit She'an green glass discs were found, probably coming from the windows of the destroyed second floor. These will be published by Gorin-Rosen.

11 The location of this find suggests that this may be evidence of trade in metals transported by Italian merchants to Egypt from the West, which had received papal censure but appears to have continued to take place.

12 There may have been a similar grille in the Holy Sepulchre. John of Wurzburg mentions an iron lattice above the altar that stood at the head of the Holy Sepulchre (John of Wurzburg 1890: 36).

13 A similar plate with a running stag and an inscription also comes from Cyprus (Enlart 1928, Atlas: Figure 154). Two additional plates, one also showing a stag, can be seen in the Byzantine church at Peristerona, west of Nicosia.

14 This practice began in the Byzantine period. A mould for ceramic ampullae was found on Mount Zion in Jerusalem in 1903 and a second mould came from the village of Siloam (Piccirillo 1994: 617, illustrations on pp. 47–50).

15 This information was very kindly given to me by Danny Syon of the Israel Antiquities Authority who discovered the Akko find.

16 This cross form was the cross of the Latin Patriarch of Jerusalem. It appears on some Crusader coins and seals as well as ampullae. There is a patriarchal cross on the plastered wall of a vaulted cistern beneath what may have been the royal palace in Jerusalem (Bahat and Broshi 1972: 103). Another example is carved on a stone in a medieval building in Nablus (Clermont-Ganneau 1896: 316).

17 For informative discussions on reliquaries see Kühnel (1994: 125–53) and Folda (1995: 97–100, 166–9, 290–4, 297–9).

18 Members of the military orders were required to shave and to be 'well tonsured' (Upton-Ward 1992: 25).

19 For sundials in Israel see Ben-Layish 1969–71.

20 See also the sculpture of the crucified Christ mentioned below (pp. 198–9).

21 Tent pegs were items made by knights in their spare time and were occasionally used for betting (Upton-Ward 1992: 83, 89).

22 Nine Men's Morris (*marelles* or *morelles* in French, *Mühlespiel* in German) is a game played on a board incised with three concentric squares divided by eight radial lines with twenty-four intersections. Each of two players has nine game pieces. They alternately place single pieces on empty intersections until all pieces are in position. Then the pieces are moved along the lines, the aim being to get three pieces in a straight line, after which the player can remove the opponent's pieces. The game concludes when one of the players has only two pieces left (Kirk 1938: 229–32).

23 Lead tokens found at 'Atlit Castle and at Vadum Jacob may also have been used in dicing (see p. 188).

24 At the end of the nineteenth century a hoard of wooden arrow-shafts was found in the Tower of David in Jerusalem. They were subsequently published in a short note as Crusader arrows (Merril 1902: 106). Clermont-Ganneau (1902: 136–7), however, objected to the dating, believing it to be too early. These arrows were 69.5 cm long and their maximum circumference, at the centre, was 3.3 cm. They had an abrupt end for the arrowhead and a bulbous end with a deep notch for the bowstring. The abrupt end may suggest that they were intended for socket-type arrowheads which is the type common in the West, thus perhaps supporting a Frankish origin, but as these arrows appear to have been lost this is mere speculation.

25 This information was kindly supplied by Alisa Baginski of the Israel Antiquities Authority and will be expanded upon in forthcoming articles by Baginski and Shamir.

26 See also Malloy *et al.* 1994.

27 A reference of 1156 to *sarracenicos de Sur* (bezants of Tyre) and a Venetian document dated 1243 that mentions a house in Tyre where coin had been struck (Metcalf 1983: 11, 12) suggest that there was a royal mint in Tyre. In addition,

according to the Syrian chronicler Ibn-Khallikan, the Franks continued to strike coins in the name of al-Amir in the three years following the conquest of Tyre in 1124 (Malloy *et al.* 1994: 39, 91, 108).

28 It is possible that this process began with the capture of Tyre in 1124 when according to Ibn Khallikan the Franks occupied the mint and used the existing dies to strike coins. See Balog and Yvon 1958: 141–2.

29 See Yvon 1961: 81–2. The term *moneta regis* denotes the royal prerogative of minting coins.

7 The fine arts

One of the principal features of the Frankish endeavours in the fine arts in the East, and one which is at the heart of all serious discussion on the subject, is the converging of different cultural influences. These are predominantly French, Italian, Byzantine and Syro-Palestinian. The particular combination of these influences and the manner in which they find expression gives a special character to Crusader art and raises the issue of whether or not it should be considered a colonial art (Hunt 1991: 69–85).

While there were probably Western artists who produced works while staying temporarily in the Latin East, in many cases the artist who produced the paintings, sculptures and other art-forms were local residents who had either been trained in the West or had local training following European traditions. Non-Frankish indigenous artists also played a part in the development of Crusader art, in architectural sculpture (Kenaan 1973: 16–75, 221–9, Plates 57–63) and particularly in mosaics and fresco painting. The considerable impact of Byzantium on the Crusader arts is discerned in almost every art-form. Kurt Weitzmann noted the polarity found in twelfth-century Crusader art, in which artists fall into one of two categories: those who attempted to ignore the local (Byzantine) style, and those who attempted to absorb it totally (Weitzmann 1966: 52). Even the works of the first group were often permeated with the Byzantine spirit.

Western and southern Europe and Byzantium are the dominant sources for style, iconography and technique. As opposed to its role in the lesser arts and crafts, Islam was a comparatively minor influence which found expression mainly in architectural ornamentation. Despite its eclectic nature, there is a certain quality to the art produced in the Latin East which gives it a unity and permits us to consider the whole under the title 'Crusader art'.

Figurative sculpture

The Romanesque sculpture of west-central France and, somewhat later, that of central and southern Italy were the main stylistic influences on the sculpture executed in the kingdom of Jerusalem (Barasch 1971: 16–65; Kühnel 1994: 34–47; Folda 1995). The French influence dates to the first half of the twelfth century and that of Italy, mainly Abruzzi and Apulia, to the later part of the twelfth century. In Cyprus the Gothic influence is much more strongly felt.

The lintels of the Church of the Holy Sepulchre

Amongst the finest examples of Frankish sculpture are two carved lintels that formed the bases of the tympana of the portals in the Church of the Holy Sepulchre in Jerusalem. Badly deteriorated, they were removed from the church in 1929 for conservation and have since been housed in the Rockefeller Museum. That they were produced locally is demonstrated by the fact that the eastern lintel is carved on the back of a Fatimid carved plaque. Each lintel has its own style and theme. The western lintel displays scenes from the life of Christ. From left to right, it shows the raising of Lazarus, Jesus meeting Martha and Mary, the preparation of the Last Supper, the entry into Jerusalem and the Last Supper. The style is that of southern France, Provence and Languedoc. The eastern lintel is decorated with floral scrolls inhabited by figures of men and birds caught in the coils of foliage. On the basis of iconography, architectural placement and style, Kühnel has compared this sculpture with works in Abruzzi and notes the similarity of the piece to reliefs in the portals of Trasacco and Celano (Kühnel 1994: 44).

The Nazareth finds

A remarkable group of carved capitals was discovered in excavations outside the northern wall of the Church of the Annunciation in 1908 (Plates 7.1–7.3). The group was found intact and unweathered where it had apparently been hidden in the twelfth century. Folda suggests that it may have been intended for an octagonal baldacchino planned to rise above an aedicule over the grotto of the Annunciation (Folda 1995: 434). These capitals were carved in the local soft, grainy limestone. They portray various scenes from the lives of the apostles, boldly sculptured in high relief, with figures representing St Peter, St Thomas, St Matthew, St Bartholomew and St James. A number of scholars have pointed to the similarity of these remarkable works to those at Plaimpied near Bourges (Boase 1938–39: 1–21; Borg 1982: 97–119). The form of the capitals at Nazareth and Plaimpied is the same, with an architectural frame of arches and turrets above figures set in concave niches. The shape of the figures and their facial expressions, the rendering of the drapery and other details all support this connection.

Other important sculptural works were found in Nazareth. In 1867 during excavations in the Church of the Annunciation a large limestone capital (0.50 m high) was found. It is an unfinished carving of two larger-than-life bearded heads. In style it resembles Burgundian sculpture, and as the stone is local one can conclude that it is the work of a Burgundian-trained sculptor working in Nazareth. This remarkable work is now in the Greek Patriarchate Museum in Jerusalem. Also from Nazareth a nearly life-size headless figure

Plate 7.1 Capital from Nazareth (courtesy of the Studium Biblicum Franciscanum)

now in the collection of the Duke of Devonshire in Chatsworth, England has been identified as representing a prophet. A second torso was found in 1955 during excavations prior to the construction of the new cathedral. It is a coarser work and appears to have been by a different hand from the other piece, although it is similar in style. Two additional torsos were found in 1968, one identifiable as St Peter. These figures were probably destined for a doorway of the cathedral.

Plate 7.2 Capital with two bearded heads from Nazareth (photograph by Ze'ev
Goldmann)

Other sculptural finds in the kingdom of Jerusalem

Figurative capitals from the west door of the Cathedral of St John in Sebaste
are now located in the Istanbul Museum. One has a scene representing
Herod's feast and the other shows the Dance of Salome. Some small pieces of
figurative sculpture were found in the excavations at Belvoir in the 1960s.
They were in all probability originally located in the first-floor chapel, which
was destroyed by Saladin in 1189. They include a winged angel, a bearded
head, and the head of a smiling youth. A small sculptured head and the

Plate 7.3 Torso from Nazareth (courtesy of the Studium Biblicum Franciscanum)

figure of an angel were found in the excavations at Montfort Castle in 1926, and another head was recently found there. None of these pieces compares in quality with those of Nazareth. Some fine figurative sculpture from the Church of St Mary Major in Jerusalem is now on display in the Greek Patriarchate Museum in Jerusalem.

Only a single example of metal sculpture is known to have survived in the Latin East, although such works are described in contemporary sources. The Russian pilgrim Abbot Daniel, who visited the kingdom in 1106–8, described a larger-than-life silver standing figure of Christ made by the Franks and placed on the baldacchino over the Holy Sepulchre (Daniel 1888: 13). A small gilded bronze Christ, its feet missing, was found in Jerusalem and is now located in the Museum of the Flagellation in Jerusalem (Plate 7.4).

The head and torso of an almost life-size figure of the crucified Christ is, if authentic, the only known example of painted wooden sculpture from the

Plate 7.4 Gilded bronze crucifix (courtesy of the Studium Biblicum Franciscanum)

Latin East (Plate 7.5). This very beautiful work of unknown provenance was purchased in Akko by Z. Goldmann.[1]

The Larnaca tympanum

Some of the finest non-figurative sculpture of the Latin East is found in the Gothic churches and other buildings in Cyprus, but virtually no figurative sculpture of the quality found in the kingdom of Jerusalem has yet come to light there. From Larnaca comes a bas-relief, now in the Pitt-Rivers

Plate 7.5 Painted wooden crucifix (courtesy of Ze'ev Goldmann)

Museum at Farnham, Dorset, which Enlart suggests may have originated in Famagusta or Paphos (Enlart 1987: 43). It decorated either a doorway or an altar. The tympanum can be divided horizontally into two sections, the upper semicircular part containing at its centre the figure of Christ in an elliptical mandorla supported by four angels. On either side are smaller panels containing various scenes. These include, on the right, the Crucifixion and the Carrying of the Cross, and on the left the Visitation, the Baptism and a scene with an enthroned angel above two donors and two fighting soldiers. The lower rectangular register of the tympanum contains the Annunciation with six apostles on either side of the Virgin Mary and, for the sake of symmetry, two representations of Gabriel. This work, a fusion of Gothic and Byzantine styles, is, in the words of Enlart, 'clumsy, heavy and incorrect' (Enlart 1987: 320). It probably dates to the end of the fourteenth century (Enlart 1987: 43).

Non-figurative ornamentation

In the ornamentation of structures with capitals, rosettes, friezes, corbels and other embellishments various Western influences are combined with indigenous Middle Eastern elements (Plates 7.6–7.9). Some of the finest works still to be seen in Jerusalem, particularly in secondary use in Muslim structures on the Temple Mount, and occasionally found further afield (the

Plate 7.6 Carved frieze from the Tomb of the Virgin Mary in Jehoshaphat (photograph by the author)

Plate 7.7 Detail from the facade of the Church of the Holy Sepulchre (courtesy of the Studium Biblicum Franciscanum)

Latrun Capitals in Istanbul, for example), came from the Temple atelier, as perhaps did a capital and cornice in secondary use on the north transept portal of St Sophia, Nicosia. The remarkable pieces believed to have originated in the Temple atelier are notable for their deep-cut 'wet-leaf' foliage and coiling. The masons developed an individual style that follows and frequently surpasses the Romanesque carvings of southern France and Italy.

Fragments on the Temple Mount

Today, several exceptional pieces from the Temple workshop are located in various locations on the Temple Mount. They probably originated in Christian buildings on the Temple Mount which were dismantled by Saladin. They include friezes and capitals on a small *minbar* (pulpit) on the edge of the platform to the south of the Dome of the Rock and twisted columns in a building to its right. Some of the finest examples are located in al-Aqsa Mosque. These include twisted columns in a *mihrab* and very fine capitals and friezes formed of acanthus leaves reused in the *dikkah* (reading podium).

Plate 7.8 Details from the façade of the Church of the Holy Sepulchre (courtesy of the Studium Biblicum Franciscanum)

Plate 7.9 Details from the southern portals of the Church of the Holy Sepulchre
(courtesy of the Studium Biblicum Franciscanum)

The Latrun capitals

Two groups of three joining capitals were found in a villager's house in the ruins of the Templar castle of Toron des Chevaliers (Latrun). They were removed to the Istanbul Museum in 1917. They are remarkably well preserved, decorated with acanthus leaves, animals and birds. The high quality of the workmanship suggests that they are also products of the Temple workshop.

Wheel windows, rose windows and window tracery

Wheel windows were the Romanesque predecessor of the Gothic rose windows, themselves developing out of the *oculi* of earlier church architecture. They adorned the western facades of churches. Wheel windows were usually not very large and consisted of a carved hub and spokes in the form of small pillars with bases and capitals which supported the surrounding arches. Wheel windows were to be found in some churches in the kingdom of Jerusalem but have not survived *in situ*. In the Tariq Bab al-Silsila in Jerusalem there is a drinking fountain called the Sabil of Suleiman which contains, amongst other *spolia*, part of a finely carved wheel window with diminutive columns, round arches and at its centre a deeply carved floriate hub (Plate 7.10). It may have originated in the Church of St Gilles, which

Plate 7.10 Wheel window, possibly from the Church of St Gilles, Jerusalem, rebuilt into a fountain (photograph by the author)

was located just to the west. A second small wheel window is located in al-Aqsa Mosque (Enlart 1927: Plate 115). In Cyprus there are rose windows from the early thirteenth century. There is a rose window in the northern end of the transept at St Sofia in Nicosia, which now lacks tracery. In the west end of the nave of St Nicholas in Famagusta there is a rose window in *rayonnant* style (Enlart 1987: 41). Rose windows dating from the second half of the fourteenth century are found in St George of the Greeks and the Nestorian church in Famagusta, and in St Catherine in Nicosia.

Diminutive capitals

Amongst the features of Romanesque and Gothic architecture introduced to the East by the Franks were diminutive capitals used to support groin-vaults, door and window frames and other features. They were placed on single or grouped columns and elbow columns, and range from extremely elaborate figurative designs to oak or vine leaves, twisted palm branches and acanthus leaves. The carving is generally deep, sometimes to the extent that the design appears three-dimensional.

Bossets

Amongst the ornaments found in buildings roofed with rib-vaults are beautifully carved keystone bossets. Some very fine examples were found at Montfort. They are decorated with vine, oak and fig leaves (Dean 1927/1982: Figs. 33–7). Enlart published drawings of the fine carved bossets at Tortosa (Enlart 1927: Plate 169).

Wall painting

The study of Frankish frescos has been greatly enhanced in recent years by the publication of a monumental work on wall painting in the kingdom of Jerusalem which appeared in 1988 (Kühnel 1988) and various other important discussions (Kühnel 1994: 47–60; Folda 1995: 91–7, 163–6, 313–18). Four major and several lesser examples of wall painting from the Crusader period survive. Gustav Kühnel discussed the paintings on the columns in the Church of Nativity in Bethlehem, the paintings in the Church of St Jeremiah in Abu Ghosh (Emmaus), the Theoctistus Monastery in the Judean Desert and the Chapel of St John the Baptist in Sebaste. Other fragmentary examples are the heads of saints found in a chapel (possibly the Church of St Abraham) excavated outside Jerusalem's Damascus Gate in 1964–66 (Hennessy 1970: 22–7) and the head of an angel from the Church of Gethsemane now located in the Museum of the Flagellation. Western influences are present in some of these works, as, for example, in the choice of saints, the iconography and the style of frescos in the Church of Nativity (Kühnel 1988: 205). But unlike manuscript illumination and icon painting, which were generally carried out by Frankish artists using Byzantine models, the wall paintings appear to have been largely the work of Byzantine artists.

Outside the kingdom of Jerusalem monumental wall painting survives at Crac des Chevaliers in the county of Tripoli, and various examples of later date survive in Cyprus.

The Church of St Jeremiah in Abu Ghosh

The paintings in this church have deteriorated badly. The decorative programme, to the extent that it survives, covers the apses in the east and the northern and southern walls. In the central apse is the *Anastasis* scene, with the central figure of Christ and groups of standing saints on either side. The northern apse has the *Deesis* scene, with a poorly preserved representation of Christ enthroned, John the Baptist to his right, and Mary to his left. The southern apse shows the three patriarchs in Paradise with the souls of the just in their laps. The northern wall of the church has the *Koimesis* scene, the apostles gathered at Mary's deathbed. On the southern wall is a Crucifixion scene. Kühnel assigns these frescos to the 'dynamic' phase of the imperial Comnenian style which dates to the third quarter of the twelfth century (Kühnel 1988: 117), and suggests that they are possibly the outcome of the direct patronage of the Emperor Manuel Comnenus (Kühnel 1988: 205).

The columns of the Church of the Nativity in Bethlehem

On twenty-eight of the columns in the Church of the Nativity in Bethlehem are frescos dating from the twelfth century. They were carried out by a number of different hands in Byzantine style and represent various figures which are identified by Greek and Latin inscriptions. The columns on the northern side of the nave include representations of St Macarius, St Antony Abbot, St Euthymius, St George, St Leonard, St Cosmos, St Damian, St Cataldus, the Virgin and Child, St John the Evangelist and a Crucifixion scene. On the south colonnade of the nave are St Theodosius, St Sabas, St Stephen, St Canute, St Olaf, St Vincent, St John the Baptist, Elijah, St Humphrey, St Fusca and Margaret of Antioch. In the colonnade between the two southern aisles are St James the Greater, St Bartholomew, St Blaise, the Virgin and Child, St Leo, St Anne, St Margaret, and another Virgin and Child. These paintings are in fact not true frescos painted with tempera pigments applied to gesso, but they were executed with pigments suspended in oil or wax and applied directly on to the smooth marble surface of the column (Folda 1995: 94). The pigments range from red and purple to brown and the background is generally cobalt blue. Stylistically they have little unity; some are mainly Byzantine in style, others Western Romanesque, and it is clear that several artists worked here over a fairly extensive period in the twelfth century and perhaps later.

The church at the Damascus Gate, Jerusalem

Excavations carried out by the British School of Archaeology in Jerusalem in 1964–65 at the Damascus Gate uncovered the remains of a small chapel on the exterior western side of the gate, within the double gate complex constructed by the Franks in the twelfth century. Fragments of frescos were found here, including parts of the Annunciation scene which had decorated the eastern wall of the chapel. The remains include the head of an angel with the face largely destroyed, a small part of the haloed head and a few fragments of other angels. On the same wall there was a painted dado made up of blue diamonds and red circles outlined in white on an ochre background. Folda dates the work, on the basis of stylistic comparisons with the frescos at Bethlehem, Abu Ghosh, and Gethsemane, to the late 1160s or early 1170s (Folda 1995: 379).

The Theoctistus Monastery in the Judean Desert

With Gustav Kühnel's recent publication, the little-known wall paintings in the Theoctistus coenobium in the Judean Desert received the first serious treatment since they were originally discussed in 1928 (Chitty 1928: 143–52; Kühnel 1988: 181–91). The paintings are located in the oratory (where they survive only in the apse), in an icon at the cave entrance, and in two hanging niches on the cliff face. The painting in the apse shows the enthroned figure of Christ with the apostles below. The scene is interpreted as Christ's Ascension. The icon shows Christ flanked by the figures of the archangels Michael and Gabriel and by St Sabas and St Gerasimus. In the larger of the two hanging niches is a Crucifixion scene, with Mary on the left of the cross, John the apostle on the right and two angels above. The smaller niche to the left has a bust of Mary with the Christ child depicted on her chest. Other figures represented in the area around the two niches are John of Damascus, Emmanuel and St Euthymius, as well as some unfinished sepia representations. Kühnel dates this work to around 1187, in part on the evidence of the unfinished sepia drawings which hint at the work being abandoned suddenly, possibly due to the defeat of the Franks at Hattin (Kühnel 1988: 191). However, there could have been other causes for the work remaining unfinished, and stylistic considerations are perhaps a more secure basis for the dating. Kühnel points out that the manneristic representation of the folds of the garments and the contorted movements are appropriate to works of the third quarter of the twelfth century.

The Church of the Agony, Gethsemane

A single very fine fragment of a fresco found here shows the head and wings of an angel, part of the scene from the Agony (Plate 7.11). It measures 85 by 30 cm. It is now in the collection of the Museum of the Flagellation in

Plate 7.11 Fresco of an angel from Gethsemane (courtesy of the Studium Biblicum Franciscanum)

Jerusalem. Bianca Kühnel notes the similarity of this work to the angel in the chapel at the Damascus Gate and to the angel rendered in mosaic on the north wall of the Church of the Nativity in Bethlehem, and considers it to be in the Byzantine tradition of the third quarter of the twelfth century (Kühnel 1991: 346).

The Grotto of the Holy Cross, Holy Sepulchre, Jerusalem

A fragmentary fresco depicting the Crucifixion is located on the lower part of a small eleventh-century apse in the Grotto of the Holy Cross. The torso and lower part of the body of the crucified Christ can be seen with parts of the Virgin and St John. It has been suggested that on the basis of style and iconography this work dates to the third quarter of the twelfth century and was perhaps the work of an Italian artist (Folda 1995: 239).

Stele of Bethphage

A large stone stele was erected at Bethphage, between the Mount of Olives and Bethany, to mark the site from which Christ began his entry into Jerusalem. In 1172 Theoderich described 'a great stone which may be seen in the chapel'. He makes no mention of the frescos and they probably post-date his visit. Folda suggests a date shortly before 1187 (Folda 1977: 262). The frescos were restored by C. Vagarini, unfortunately rather heavily. They show scenes from the Gospel of St Matthew and the Raising of Lazarus. The Romanesque tradition is combined with Byzantine iconography, notable in the drapery of Lazarus and the posture of Christ blessing in the Greek manner.

The Crypt of St John the Baptist in Sebaste

Poorly preserved remnants of wall paintings decorate the apse of the crypt in the Greek monastery church in Sebaste. They have been dated by Kühnel to the third quarter of the twelfth century. The style is typical of Middle Byzantine art (Kühnel 1988: 203). In the centre of the east wall is a niche divided into two parts by a stone shelf. Two kneeling angels are depicted on either side of it. On the upper part of the niche was a scene of the decapitation of John the Baptist, of which can be seen a figure in a red tunic and white coat with his arm stretched above a second figure, apparently the saint. In the lower niche two men are shown digging while four other figures look on. This scene represents the Invention of the Baptist's Head and the Second Martyrdom of the Body of the Saint.

Crac des Chevaliers

In the main chapel of this castle in the county of Tripoli and in a secondary small chapel outside the main entrance to the castle, fragmentary remains of frescos have been found. In the main chapel is part of the scene of the Presentation of Christ in the Temple. It has been dated to around 1200 (Folda 1995: 402). A figure of St Pantaleon and next to it the Virgin and Child (*Hodegetria*) were painted on the western wall of the outer chapel, and the mounted figure of St George, of which all that survives are the horse's legs, was on the north wall. The different stages of this work date from between 1170 and 1200.

The Margat Castle Pentecost

In the chapel of Margat Castle to the south of the principality of Antioch, frescos have survived, mainly on the vault. A Pentecost scene with the twelve apostles was recently discovered there (Folda 1982b: 196–210, Plates 28–38). These poorly preserved frescos date from between the construction of the chapel in 1186–87 and the loss of the castle to the Mamluks in 1285, and Folda suggests on the basis of the style (that of a non-Byzantine artist painting in the Byzantine manner) that they fall into the final years of the twelfth century up to 1202 (Folda 1982b: 208).

Cyprus

None of the major frescos that once existed in the cathedrals of St Sofia in Nicosia and St Nicholas of Famagusta can be seen today. Fragmentary remains can be seen in the churches of St Anne, St George of the Greeks, and the Nestorians in Famagusta. The Italo-Byzantine influence seems to have been the rule here, as in the frescos of the mainland. Boase points out that the smaller churches in the Troodos mountains contain the best surviving examples of Frankish frescos (Boase 1977d: 189), notably the Chapel of the Virgin above the village of Moutoullas which has late thirteenth-century frescos, fourteenth-century examples in a small church in Pelendria, the late fifteenth-century frescos in the Church of the Archangel Michael at Pedhoulas, and the Chapel of the Virgin at Kakopetria which has frescos dating from 1520.

Mosaics

Two examples of mosaics from the Crusader period have survived, a small fragment of the mosaics which originally decorated the interior of the Church of the Holy Sepulchre in Jerusalem and a much larger example of wall mosaics in the Church of the Nativity in Bethlehem.

The Church of the Holy Sepulchre

The German pilgrim Theoderich, who visited the Holy Land in around 1172, gives a detailed description of the rich mosaics that at the time decorated the Church of the Holy Sepulchre. He describes the interior, which 'glows with mosaics of incomparable beauty'.[2] Only a single fragment of these fine mosaics has survived. A medallion in the vault of the Chapel of Calvary shows Christ ascending to heaven (Kühnel 1997a, 1997b) (Plate 7.12). The elongated figure of Christ, the loose flowing drapery and the use of colour help to date it to the twelfth-century. The iconography suggests that the artist was possibly Frankish but trained in the Byzantine school.

Plate 7.12 Mosaic from the Chapel of Golgotha, in the Church of the Holy Sepulchre (photograph by the author)

The Church of the Nativity, Bethlehem

The most important wall mosaics surviving from the Crusader period are in the Church of the Nativity in Bethlehem. Amongst the mosaics that have survived in this church are scenes from the Life of Christ in the transepts, the Nativity scene in the grotto, the Seven Oecumenical Councils of the Church on the south wall of the nave and the Six Provincial Councils on the north wall. Below the councils on the south wall are several extant portraits of the Ancestors of Christ and between the clerestory windows are angels. The Tree of Jesse was on the west wall of the nave. These works are carried out in Byzantine style and with Byzantine iconography. The mosaicists, who left their signatures, included a Syrian Orthodox named Basilius, a Venetian named Zan and a monk called Ephraim.

Manuscript illumination

The medieval art of manuscript illumination was represented in the Latin East by works produced in two important scriptoria in Jerusalem and Akko. The twelfth- and thirteenth-century scriptorium in Jerusalem belonged to the Church of the Holy Sepulchre and that of Akko was probably founded by Louis IX during his residency in the city between 1250 and 1254.

The first major study of Crusader manuscript painting was published by Hugo Buchthal in 1957 and other more recent publications have expanded on the subject, most notably those of Folda (1976, 1995: 100–5, 137–63).

The scriptorium of the Holy Sepulchre, Jerusalem

The scriptorium in Jerusalem may have been located in the complex of conventual buildings on the northern and eastern side of the Church of the Holy Sepulchre. It undoubtedly produced during the twelfth century and in the short period of Frankish rule in the thirteenth century a considerable body of important and lesser works, of which only a handful survive. A major work of this scriptorium is the psalter which has been identified as the possession of Queen Melisende (Buchthal 1957: 1). Within the remarkable ivory covers of Queen Melisende's psalter (see p. 183) are illuminations including a New Testament cycle, signs of the zodiac, eight full-page initials and the portraits of nine saints. These works are by a number of different artists. The cycle is signed, 'BASILIUS ME FECIT' (Basilius made me), but the artist was apparently a Frank despite his name. Whereas he follows Byzantine models, sometimes quite closely, the iconography and style of the cycle work are not characteristically Byzantine and the use of full-page frontispieces is typical of the Latin West, particularly England, rather than the Byzantine East (Buchthal 1957: 2). Buchthal points to the tradition of Romanesque craftsmanship that permeates this work and suggests that Basilius was trained in the Latin West but spent some time in Constantinople (Buchthal 1957: 9).

Two other works from this scriptorium are the Sacramentary and the Missal of the Holy Sepulchre. These two works date from just before the middle of the twelfth century (Buchthal 1957: 14). The Sacramentary, which is the earlier of the two, incorporates 'Franco-Saxon' interlace and elements pointing to an English source, but evidence of a Byzantine influence is also seen in the more realistic manner in which human anatomy is represented (Buchthal 1957: 15–16). On the other hand, amongst other influences the Missal shows a mixture of northern European and Italian elements (Buchthal 1957: 16).

Another work from Jerusalem, the Gospel of St John in Paris, probably dates from between 1130 and 1135 (Buchthal 1957: 24). It too is an imitation of a Byzantine model by a Latin artist. Two other Gospels, one in Paris and another in the Vatican which are very similar to one another, have been dated to the third quarter of the twelfth century, either towards the end of the reign of Baldwin III (1143–63) or during the reign of Amalric (1163–74) (Buchthal 1957: 25, 33). They are the only surviving examples of work from the Jerusalem scriptorium in the immediate period leading up to the fall of Jerusalem in 1187. The illuminations include portraits of the evangelists and various initials. The models are Byzantine and some of the portraits are, to quote Buchthal, 'the closest copies of Byzantine work ever attempted by medieval Latin artists' (Buchthal 1957: 28). However, the workmanship of the illuminations is poor and there is no relationship between the subject matter and the illustrations. In some of the initials there is evidence for a western 'Umbro-Roman' influence.

Three surviving manuscripts from the scriptorium of the Church of the Holy Sepulchre date from the short period of Frankish rule in Jerusalem during the thirteenth century (1229–44). One of these is the Riccardiana Psalter, which was written for a noble lady. As the litany mentions English saints and displays a German form of illustration (scenes from the Life of Christ which bear no relation to the subject matter of the accompanying text), Buchthal suggests that it was commissioned by the German Emperor Frederick II for his English wife, Isabel (Buchthal 1957: 41). He dates it to 1235–37. The layout is Western but the iconography is generally Byzantine, with influence of Norman Sicily. However, there is no longer any attempt at the painstaking imitation of Byzantine manuscript art, as had been prevalent in the manuscript painting of the Jerusalem scriptorium in the previous century (Buchthal 1957: 43). The artist would appear to have been a Sicilian or someone who was trained in Sicily. Two other works, the Egerton Sacramentary and the Pontifical of Apamea, are inferior pieces in a debased style which were carried out by a single hand in the same period as the Riccardiana Psalter. Buchthal suggests that they are probably more typical of the products of the scriptorium at this time than is the Psalter.

The scriptorium at Akko

Whereas we can assume that the scriptorium of the Holy Sepulchre was located somewhere in the conventual complex to the north and east of the Church of the Holy Sepulchre, we can only guess at the location of the scriptorium at Akko. It may have been in the house of the canons of the Holy Sepulchre, which was probably located east of the quarter of the Hospitallers of St John. According to Dichter (1979: 59), a scriptorium was attached to the Church of the Holy Cross, the cathedral church of Akko, which was also located east of the Hospitaller's Quarter.

A number of surviving works have been identified as deriving from Akko in the thirteenth century. One of these is the Missal in Naples, an incomplete and poorly preserved work of provincial character. It may be the earliest surviving example of illumination from the new capital of Akko, possibly made around 1200. It contains two full-page miniatures, a Crucifixion and a Maiestas Domini, as well as a number of initials. They were the work of a southern Italian master working in the tradition of the scriptorium of the Holy Sepulchre (Buchthal 1957: 34). One of the finest works, the Arsenal Bible, is preserved in the Bibliothèque de l'Arsenal in Paris. It is an Old French translation of twenty books selected from the Old Testament, each with a frontispiece miniature and an illuminated initial. The miniatures are in the form of cycles formed of small scenes, which can be connected in varying degrees to Western and Byzantine models (Weiss 1998). The Missal in Perugia, which was written in French, dates from the third quarter of the thirteenth century (Buchthal 1957: 48). The artist of the full-page miniature illuminating the Canon appears to have been a Venetian and the half-page illumination shows a Venetian influence but also a conscious attempt to work in the tradition of the School of the Holy Sepulchre (Buchthal 1957: 49). The initials in this work, however, are by a different hand, perhaps of French origin (Buchthal 1957: 51). Another important work, the Egerton Missal which is now housed in the British Museum (Catalogue no. 13), has a full-page Crucifixion which is a replica of one in the Perugia Missal but with a slightly more linear representation of the draperies. It is in a poor state of preservation.

A manuscript in the Biblioteca Capitolare in Padua (Catalogue no. 13) contains a psalter, the Book of Daniel, the Minor Prophets and the Maccabees. This work dates from the third quarter of the thirteenth century. The cycle illuminating the psalter follows those found in psalters and bibles from mid-thirteenth-century Paris, as do other illustrations in this manuscript, but there is also evidence of English traditions from the beginning of the thirteenth century (Buchthal 1957: 52). The initials bear a resemblance to those in the Perugia Missal but are of better quality. The technique of some of the illustrations in this work follows Byzantine traditions but it is clear that the work was that of an illuminator trained in a French scriptorium.

Copies of the *Histoire Universelle*, a popular work intended for the lay public, are now situated in Dijon, Brussels and the British Museum. On the basis of their style they have been identified as works of the scriptorium of Akko. Various illuminated copies of the French translation of William of Tyre's work (*History of Deeds Done Beyond the Sea*) and of the French continuation of it were made in Akko in the later part of the thirteenth century.[3]

In Cilician Armenia the long-established school of manuscript illumination followed strong Byzantine traditions but in the Crusader period Western influence is found in the choice of motifs (Boase 1977d: 137).

Icons

The most important collection of icons of the Crusader period is in the monastery of St Catherine in Sinai (Weitzmann 1963: 179–203). Kurt Weitzmann attributed forty-two icons to the kingdom of Akko, with the vast majority (thirty-nine) coming from the ateliers of Akko. French, Venetian and perhaps southern Italian or Cypriot traditions are evident amongst these workshops. Some of the icons are the work of artists who had come to the East but continued to work in the style of their homeland. An icon from St Catherine's Monastery which dates from the first half of the twelfth century shows Christ enthroned and holding an open book. It was carried out in the style of northern France with an English influence (Weitzmann 1966: 52, Plate 1). However, the proportions are more realistic than those found in works from northern France and England, and there is a clear affinity with Byzantine art (Weitzmann 1966: 53). Other icons are by artists who had absorbed the local style at the expense of their own traditions. For example, an icon showing the Crucifixion, also from Sinai, has Byzantine iconography but betrays the Western origins of the artist through the presence of certain elements of Romanesque stylization, such as a stiffness and lack of articulation in the human figures (Weitzmann 1966: Plate 5). In such works the proportions of the figures (thickset with oversized heads), and the facial expressions which lack emotion, fall short of the Byzantine models (Weitzmann 1966: 54). A less effective treatment of the highlights and the occasional illustration of Western costumes are additional evidence in identifying the artist as a Westerner.

The vast majority of icons from the Latin East are from the second half of the thirteenth century. Various workshops with artists of French or Italian (Venetian) origin were producing icons in Akko, particularly in the later part of the thirteenth century. These workshops appear to have been in close contact with the scriptoria producing miniature paintings. Some masters may have been working in both media (Weitzmann 1966: 74).

Notes

1 According to Goldmann the sculpture was sold to the dealer in Akko by UNIFIL soldiers and may have come from somewhere in Lebanon.
2 Theoderich 1891: 11–12.
3 William apparently died in 1185 and his work ends in 1184, but French continuations carry it up to the middle of the thirteenth century.

8 Building techniques and materials

The construction methods used by the Franks combined Western techniques brought to the East by the new settlers with techniques which they encountered in the East. The manner in which they applied Western or Eastern methods depended on the type of building they were constructing. In churches the Franks followed Western traditions with only limited use of Eastern building practices, such as the use of flat rather than gabled roofs and pointed arches. In urban domestic architecture, although Eastern layout was commonly adopted, there was restricted use of local construction methods and decorative elements such as interlocked or joggled voussoirs in arches and *ablaq* (alternating use of dark and light-coloured stone which is occasionally found in Frankish buildings but became popular in Mamluk architecture). In newly founded villages there is little that can be said to be local or Eastern. The masonry of all types of buildings was carried out by the methods in use in western Europe: fine diagonal tooling together with widespread use of masons' marks (Plates 8.1 and 8.2). The combination of fieldstone construction with drafted quoins, window frames and door frames is another technique not found in local architecture prior to the twelfth century.

Mortar and plaster

The mortar used in Frankish buildings varies in quality, from the coarse mud mortar used for the core of rubble-filled walls of domestic buildings to the hard white mortar found in fine masonry and the extremely hard mortar used in fortifications. The latter is so hard that in sandstone construction such as the walls of Ascalon and Caesarea it remains solid long after the ashlar facings have worn away, and at Vadum Jacob, where the ashlars have been robbed, the core still stands to a height of six or seven metres.

Plaster was made from lime and sand mixed with water with occasional carbonized organic material. Potsherds were added to hydraulic plaster that lined cisterns. Plaster was generally applied in at least two layers, the uppermost one being smoother and finer. 'Fish scale' or 'herringbone' trowel incisions were often applied to give the surfaces a better grip. Plaster was occasionally used in a decorative manner by moulding, incision, painting or a combination of these. Church walls and ceilings were sometimes decorated with frescos, but in general plaster was used in a purely functional manner and the remarkable use of stucco ornamentation found in Islamic buildings is unknown.

Wood

Apart from the scaffolding used in the construction of vaults, there was only limited use of wood in Frankish buildings. Evidence of scaffolding for barrel vaults can be seen in the presence of putlog holes. These are holes in the side walls, at the base or spring of the vault, into which the wooden frame was placed. Window frames and shutters and door panels were certainly made of wood but have not survived. Staircases were occasionally wooden; at Chastel Rouge a wooden staircase originally led to the first-floor doorway. In a Frankish building at Akhziv (Chastel Imbert) a wooden staircase gave access to an opening high in one of the walls, from where a stone staircase continued inside the thickness of the wall. In castles and city gates there were wooden drawbridges, and towers had wooden hoardings, but only the stone supports have survived.

Stone

Whereas in the northern principalities there was a reasonably good supply of timber for construction, in the kingdom of Jerusalem there were few forests and the native trees were small and of little use in construction. Building stone, however, was plentiful throughout the Latin East and was in any case better suited to the climate, retaining the cool night temperatures well into the heat of the day. Various types of stone were available in different regions. In the hilly interior there were different qualities of limestone, including a soft and inferior building stone known locally as *nari* as well as harder limestone. In the eastern highlands volcanic basalt was available. A hard stone to work, it was generally used for fieldstone construction and was occasionally combined with limestone to achieve a decorative quality perhaps best seen at Margat Castle. The Levantine coast is lined with a double ridge of cross-bedded, wind-laid calcareous sandstone known locally as *kurkar* (eolianite), which is formed from deposits of Nile sands. *Kurkar* has always served as the principal building material in the coastal cities.

Stone was generally quarried on or very near to the construction site. In some buildings a finer-quality stone was brought in from more distant quarries for use in decorative elements. In many sites marble or granite *spolia* from ancient buildings were available and these were used for both decorative and functional construction. The Frankish adage that a castle destroyed is a castle half built finds testimony in many of their buildings. In the Land Castle at Sidon the ancient *vomitoria* of the Roman theatre formed the base of the castle, at Beit She'an and Beit Govrin amphitheatre seats were reused in the castle walls, and a Roman sarcophagus was built into the walls of the tower at Saffuriya. At Ascalon and Caesarea granite and marble columns were reused as lateral ties in the fortification walls.

A number of quarries have been identified and surveyed over the years at sites including Montfort and Destroit, and most recently at Nebi Samwil, Vadum Jacob and Blanchegarde.[1] The quarrying technique that can be observed in these quarries appears to differ little from that of earlier periods. With the use of hammers and iron chisels the stone was cut into cubes and then tooled on the quarry site. To facilitate the process of freeing the stone, quarries were often located at sites where a limestone bed only about one metre thick lay on a harder layer of basalt or a softer layer of chalk. Vertical V-shaped channels were cut through the limestone down to the level of the harder or softer stone, from which it could be pried free with relative ease. This technique can clearly be seen at Vadum Jacob, where the limestone bed lies on basalt, and at Blanchegarde, where soft chalk is located under the harder limestone.

Treatment of the stone

Once it was freed from its surroundings, the ashlar was shaped by the mason and then carefully tooled to give it a smooth finish (Plate 8.1). Ellenblum noted that this often took place in the quarry rather than at the building site, and worked stones are occasionally found on quarry sites. The quality of the tooling varied with the type of building under construction. In the case of fortification walls and rural domestic buildings the tooling was generally fairly coarse, whereas in churches and urban public and domestic buildings the workmanship was usually very fine. The Franks introduced to the East a method of dressing stone with fine diagonal striations, particularly common from the thirteenth century on in France and England (Braun 1968: 65). Clermont-Ganneau was the first to recognize its use in the East, identify it as a characteristic of Frankish construction and consequently realize its value as a means of identifying Frankish buildings (Clermont-Ganneau 1899: 40).

In the doorway of the now destroyed farmhouse at Har Hozevim, Jerusalem, a number of unfinished stones displayed this surface treatment. From these examples we can see the stages of the tooling process. The stone was first roughly smoothed with a tool which left round impressions about 4 mm wide and 2 cm long and 2–3 cm apart. Subsequently similar but finer tooling was carried out, leaving impressions 3 mm wide and 1 cm long and spaced about 3 mm apart. In the final stage a serrated tool was applied to the surface leaving impressions of about 2.5–3 cm long but carried out consecutively, so that they appear as continual diagonal lines.

Other techniques frequently used by Frankish masons involved tooling of the entire surface of the stone except for the margins of the face (usually about 10 cm wide), and in other cases tooling only the margins and leaving

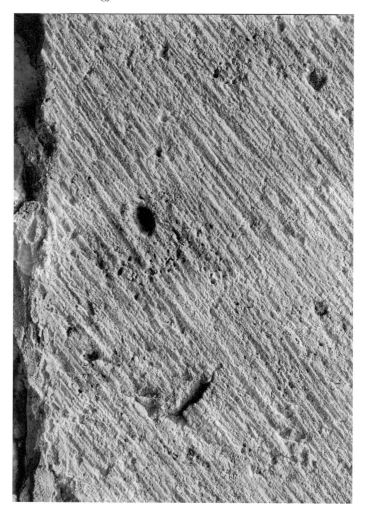

Plate 8.1 Frankish stonework: diagonal tooling (photograph by the author)

the remainder of the stone unworked as a rough, pronounced boss. The use of marginally tooled stones is not limited to the medieval period, but the Franks do seem to have been responsible for cases where it is restricted to the quoins, window frames and door frames, with the remainder of the construction being of roughly worked fieldstone (Ellenblum 1992: 72).

Masons' marks

Letters and symbols are frequently found incised on the surface of worked stones in Frankish buildings (Plate 8.2). Various interpretations have been

Plate 8.2 Frankish stonework: masons' marks (photograph by the author)

suggested for the function of these marks, including the possibility that they were quality marks made by masons accepting responsibility for the accuracy of stones they had hewn (Braun 1968: 64), or that they were assembly marks labelling stones prepared at distant quarries for positioning in a building (Ellenblum forthcoming). In most cases, however, they appear simply to have been the tallies of individual masons that enabled them to identify and count the stones they had cut in a certain period in order to receive payment for their labour. The use of masons' marks in Frankish buildings was first recorded in 1669 by the Franciscan Father Morone da Maleo (da Maleo 1669: 209).[2] Their importance in identifying Frankish construction was once again first noticed by Clermont-Ganneau (1899: 1–38).

Construction

In roof construction the Franks generally adopted the flat roofs that are typical of Eastern architecture. This is true even of buildings which in other aspects were typically Western, such as churches. There is, however, occasional evidence for the use of gabled tiled roofs. We find them in a building constructed by the Templars beside the *Templum Domini* in Jerusalem which Theoderich described as having a high-pitched roof, contrary to the local custom (Theoderich 1891: 31). Roof-tiles have occasionally been found in Frankish buildings such as at the farmhouse at Har Hozevim near Jerusalem. Here, as in earlier periods, large, flat, rectangular tiles with raised edges (*tegulae*) were used together with narrower, arched riders (*imbrices*). The tiles were set in place and sealed with plaster.

Domed roofs are unusual in Frankish buildings except for occasional use in churches, where the transept crosses the nave, and in small constructions such as ovens. For roof construction, both in domestic and in monumental buildings, the Franks generally employed vaults. They adopted the slightly pointed Eastern arch before it became popular in Western Gothic architecture; it became one of the distinguishing features of Romanesque architecture in the Latin East, while in Western Romanesque arches and vaults remained rounded. The Franks used both groin vaults (cross vaults) and barrel vaults (tunnel vaults). The barrel vault, which has been described as 'a continuous arch resting on the side walls of a building' (Mitchell and Mitchell 1908: 292), was used to cover rectangular spaces. It was comparatively easy to construct but had some disadvantages: it was limited to a certain width, about 7 m, and the side walls had to be extremely thick in order to support the weight and downward thrust of the superstructure. This necessitated limiting or avoiding altogether the opening of doors and windows in the side walls. Consequently, this type of construction was preferred for cellars or ground floors but not for upper storeys. In order to construct a barrel vault, continuous, half-wheel-shaped wooden frames were inserted into the upper part of the side walls on to which a wooden vault was constructed. On this the stone vault was built, and after its completion the framing was removed and the holes made in the side walls to support the framework (putlog holes) were blocked.

In the excavation of the farmhouse at Har Hozevim in Jerusalem it was possible to examine the make-up of a typical barrel vault. A cross-section of the collapsed main vault was exposed. It contained seven distinct layers: a grey plaster which covers the interior of the vault, a layer of large, roughly shaped, vertically placed stones which was bonded with the same grey mortar, a fill of *terra rossa* and fieldstone, a layer of yellowish, sandy gravel, a thin layer of *terra rossa*, a second thin, yellowish, sand layer, and finally a layer of grey plaster which apparently formed the floor of the upper storey.

With the groin vault the thrust was concentrated on the piers; this meant that, unlike with barrel vaults, the walls could have large openings on all sides. Groin vaults were usually constructed of brick-shaped stones of varying size set in mortar and covered with plaster. In addition to its attractive appearance, the advantage of the groin vault lies in the fact that the limitation to its dimensions could be overcome by using several connected groin-vaulted bays supported on piers. In Gothic architecture the rib-vault was often used; it is so-called because the *arris* (the meeting apex of two vault planes) is projected in a rib-like form (Plate 8.3). The ribs were often supported on small 'elbow' columns that extend out from a wall and immediately bend at a right angle, supporting a small capital which in turn supports the rib of the vault. At the junction of the ribs at the centre of the vault there was often an elaborately carved keystone bosset.

Plate 8.3 Rib-vaulting in Crac des Chevaliers (photograph by Jonathan Phillips)

Another means of roofing occasionally employed by the Franks was a flat wooden roof supported on stone transverse arches. This was easier to construct than stone vaulting but had neither the strength of the barrel vault nor the beauty of the groin vault, and its construction was dependent on the availability of timber. More often transverse arches were used to strengthen barrel vaults and to support the divisions between naves and aisles in churches or between bays in groin-vaulted halls.

The construction of walls in Frankish buildings, particularly the side walls of barrel vaults, was carried out by building an outer and an inner wall of solid ashlar masonry (or alternatively of fieldstone with marginally drafted quoins) and then filling the space between the two walls with rubble and mud mortar. Floors in public buildings were often constructed of well-cut pavers. In much private architecture, however, floors were of either packed earth or lime, or if the building was constructed directly on the bedrock the builder simply worked the rock to a reasonably smooth finish and occasionally covered it with a lime surface.

In Frankish architecture doors and windows have both rounded and pointed arches or have a flat lintel. Occasionally there is use of interlocked or joggled voussoirs, a technique which gained great popularity in Mamluk architecture. Shallow relieving arches were frequently used to take the weight off monolithic stone lintels. Embrasure windows are characteristic of both

Plate 8.4 Moulded arch on the door of St Anne's Church, Jerusalem (photograph by Yael Sternheim)

public and private buildings, as are double windows. The use of mouldings (hood mouldings or drip mouldings over doors and windows, cornice mouldings and mouldings on imposts) was a popular means of accentuating the architectural form (Plate 8.4). As in the West, windows may have been covered by wooden shutters or oiled leather, but certainly glass was also used. Fragments of plate glass are occasionally found and circular panes of blown glass about 20 cm in diameter, generally greenish in colour, were occasionally used (Benvenisti 1970: 386). Examples of such panes have been recovered at Beit She'an (see p. 190, n. 10). Doors had wooden panels, usually two, and were supported by an axle which fitted into sockets behind the thresholds and lintels. The sockets were lined with bronze, lead or iron to facilitate the movement of the doors.[3] Shallow channels on the thresholds allowed the axle post to be slipped into place; these channels were necessary because the height of the axle post was greater than that of the door. The doors opened inward and could be secured by means of a bolt mechanism and a wooden beam which was drawn out of a channel in the side wall.

Staircases were constructed either of wood, in which case they have not survived, or of stone, and were carried on half-arches. In the kingdom of Jerusalem there is little use of the spiral staircase which is common in the West. In castles, churches and manor houses, staircases were often built within the thickness of walls in order to save space. Cisterns were present in most buildings and deemed a necessity in castles and private dwellings. They were fed from pipes leading from catchment areas such as roofs and paved courtyards. The cisterns were usually barrel-vaulted or, if cut into the bedrock, bell-shaped. They were lined with hydraulic plaster and were often attached to a sump shaft.

Notes

1 Publication of the latter three sites is now under way.
2 Masons' marks have been discussed by Clermont-Ganneau in some detail. See Clermont-Ganneau 1899: 4–38, and for a more up-to-date discussion see Pringle 1981: 173–99.
3 At Vadum Jacob lead was found in some of the door sockets.

9 Burials

Burial customs

The Franks buried their dead in quite shallow graves. As grave goods are comparatively rare, there was no need for the deep burials that are intended to thwart grave-robbing. The body was laid on its back with an east–west orientation, the head to the west, facing upwards. There was often an earthen or stone pillow to support the head. The arms were either clasped across the body or with the left arm across the chest and the right arm across the waist (Bull 1987: 8). In churchyard burials at Tel Jezreel the hands were placed on the pelvis. In Templar burials the right hand was placed over the heart and the left arm extended across the abdomen. Ankles were sometimes placed close together (Bradley 1994: 63–4).

Not all Christians were buried with such care. In the battlefield, circumstances often necessitated mass burials in trenches, and in Jerusalem poor pilgrims who died in the hospital were simply cast into a charnel pit.

Anthropological research

Studies of skeletal remains, including the examination of calcium and fluoride levels in bones, can provide information on physical appearance, diet, diseases, injuries and cause of death. Unfortunately, in recent years religious sentiments have brought anthropological research in Israel to an almost complete standstill. Even before this, relatively little work was carried out on human remains of Frankish date. One of the few exceptions is a discussion of remains from tombs in Parva Mahumeria (al-Qubeiba) published in 1947 by Bagatti (1993: 77–9). More recent work includes burials from cist graves in the nave of the church at Yoqne'am (Smith and Sabari 1996: 242–5) and as yet unpublished Frankish burials have been found at Caesarea. The most important discussion to date is that of the human remains uncovered in excavations at Tel Jezreel (Bradley 1994; Mitchell 1994). This excavation provided evidence of high infant mortality which was no doubt typical of this period. Amongst the diseases of the individuals buried here are meningitis, anaemia, enthesopathy and periostitis in infants, and osteomyelitis and gout in adults (Mitchell 1994: 67–70).

Cemeteries

A number of medieval cemeteries are known, either through the survival of burial structures, sarcophagi and tombstones or through rediscovery during excavations. The finest example is located outside the walls of the faubourg at 'Atlit to the north-east of the castle. It is a walled, trapezoid-shaped area (approximately 85–95 × 50–70 m) containing 1,700 graves, most of which are aligned in an approximate east–west orientation. This important site has not yet been properly examined.[1] Some impressive monolithic tombstones are located here, but most of the grave markers are of sandstone rubble. One interesting feature that can best be seen in aerial photographs is that the tomb markers on the southern side of the cemetery appear to be much broader than those on the north side. This may point to a change in the way these markers were constructed, constituting evidence of two distinct periods of burial in the graveyard. In general, the impression one gets from an examination of the layout of the tombs is that there was no great attempt at order, a fact which may point to these burials having taken place over an extended period (1217–91). However, here and there one can make out a fairly orderly row of graves, possibly connected to a particular event.

On the twelfth-century maps of Akko accompanying the *Chronica Historia Anglorum Majori* of Matthew of Paris, the cemetery of St Nicholas appears outside the city on the north side, to the east of the suburb of Montmusard. It is depicted beside the Church of St Nicholas as rows of tombstones together with the inscription 'Le cimitire Seint Nicholas u hom enterre les mortz' (Saint Nicholas cemetery where they bury the dead). On Sanudo's map St Nicholas' Gate is in the eastern wall of the city and the cemetery may actually have been here rather than where Paris places it, possibly at the site of the Muslim cemetery near the ancient mound. Some apparently medieval tomb markers may still be seen there (Kedar 1997: Figure 21).

Other cemeteries in Akko are mentioned in medieval sources. These include the cemetery of St Michael, which may have been located in an open area near the gate of that name in the south-western corner of Montmusard (Dichter 1979: 92)[2] and, also in Montmusard, the cemetery of the Carmelites (Dichter 1979: 92). The Knights Hospitallers of St Thomas may have had a cemetery outside the northern wall of Montmusard (Dichter 1979: 110).

Several cemeteries are known in Jerusalem. One is to the west of the city walls in the vicinity of the pool of Mamilla. The cartulary of the Holy Sepulchre mentions a church and cemetery outside David's Gate beside the road to Bethlehem.[3] Clermont-Ganneau argued convincingly for this having been in the area of the existing Muslim cemetery and the Mamilla pool, pointing out that the Bethlehem road, which is now located further south, previously cut across in the direction of the pool before turning to the south. Frankish sarcophagi may still be seen in this cemetery (see pp. 234–5). Those Crusaders who fell during the siege of Jerusalem in 1099 were buried outside the eastern wall of the Temple Mount near the Golden Gate. In the twelfth century this graveyard was one of the stations in the procession held on 15 July each year to mark the anniversary of the conquest of the Holy City in 1099. There is no visible evidence of this site today.

The practice of burying the dead next to the parish church rather than at some distance from the living community was one that had developed in the West some time between the early Middle Ages and the twelfth century (Duby 1991: 44). It appears also to have been adopted in the Latin East, where churchyard burials are known at Caesarea, Jezreel and al-Qubeiba, as well as in Nazareth, Akko and Jerusalem. In the seventeenth-century engraving of the ruins of the Church of St Andrew in Akko drawn by Cornelius Le Bruyn in 1681, one can quite distinctly make out a number of tombstones in the churchyard. In the faubourg at 'Atlit, burials were found on the northern side of the churchyard (Johns 1997: 80–1). A medieval graveyard with stone tomb markers was excavated beside the basilica in Nazareth (Bagatti *et al*. 1954–55; Bagatti 1984). With high infant mortality, children were sometimes buried in a separate area in the cemetery; a children's plot was excavated in the churchyard cemetery at Jezreel (Mitchell 1994: 67–71).

Burials inside churches are known at the Church of the Holy Sepulchre and the Church of St Mary in Jehoshaphat, in the nave of the faubourg church at 'Atlit, in the Cathedral of St Peter in Caesarea, the church in Yoqne'am and in the small parish church at al-Qubeiba.

Tombs

Enlart divided the tombs in the kingdom of Cyprus into three categories: carved slabs, sarcophagi and painted tombs (Enlart 1987: 361). The same division also applies to the mainland, though we should add chamber tombs, niche tombs and communal burial structures.

Chamber tombs

The Franks constructed beautiful chamber tombs (*aedicules*) over the Tomb of Christ and the Tomb of the Virgin Mary. This was mainly in order to make the rather unimpressive remains as beautiful as their importance demanded. There was also a practical reason for covering the remains: pilgrims habitually broke pieces off the tombs for keepsakes,[4] and marble encasings made this more difficult. The Tomb of Christ in the Church of the Holy Sepulchre had originally been a typical Second Temple period burial cave, but by the twelfth century little was left of it. A tomb chamber was built over the remains, and early in the twelfth century the Franks renewed it with a new *aedicule*. The Russian Abbot Daniel (1888: 13) described the new structure as being constructed

> with beautiful marble, like a raised platform and surrounded by twelve columns of similar marble. It is surmounted by a beautiful turret resting

on pillars, and terminating in a cupola, covered with silver-gilt plates which bears on its summit a figure of Christ in silver.

The other chamber tomb, that of the Virgin Mary, is located in the subterranean church of St Mary in Jehoshaphat. The Franks rebuilt the tomb, which at the time of Abbot Daniel's visit (1106–7) was in ruins. At the end of the sixteenth century the structure built by the Franks was dismantled. However, on the basis of pilgrim accounts and the remains exposed during work on the tomb in 1972, Michele Piccirillo has attempted to describe the original appearance of the structure (Piccirillo 1975: 73–82, Figure 19). The Franks constructed a square chamber, each side measuring 3.36 m. Piccirillo estimates the chamber to be about 2.72 m high. Excavators found sixteen column bases, but the twenty columns mentioned by Theoderich may have included double columns on the corners.[5] The columns supported capitals which in turn supported pointed arches, four on each side. Above the arches the upper part of the chamber was decorated with a carved and gilded inscription and above it the *limbum* (cornice). On the roof of the chamber was a *ciborium* (canopy) supported on six double columns and covered by a dome with a gilded cross above.

Inside, the sepulchral bench was covered on the front with a marble *transenna* (a grille 66 cm high and 2.04 m long) with three holes through which the stone could be seen and touched but which made it difficult to break off large pieces (Plate 9.1).[6] The *transenna*, which is still in place, was decorated with a cornice of acanthus leaves. The top of the bench was covered with a marble slab to form an altar.

Niche tombs

In churches, the tombs of important personages were occasionally placed in blind arched niches or shallow vaulted chambers. The tomb of Queen Melisende (d. 1161) in the Church of St Mary in Jehoshaphat is placed in a deep chamber (3.87 m long, 1.58 m wide and 2.69 m high) on the eastern side of the staircase leading down to the chamber of the Tomb of the Virgin. The vault has a cupola above it with two windows (one of which is now blocked). On the eastern wall of the chamber at the height of 0.85 m is an *arcosolium*, 1.85 m wide and 91 cm high. The decoration of this tomb is low-key, restricted to the simply carved voussoirs of the entrance arch.

Enlart illustrates three elaborate Gothic niche tombs in Cyprus: the Tomb of the Abbess Eschive of Dampierre (d. 1340) (Enlart 1987: 366–7, Figure 332), the Tomb of St Mammas at Morphou (Enlart 1987: 367–70, Figure 333) and a tomb niche in Famagusta Cathedral (Enlart 1987: 370–1, Figure 335). All three are finely decorated with floriate ornamentation.

Plate 9.1 Transenna of the tomb of the Virgin Mary in Jehoshaphat
(courtesy of the Studium Biblicum Franciscanum)

Carved slab tomb markers

Carved stone slabs used as tomb markers are quite common in the Latin East.
In their simplest form they lack decoration and inscriptions, although it is
likely that such markers originally had some sort of painted inscription which
has worn off. The same is probably true of markers which have no inscription
but have some form of design such as a cross, a coat of arms or tools of a certain
trade carved on them. Other examples have a few lines of inscription. The
tomb markers of knights and bishops are the most elaborate of this type. They
generally have an effigy carved in low relief shown standing under a simple or
more often trilobed arch with an inscription and pillars on either side.

Many of the tombs in the cemetery at 'Atlit are marked by piles of plaster
rubble but a number of them are covered with whitewashed monolithic sandstone markers, either flat or gabled in form. None of these markers have
inscriptions, but some display incised designs showing various forms of
crosses or symbols of the profession of the deceased, the tools of his trade,
together with a cross. A single upright headstone is decorated with a cross
and a crossbow. Between the tombstones Johns found broken ceramic bowls
which he suggests may have held flowers (Johns 1997: 92).

Elsewhere, the custom of recalling the profession of the deceased on his
tombstone is repeated, even when that profession was as lowly (in medieval
eyes) as that of tanner. A twelfth-century marble tombstone that belonged to

a *coriparius* (tanner) from Akko was found in Gethsemane during excavations conducted in 1912–20 (Orfali 1924: 15–17, Figure 10). It measures 42 × 19 cm with letters 4 cm high. The inscription is interpreted as reading '[HIC] IACET [CORPUS] LAMBERTI CORIPARII DE ACON' (Here lies [the body of] Lamberti, tanner, of Akko).

Like the kings, lesser nobles vied for burial as close as possible to the sacred sites. In front of the eastern door of the Church of the Holy Sepulchre and very near to the royal tombs there is a tombstone over the grave of a knight named Philippe of Aubigné. It was discovered in 1867 when a stone bench was removed from the right-hand side of the door (Clermont-Ganneau 1899: 106–12). It is trapezoid in shape with bevelled edges and bears a three-line Latin inscription and a large coat of arms. The inscription reads 'HIC IACET PHILIPPVS DE AVBIGNI CVIVS ANIMA REQVIESCAT IN PACE AMEN' (Here lies Philippe d'Aubigné. May his soul rest in peace. Amen). Apparently Philippe d'Aubigné was an English knight, the tutor of King Henry III, who died in the Holy Land while on pilgrimage in 1236.

It is possible that burials were also made on the Temple Mount in Jerusalem, perhaps of Augustinian monks and knights of the Order of the Templars who had their headquarters there. In 1881 Clermont-Ganneau discovered a piece of a large tombstone reused in one of the piers at the entrance to the Temple Mount from the Tariq Bab al-Silsila (Clermont-Ganneau 1899: 129–30). It contains part of an inscription reading '[HIC IA]CET DROGO DE BUS . . . ' ([Here li]es Drogo de Bus . . .).

Part of a trapezoid-shaped tombstone with the short inscription 'HIC REQVIESCIT IOH[ANNE]S DE VALENCINUS' (Here rests Joh[anne]s of Valencinus) is now located in the grounds of the Church of St Anne (Plate 9.2). It was found in 1874 during the removal of stones, many of Frankish date, from the grounds between the Protestant school and the English cemetery on the south-west side of Mount Zion. Clermont-Ganneau suggested that the absence of a cross on this stone may mean that it was unfinished and, because of its general similarity to the tombstone of Philippe d'Aubigné, tentatively dated it to the short period of restored Frankish rule between 1229 and 1244 (Clermont-Ganneau 1899: 276–9). If this was the case, it is possible that a tombstone carvers' plot was located on Mount Zion in the thirteenth century, probably adjacent to a cemetery. Another stone of uncertain provenance in Jerusalem was found by Clermont-Ganneau. It bears the inscription 'HIC JACET IOANNES DE LA ROCHELLE, FRATER ADE DE LA ROCHELE CUJUS ANIMA REQUIESCAT IN PACE. AMEN' (Here lies John of la Rochelle, brother of Adam of La Rochelle, may his soul rest in peace. Amen) (Clermont-Ganneau 1899, vol. I: 231–2).

Of the type with incised effigy and inscription there is a thirteenth-century marble tombstone of a bishop (d. 1258), now in the Ustinow Collection in the University of Oslo, which was found 2.5 km north-east of Jaffa in about 1874. The incised design shows a bishop in his regalia including mitre and pastoral staff, and above him to his right an angel waving

Plate 9.2 Tombstone of Johannes of Valencinus (photograph by the author)

a censer[?]. The inscription reads '[ANNO D(OMI)NI MILLESIM]O DUCENTES-
IMO QUI(N)QUAGESIMO OCTAUO, IN FESTO SANCTORUM [OMNIUM, or
C . . . , or M . . .]' (In the year of our Lord one thousand two hundred and
fifty-eight, in the day of the feast of the saints...) (Clermont-Ganneau 1874:
270–4, 1876, 1896: II, 152–4; de Sandoli 1974: 258–9, no. 348; Pringle
1993b: 269, CXC). This piece was found near the tomb of Sheikh Murad. It
was probably originally located in one of the principal churches of Jaffa.

Another incised tombstone, believed to be that of Archbishop William of
Nazareth (d. 1290), was found in Akko in 1962 (Prawer 1974: 241–51). It
is the lower third of the stone preserved to 92 cm high, 112 cm wide and is
4 cm thick. Prawer estimated the original height as 2 m. The figure of an
archbishop holding a crosier and standing between two columns is incised
on it. On the lower left is a small kneeling figure and around the edges of
the slab is an inscription carved in French which gives the date 31 July 1290,
just one year before the fall of Akko.

In Cyprus there are a number of tombstones of this type, many of which
can be seen in the castle museum at Limassol and some of which were
published and illustrated by Enlart (1987: 361–2, Figs. 322, 323, 324). One
is the tombstone of a knight named Brochard of Charpignie. A large heraldic
shield fills the central part of the stone. The knight is dressed in a hauberk
and helmet with a sword and a spear. He stands on two fish and between
his legs a dog can be seen sitting on a column. Enlart also published the
tombstone of a woman shown clothed in a long flowing dress and a simple
head-covering, her head resting on a pillow.

Sarcophagi

As in the West, royalty were buried *ad sanctos* (amongst the saints) in the two
most holy sites: the Church of the Holy Sepulchre and in the Church of the
Virgin Mary in Jehoshaphat. Until the fire of 1808 the tombs of the first
eight rulers of the kingdom of Jerusalem were located in the Church of
the Holy Sepulchre, beside the Chapel of Adam below Golgotha. Of these
monuments only that of Baldwin V, which was in the form of an elaborately
carved sarcophagus, is known to have survived in fragmentary form. An
attempt has been made by Zehava Jacoby to reconstruct it from surviving
fragments and on the basis of drawings made before its destruction; it is now
on display in the Greek Patriarchate Museum in Jerusalem. Baldwin V died
in August 1186, one year before Hattin, at the age of 9. The tomb must
obviously date from between his death and the loss of Jerusalem in 1187. It
is an ornate structure decorated on three horizontal planes: a chest-like part
at the base, a central section decorated with twisted columns and elaborate
capitals supporting the upper part which has Christ's figure flanked by angels
and conchoid niches between them. The entablature at the top and the lower
chest are decorated with wet-leaf acanthus. On the top was a slab with the
inscribed epitaph. The other royal tombs were comparatively simple affairs

formed of rectangular blocks of marble on which a number of small columns supported a large gable-shaped stone. The upper sides of the top epitaphs were engraved and on the ends of the stones there were carved crosses. A fragment probably originating in one of the tombs, consisting of a group of small, twisted pillars, is now on display in the Museum of the Flagellation in Jerusalem.

In the past a number of Frankish sarcophagi could be seen in the cemetery of Mamilla in Jerusalem; these were recorded at the end of the nineteenth century by Clermont-Ganneau. He described, apart from the two fine Gothic-style monuments that can still be seen, a number of lesser markers, many of them 'hewn into a prismatic shape, with a shelving ridge, sometimes connected with a base' (Clermont-Ganneau 1899, vol. I: 279–90). In 1955 several of these tombs were unfortunately bulldozed aside during work on the new Mamilla Park and only one or two examples, which remain largely buried, can be traced today. However, the two finest tombs in the cemetery have fortunately survived more or less intact, one of them because it was reused and is situated within a Mamluk funerary chapel known as the al-Kebekiyeh, the other simply by good fortune and perhaps because of its large size, which made it difficult to carry away (Plate 9.3). In the clearance work the latter tomb was moved from its original position and its lid was overturned but subsequently replaced. These two monuments are similar to one another but not identical. They are carved in the form of gabled buildings with blind-arched facades. They may possibly have been the tombs

Plate 9.3 Sarcophagus in the burial ground of the canons of the Holy Sepulchre in Mamilla, Jerusalem (photograph by the author)

of priors of the Church of the Holy Sepulchre. What appear to be sarcophagi, also in the shape of gabled buildings, can be seen in a sixteenth-century drawing of the Church of St Andrew in Akko.

In the village of Parva Mahumeria (al-Qubeiba) excavations revealed a number of large tombstones, some of them *in situ* inside the church. One of these tombs may have been that identified in the fifteenth and sixteenth centuries as that of St Cleophas (Bagatti 1993: 78, Plates 2 and 9:1). These tombs had prismatic covers similar to some of the sarcophagi or markers in the Mamilla cemetery. Like the royal tombs in the Church of the Holy Sepulchre, the covers have crosses carved on them (Bagatti 1993: Figure

Plate 9.4 The charnel-house at Hakeldama, Jerusalem (photograph by Amit Re'em)

8:10–14, Plate 9: 1,2). Also possibly similar were the tombs in the cemetery of St Nicholas in Akko which appear on Matthew of Paris' map.

In Cyprus some very elaborate Frankish sarcophagi have survived. Enlart illustrates a number of these, decorated with Gothic arches, heraldic shields and figurative and floral designs (Enlart 1987: Figs. 325, 329, 330, 331).

Painted tombs

In the kingdom of Jerusalem only a single example of a painted tomb is recorded. This is a stone in the cemetery at 'Atlit. It has a carved shield shape that originally held a heraldic shield in coloured plaster. It is possible that many of the stones which were not inscribed with incised epitaphs originally had painted epitaphs, and perhaps painted decoration as well.

Communal burials

William of Tyre and Raymond d'Aguilers noted that in Jerusalem pilgrims were buried beyond the city walls in the field of Acheldama (William of Tyre 1986: 8.2; Raymond d'Aguilers 1846: 354), where a large, barrel-vaulted Frankish charnel-house can still be seen (Plate 9.4). This is partly a natural cave which has been expanded and partly a barrel-vaulted construction. The slightly pointed barrel vault measures about 9 × 6 m and is about 10 m high. It is supported by a pier constructed of marginally drafted stones. On the roof there are nine openings through which bodies of the dead could be lowered into the chamber. Dead pilgrims from the Hospital of St John were brought to this charnel-house for burial. According to medieval descriptions, the bodies decomposed in only three days.

Notes

1 Renewed excavations on some of the tombs are planned.
2 Alternatively St Michael cemetery may have been part of the cemetery of St Nicholas.
3 'Praeterea ecclesiam et cimiterium extra partam David, juxta viam qua itur Bethleem' (Bresc-Bautier 1984: no. 170).
4 Abbot Daniel describes the keeper of Christ's tomb furtively breaking off a piece of the sacred rock to give him as a memorial (Daniel 1888: 81).
5 As Piccirillo suggests, however, twenty was a hasty estimate by Theoderich for five columns on four sides, forgetting that the corner columns were shared.
6 The top of the bench shows clear evidence of the damage caused before this arrangement was made.

Postscript

Crusader archaeology and art-historical research dealing with the material culture of the Latin East has made major strides in recent years. The list of sites excavated over the past few years or being excavated at present is long. In Israel recent and ongoing excavations include Frankish sites in Akko and Jerusalem, the castles of Belmont, Beit Govrin, Beit She'an, Blanchegarde, Caesarea, Jaffa, Jerusalem, the Red Tower and Vadum Jacob; this is only a partial list. Important work has been carried out in Cyprus, particularly at Saranda Kolones Castle and at the sugar refinery of Kouklia. Castles have received considerable attention over the years, resulting in some important studies (Ellenblum 1996; Kennedy 1994; Pringle 1986b, 1989, 1994b, 1994c). Major surveys of ecclesiastical and lay buildings have been carried out (Pringle 1993b, 1997, 1998). The study of Frankish art has been greatly enhanced with the recent publication of major studies and surveys (Folda 1995; Jacoby 1979, 1982; Kenaan 1973, 1979; Kenaan-Kedar 1992; G. Kühnel 1988; B. Kühnel 1979, 1991, 1994). A number of studies of Frankish coins and ceramics have been published (Boas 1994; Glücksmann and Kool 1995; Megaw 1968, 1975, 1989; Metcalf 1995; Pringle 1982, 1984b, 1985c, 1987; Stern 1997). There are, however, still many areas that remain untouched. Very little work has been done on human, animal and plant remains. The use of aerial photography, particularly the study of early photographs, introduced and used to great effect by Kedar, has led to some important discoveries (Boas 1997; Kedar and Pringle 1985; Kedar 1997) and has considerable potential, justifying broader use. Pioneering studies of glass and textiles have been made (Baginski and Shamir 1994a, 1994b, 1998; Gorin-Rosen 1997). However, in these and other fields the surface has barely been scratched. Nonetheless, the momentum has picked up and if the present rate of research and publication continues, the future of this field looks bright.

Bibliography

Medieval and later sources

Benjamin of Tudela (1907) 'The Travels of Rabbi Benjamin of Tudela', trans. Asher, in *Early Travels in Palestine* (1848), ed. T. Wright, pp. 63–126, New York.

Bresc-Bautier, G. (1984) 'Le Cartulaire du chapitre du Saint-Sepulcre de Jerusalem', *DRHC*, Paris.

Bruhn, C. van (1702) *A Voyage to the Levant*, trans. W.J. London, London.

Burchard of Mount Sion (1864) *Descriptio Terrae Sanctae*, ed. J.C.M. Laurent, *Peregrinatores Medii Aeui Quatuor*, Leipzig, pp. 1–100, *PPTS*, vol. 12.

City of Jerusalem (1888) trans. C.R. Conder, *PPTS*, vol. 6.

Curzon, H. de (ed.) (1886) 'La Règle du Temple' (reprinted 1977), ed. and trans. L. Dailliez, Société de l'Histoire de France, Paris.

Daniel (1888) 'The Pilgrimage of the Russian Abbot Daniel in the Holy Land', trans. de Khitrowa, *PPTS*, vol. 4.

Delaville Le Roulx, J. (1894–1906) *Cartulaire général de l'ordre des Hospitaliers de S Jean de Jérusalem, (1100–1300)*, 4 vols, Paris.

Desimoni, C. (1884) 'Quatre titres de propriétes des génois à Acre et à Tyr', ed. Comte de Riant, *Archives de l'Orient Latin* II, B, pp. 213–30, Paris.

Fulcher of Chartres (1913) 'Historia Hierosolymitana', ed. H. Hagenmeyer, Heidelberg.

—— (1969) *A History of the Expedition to Jerusalem, 1095–1127*, trans. F.R. Ryan, Knoxville.

Gabrieli, F. (1989) *Arab Historians of the Crusades*, trans. E.J. Costello, New York. (First published 1969.)

'Gestes des Chiprois' (1887) *Publications de la Société de l'Orient Latin, Série Historique*, ed. G. Raynaud, Geneva.

Ibn Jubair (1951) *The Travels of Ibn Jubair*, trans. R.J.C. Broadhurst, London.

'Itinerarium peregrinorum et gesta Regis Ricardi' (1864) ed. W.B. Stubbs, *Roll Series* 38, vol. I, London.

Jacques de Vitry (1896) *A History of Jerusalem. A.D. 1180* (erronious date), trans. A. Stewart, *PPTS*, vol. 11.

John of Wurzburg (1890) 'Description of the Holy Land', trans. A. Stewart, *PPTS*, vol. 5.

Joinville, J. de (1921) *Chronicle of the Crusade of St. Louis*, London, New York.

King, E.J. (1934) *The Rule, Statutes and Customs of the Hospitallers 1099–1310*, London

Le Strange, G. (1890) *Palestine Under the Moslems*, London.

Ludolf of Suchen (1895) 'Description of the Holy Land', trans. A. Stewart, *PPTS*, vol. 12.

Lyons, U., Lyons, M.C. and Riley Smith, J.S.C. (1971) *Ayyubids, Mamluks and Crusaders. Selections from the Tarikh al-Duwal Wa'l-Muluk of Ibn al-Furat*, vol. 2, Cambridge.

Maalouf A. (1984) *The Crusades through Arab Eyes*, trans. J. Rothschild, London.

Mujir al-Din (1876) *Histoire de Jérusalem et d'Hebron. Fragments de la Chronique de Moudjir-ed-dyn*, trans. Henry Sauvaire, Paris.

Pococke, R. (1743–5) *A Description of the East and Some Other Countries*, 2 vols, London.

Raymond d'Aguilers (1846) 'Le "liber" de Raymond d'Aguilers', in *Documents relatifs à l'histoire de croisades*, eds J.H. and L.L. Hill, Paris.

Sanudo, M. (1972) *Liber Secretorum Fidelium Crucis Marinus Sanutus* (reproduction of Hanover 1611 edition).

Strehlke, E. (1869) (reprinted 1975) *Tabulae Ordinis Theutonici*, Berlin.

Tafel G.L. Fr. and Thomas G.M. (eds) (1856–57) *Urkunden zur älteren Handels- und Staatsgeschichte der Republik Venedig*, Vienna.

Theoderich (1891) 'Theoderich's Description of the Holy Places', trans. A. Stewart, *PPTS*, vol. 5.

Upton-Ward, J.M. (trans.) (1992) *The Rule of the Temple*, Woodbridge.

Wilbrand, Count of Oldenburg (1908) *Excerpta Cypria*, Cambridge.

William of Tyre (1986) *Guillaume de Tyr, Chronique*, ed. R.B.C. Huygens, *Corpus Christianorum, Continuatio Mediaevalis* LXIII, Turnhout.

General

Atiya, A. (1962) *Crusade, Commerce and Culture*, Indiana.

Baedeker, K. (1876) *Palestine and Syria. Handbook for Travellers*, Leipzig.

Benvenisti, M. (1970) *The Crusaders in the Holy Land*, Jerusalem.

Boas, A.J. (1995) 'Domestic Architecture in the Frankish Kingdom of Jerusalem', unpublished Ph.D dissertation, The Hebrew University of Jerusalem.

—— (1998) 'The Franklin Period: A Unique Medieval Society Emerges', *Near Eastern Archaeology* 61.3: 138–73.

Broughton (1986) *Dictionary of Medieval Knighthood and Chivalry: Concepts and Terms*, London, Westport, CT, New York.

Bull, B. (1994) *Syria. A Historical and Architectural Guide*, Buckhurst Hill.

Clermont-Ganneau, C. (1892) 'Archaeological and Epigraphic Notes on Palestine', *Palestine Exploration Quarterly* 24: 109–114.

—— (1896–99) *Archaeological Researches in Palestine*, 2 vols, London.

Conder, C.R. and Kitchener, H.H. (1881–83) *The Survey of Western Palestine*, 3 vols, London.

Coureas, N. and Riley-Smith, J. (eds) (1995) *Cyprus and the Crusades*, Nicosia.

Duby, G. (1991) *France in the Middle Ages, 987–1460*, trans. J. Vale, Oxford and Cambridge, MA.

Enlart, C. (1987) *Gothic Art and the Renaissance in Cyprus*, trans. D. Hunt, London.

Gimpel, J. (1988) *The Medieval Machine. The Industrial Revolution of the Middle Ages*, 2nd edn, Cambridge.

Goitein, S.D. (1967) *A Mediterranean Society*, vol. 1, 'Economic Foundations', Berkeley and Los Angeles.

Hill, G. (1948) *A History of Cyprus*, vol. 2, 'The Frankish Period 1192–1432', Cambridge.

Hirschfeld, Y. (1995) *The Palestinian Dwelling in the Roman-Byzantine Period*, Jerusalem.

Holmes, U.T. (1977) 'Life Amongst the Europeans in Palestine and Syria in the Twelfth and Thirteenth Century', in K.M. Setton (general ed.) *A History of the Crusades*, vol. 4, pp. 3–35, ed. H.W. Hazard, Madison, WI.

Jeffery, G. (1918) *A Description of the Historic Monuments of Cyprus*, Nicosia.

Johns, C.N. (1937) *Palestine of the Crusaders: A Map of the Country on Scale 1:350,000 with Historical Introduction & Gazetteer*, Jaffa.

Kedar, B.Z. (ed.) (1987) *The Crusaders in their Kingdom* (Hebrew), Jerusalem.

—— (1990) 'The Subjected Muslims of the Frankish Levant', in James M. Powell (ed.) *Muslims Under Latin Rule, 1100–1300*, pp. 135–74, Princeton, NJ.

—— (ed.) (1992) *The Horns of Hattin*, Jerusalem.

Kedar, B.Z., Mayer, H.E. and Smail, R.C. (eds) (1982) *Outremer: Studies in the History of the Crusading Kingdom of Jerusalem, Presented to Joshua Prawer*, Jerusalem.

Kochavi, M. (ed.) (1972) 'Judaea, Samaria and the Golan: Archaeological Survey 1967–68', *Archaeological Survey of Israel*, vol. I, Jerusalem.

Lyons, M.C. and Jackson, D.E.P. (1997) *Saladin. The Politics of Holy War*, Cambridge.

Magen, Y. and Dadon, M. (forthcoming) 'Excavations at Nebi Samwil' (provisional title), *Atiqot*.

Maitland, F.W. (1926) *The Constitutional History of England*, Cambridge.

Mayer, H.E. (1988) *The Crusades*, trans. J. Gillingham, 2nd edn, Oxford.

Peled, A. and Friedman, Y. (1987) 'Did the Crusaders Build Roads?' (Hebrew), *Qadmoniot* 20: 119–23.

Pirenne, H. (1936) *Economic and Social History of Medieval Europe*, trans. I.E. Clegg, London.

Prawer, J. (1969/72) *Histoire du royaume latin de Jérusalem*, trans. G. Nahon, 2 vols, Paris.

—— (1972) *The Latin Kingdom of Jerusalem. European Colonialism in the Middle Ages*, London.

—— (1975) *Histoire du royaume latin de Jérusalem*, 2nd edn, 2 vols, Paris.

—— (1980) *Crusader Institutions*, Oxford.

Prawer, J. and Benvenisti, M. (1970) 'Palestine Under the Crusaders', in *Atlas of Israel* sheet IX/10, Jerusalem and Amsterdam.

Prawer, J. and Ben-Shammai, H. (eds) (1991) *The History of Jerusalem. Crusaders and Ayyubids (1099–1250)* (Hebrew), Jerusalem.

Pringle, D. (1997) *Secular Buildings in the Crusader Kingdom of Jerusalem*, Cambridge.

Prutz, H. (1883) *Kulturgeschichte der Kreuzzüge*, Berlin.

Pryor, J.H. (1988) 'In Subsidium Terrae Sanctae: Exports of Foodstuffs and War Materials from the Kingdom of Sicily to the Kingdom of Jerusalem, 1265–1284', *Asian and African Studies* 22: 127–146.

Reynolds, S. (1994) *Fiefs and Vassals*, Oxford.

Richard, J. (1972) *The Latin Kingdom of Jerusalem*, trans. J. Shirley, 2 vols, Amsterdam, New York and Oxford.

Riley-Smith, J. (1967) *The Knights of St John in Jerusalem and Cyprus, c. 1050–1310*, London.

—— (ed.) (1973) *The Feudal Nobility and the Kingdom of Jerusalem, 1174–1277*, London.

—— (1987) *The Crusades*, London.

—— (ed.) (1995) *The Oxford Illustrated History of the Crusades*, Oxford.

Runciman, S. (1951–4) *A History of the Crusades*, 3 vols, Cambridge.

Salzman, L.F. (1926) *English Life in the Middle Ages*, Oxford.

Setton, K.M. (gen. ed.) (1969–89) *A History of the Crusades*, 2nd edn, 6 vols, Madison, WI.

The crusader city

Avigad, N. (1980) *Discovering Jerusalem*, Jerusalem.

Avissar, M. (1995) 'Tel Yoqne'am. The Crusader Acropolis' (Hebrew), *Hadashot Arkheologiot* 103: 36–7, Figure 36.

Avissar, M. and Stern, E. (1995) 'Akko, the Citadel', *ESI* 14: 22–25.

Avissar, M. and Stern, E. (1996) 'Akko, the Old City' (Hebrew), *Hadashot Arkheologiot* 106: 20–1.

Bagatti, B. (1952) *Gli antichi edifci sacri di Betlemme*, Jerusalem.

Bahat, D. (1991) 'Topography and Archaeology [of Jerusalem]. Crusader Period. (Hebrew)', in J. Prawer (ed.) *The History of Jerusalem*, pp. 68–119, Jerusalem.

—— (1992) 'The Topography and Toponomy of Jerusalem in the Crusader Period', unpublished Ph.D dissertation, The Hebrew University of Jerusalem.

Bahat, D. and Broshi, M. (1972) 'Excavations in the Armenian Gardens' (Hebrew), *Qadmoniot* 5 (3–4): 102–3.

—— (1975) 'Excavations in the Armenian Gardens', in Y. Yadin (ed.) *Jerusalem Revealed. Archaeology in the Holy City, 1968–1974*, p. 55, Jerusalem.

Ben-Dov, M. (1978) 'Banias – A Medieval Fortress Town' (Hebrew), *Qadmoniot* 11.1: 29–33.

—— (1982) *The Dig at the Temple Mount*, Jerusalem.

Ben-Tor, A. and Rosenthal, R. (1978) 'The First Season of Excavations at Tel Yoqne'am, 1977', *IEJ* 28: 57–82.

Ben-Tor, A., Avissar, M. and Portugali, Y. (eds) (1996) *Yoqne'am I The Late Periods, Qedem Reports*, 3, Jerusalem.

Ben-Tor, A., Portugali, Y. and Avissar, M. (1979) 'The Excavations at Tel Yoqne'am 1978', *IEJ* 29: 65–72.

Boas, A.J. (1997) 'A Rediscovered Market Street in Frankish Acre', *Atiqot* 31: 181–6.
—— (forthcoming) 'Survey of Frankish Domestic Buildings in Jerusalem, Acre, Akhziv, Motza and Lifta', *Atiqot*.
Bull, R.J. (1987) *The Joint Expedition to Caesarea Maritima Preliminary Reports*, Microfiche, Drew University, Madison, WI.
Burgoyne, M.H. and Richards, D.S. (1987) *Mamluk Jerusalem: An Architectural Study*, London.
Chehab, M.H. (1979) 'Tyr à l'époque des croisades', *BMB* 31.
Dichter, B. (1973) *The Maps of Acre*, Acre.
—— (1979) *The Orders and Churches of Crusader Acre*, Acre.
Dothan, M. (1976) 'Akko: Excavation Report, First Season, 1973–4', *BASOR* 224: 1–48.
Ellenblum, R. (1987) 'The Crusader Road to Jerusalem' (Hebrew), in Y. Ben-Artzi and H. Goren (eds) *Historical-Geographical Studies in the Settlement of Eretz Israel*, Jerusalem.
Gertwagen, R. (1996) 'The Crusader Port of Acre: Layout and Problems of Maintenance', in M. Balard (ed.) *Autour de la Première Croisade. Actes du Colloque de la Society for the Study of the Crusades and the Latin East (Clermont-Ferrand, 22–25 juin 1995)*, pp. 553–82, Paris.
Goldmann, Z. (1993) 'Acco: Excavations in the Modern City [II]', in E. Stern (ed.) *NEAEHL*, vol. I, pp. 24–7, Jerusalem.
—— (1994) *Akko in the Time of the Crusades. The Convent of the Order of St. John*, Akko.
Frankel, R. (1980) 'Three Crusader Boundary Stones from Kibbutz Shomrat', *IEJ* 30: 199–201.
—— (1987) 'The North-Western Corner of Crusader Acre', *IEJ* 37.4: 256–61, Plates 31a, b; 32a.
Hartal, M. (1993) Akko, *Hadashot Arkheologiot* 100: 1–20.
Holum, K., Hohlfelder, R.L., Bull, R.J. and Raban, A. (1988) *King Herod's Dream*, London, New York.
Jacoby, D. (1970) 'Crusader Acre in the Thirteenth Century: Urban Layout and Topography', pp. 1–45 in *Studi medievali*, 3a serie.
—— (1982) 'Montmusard, Suburb of Crusader Acre: The First Stage of its Development', in B.Z. Kedar, H.E. Mayer and R.C. Smail (eds) *Outremer. Studies in the History of the Crusading Kingdom of Jerusalem*, pp. 205–17.
—— (1989) 'The Rise of a New Emporium in the Eastern Mediterranean: Famagusta in the Late Thirteenth Century', in *Studies on the Crusader States and on Venetian Expansion*, Northampton (Meletai kai hypomnemata, Hidryma archiepiskopou Makariou III, Nicosia, 1984).
—— (1993) 'Three Notes on Crusader Acre', *ZDPV* 109.1: 83–96.
Kaplan, J. (1966) 'Tel Aviv – Yafo', *IEJ* 16: 282–3.
—— (1976) 'Jaffa', in M. Avi-Yonah and E. Stern (eds) *EAEHL*, vol. 2, pp. 532–41, Jerusalem.
Kedar, B.Z. (1996) 'The Frankish Period: Cain's Mountain', in Ben-Tor, A., Avissar, M. and Portugali, Y. (eds) *Yogne'am I The Late Periods, Qedem Reports 3*, pp. 3–7, Jerusalem.

—— (1997) 'The Outer Walls of Frankish Acre', *Atiqot* 31: 157–80.

Kedar, B.Z. and Stern, E. (1995) 'A Vaulted East–West Street in Acre's Genoese Quarter?', *Atiqot* 26: 105–11.

Kesten, A. (1962) *Acre, The Old City Surveys and Plans*, Acre: Department for Landscaping and the Preservation of Historical Sites.

—— (1993) *The Old City of Acre, Re-examination and Conclusions, 1993*, Acre.

Kool, R. (1997) 'The Genoese Quarter in Thirteenth Century Acre: A Reinterpretation of its Layout', *Atiqot* 31: 187–200.

Linder, E. and Raban, A. (1965) 'Underwater Survey in the Harbour of Acre (1964)', in *Western Galilee and the Coast of Galilee*, pp. 180–94, Jerusalem.

Makhouly, N. and Johns, C.N. (1946) *Guide to Acre*, Jerusalem.

Negev, A. (1960a) 'Caesarea', *IEJ* 10: 127, 264–5.

—— (1960b) 'Caesarea Maritima', *CNI* 11.4: 17–22.

—— (1961a) 'Caesarea', *IEJ* 11: 81–3.

—— (1961b) 'Césarée Maritima', *Bible et Terre Sainte* 41: 13–15.

—— (1962) 'Césarée Maritima', *Revue Biblique* 69: 412–15, Plates XLVI–XLVII.

Patrich, J. (1984) 'The Structure of the Muristan Quarter of Jerusalem in the Crusader Period' (Hebrew), *Cathedra* 33: 3–16.

Peters, F.E. (1985) *Jerusalem*, Princeton.

Pierotti, P. (n.d.) *Pisa e Accon*, Pisa.

Pringle, R.D. (1991a) 'Crusader Jerusalem', *BAIAS* 10 (1990–1), 105–13.

—— (1995) 'Town Defences in the Crusader Kingdom of Jerusalem', in I. Corfis and M. Wolfe (eds) *The Medieval City Under Siege*, pp. 69–121, Woodbridge.

Raban, A. (1989) *The Harbours of Caesarea Maritima: Results of the Caesarea Ancient Harbour Excavations Project, 1980–1985*, ed. J.P. Oleson, vol. 1: 'The Site and the Excavations', 2 vols, Center for Maritime Studies, University of Haifa, Publication no. III/*BAR* 491.

Rey, M.E.G. (1883) *Les colonies Franques de Syrie aux XII-ème et XIII-ème siècles*, Paris.

Roll, I. and Ayalon, E. (1977) *Apollonia/Arsuf 1977*, Israel Deparment of Antiquities and Museums, Tel Aviv University.

—— (1982) 'Apollonia/Arsur – a coastal town in the southern Sharon Plain' (Hebrew), *Qadmoniot* 57.1: 16–22.

—— (1989) *Apollonia and Southern Sharon* (Hebrew), Tel Aviv.

Roll, I. and Ayalon, A. (1993) 'Apollonia – Arsuf', in E. Stern (ed.) *NEAEHL*, vol. 1, pp. 72–5, Jerusalem.

—— (1996) 'Medieval Apollonia-Arsuf: A Fortified Coastal Town in the Levant of the Early Muslim and Crusader Periods', in M. Balard (ed.) *Autour de la Première Croisade. Actes du Colloque de la Society for the Study of the Crusades and the Latin East (Clermont-Ferrand, 22–25 juin 1995)*, pp. 595–606, Paris.

Schick, C. (1902) 'The Muristan, or the Site of the Hospital of St John at Jerusalem', *PEFQS* 34: 42–6.

Shaefer, K.R. (1985) *Jerusalem in the Ayyubid and Mamluk Eras*, Ann Arbor, MI.

Shapiro, S. (1978) 'Crusader Jaffa', *Jerusalem Post* (27 February): 7.

Stern, E. (forthcoming) 'Underground Passage in the Templar Quarter, "Akko"', *Atiqot*.

Syon, D. and Tatcher, A. (1998) 'Akko, Hanyon Ha-Abirim' (Hebrew), *Hadashot Arkheologiot* 108: 17–24.

Ussishkin, D. and Woodhead, J. (1994) 'Excavations at Tel Jezreel 1992–1993, Second Preliminary Report', *Levant* 26: 1–71.

Vann, R.L. (ed.) (1992) 'Caesarea Papers', *Journal of Roman Archaeology*, Supplementary Series No. 5, gen. ed. J.H. Humphrey.

Vincent, H. and Abel, F.M. (1914–26) *Jerusalem Nouvelle*, vol. 2, Paris.

The rural landscape

Abel, F.M. (1926) 'Les deux 'Mahomerie', el-Bireh, el-Qoubeibeh', *RB* 35: 272–83.

Amiry, S. and Tamari, V. (1989) *The Palestinian Village Home*, London.

Ashtor, E. (1976) *A Social and Economic History of the Near East in the Middle Ages*, London.

—— (1977) 'Levantine Sugar Industry in the Latter Middle Ages – An Example of Technological Decline', *Israel Oriental Studies* 7: 226–80.

Avitzur, S. (1976) *Man and his Work. Historical Atlas of Tools and Workshops in the Holy Land*, Jerusalem.

Bagatti, B. (1947) *I monumenti di Emmaus il Qubeibeh e dei dintorni*, Jerusalem.

—— (1971) *Antichi villaggi cristiani di Galilea*, SBF, Coll. min., vol. 13, Jerusalem.

—— (1979) *Antichi villaggi cristiani di Samaria*, SBF, Coll. min., vol. 19, Jerusalem.

—— (1983) *Antichi villaggi cristiani della Giudea e del Neghev*, SBF, Coll. min., vol. 24, Jerusalem.

—— (1993) *Emmaus-Qubeibeh*, English trans. R. Bonanno, Jerusalem.

Bennett, H.S. (1969) *Life on the English Manor*, Cambridge.

Benvenisti, M. (1982) 'Bovaria-Babriyya: A Frankish Residue on the Map of Palestine', in B.Z. Kedar, H.E. Mayer and R.C. Smail (eds) *Outremer: Studies in the History of the Crusading Kingdom of Jerusalem*, pp. 130–52, Jerusalem.

Boas, A.J. (1996) 'A Recently Discovered Frankish Village at Ramot Allon, Jerusalem', in M. Balard (ed.) *Autour de la Première Croisade. Actes du Colloque de la Society for the Study of the Crusades and the Latin East (Clermont-Ferrand, 22–25 juin 1995)*, pp. 583–94, Paris.

Cahen, C. (1950–51) 'Notes sur l'histoire des croisades et de l'Orient latin, 2: Le régime rural au temps de la domination franque,' *Bulletin de la Faculté des lettres de Strasbourg* 29: 286–310.

Cartledge, J. (1986) 'Faunal Remains', in D. Pringle, *The Red Tower*, pp. 176–86, London.

De Vaux, R. and Stéve, A.M. (1950) *Fouilles à Qaryet el-'Enab, Abu-Ghosh, Palestine*, Paris.

Duby, G. (ed.) (1975) *Histoire de la France rurale*, vol. 1, Seuil.

Ellenblum, R. (1991) *Frankish Rural Settlement in Palestine in the Crusader Period*, unpublished Ph.D. dissertation, The Hebrew University of Jerusalem.

—— (1996) 'Colonization Activities in the Frankish East: The Example of Castellum Regis (Mi'ilya)', *The English Historical Review*.

—— (1998) *Frankish Rural Settlement in the Latin Kingdom of Jerusalem*, Cambridge.

Ellenblum, R., Rubin, R. and Solar, G. (1996) 'Khirbat al-Lawza, a Frankish Farm House in the Judean Hills in Central Palestine', *Levant* 28: 189–98.

Hubbard, R.N.L.B. and McKay, J. (1986) 'Medieval Plant Remains', in D. Pringle, *The Red Tower*, pp. 187–91, London.

Kletter, R. (1996) 'Jerusalem, Har Hozevim', *ESI* 15: 70–1.

Kolska Horowitz, L. and Dahan, E. (1996) 'Animal Husbandry Practices During the Historic Periods', *Yoqne'am I, The Late Periods, Qedem Reports* 3, Jerusalem, pp. 246–55.

Latron, L. (1936) *La vie rurale en Syrie et au Liban*, Mémoires de l'Institut francais de Damas, Beirut.

Maier, F.G. and von Wartburg, M.L. (1983) 'Excavations at Kouklia (Palaepaphos) Twelfth Preliminary Report: Season 1981 and 1982', *RDAC*: 300–14, Plates XLVIII–LII.

—— (1986) 'Excavations at Kouklia (Palaepaphos) Fourteenth Preliminary Report: Season 1985', *RDAC*: 55–61, Plates XII–XV.

May, N. (1997) 'Jerusalem, Har Hozevim' (Hebrew), *Hadashot Arkheologiot* 107: 81–4.

Onn, A. and Rapuano, Y. (1995) 'Jerusalem, Khirbet el-Burj', *ESI* 14: 88–90.

Porat, Y. (1986) 'Nethanya ('Umm Khalid)', *ESI* 5: 85–6, Figure 44.

—— (1989) 'Arsuf Castle', *ESI* 7–8: 198.

Porëe, B. (1995) 'Les moulins et fabriques a sucre de Palestine et de Chypre', in N. Coureas and J. Riley-Smith (eds) *Cyprus and the Crusades. Papers given at the International Conference 'Cyprus and the Crusades', Nicosia, 6–9 September 1994*, pp. 377–510, Nicosia.

Prawer, J. (1952) 'Étude de Quelques problèmes agraires et sociaux d'une seigneurie croisée au XIIIe siècle', *Byzantion* 22: 5–61; XXIII (1953): 143–70. Revised English version in *Crusader Institutions*, 'Palestinian Agriculture and the Crusader Rural System', pp. 143–200.

Preston, H.G. (1903) *Rural Conditions in the Latin Kingdom of Jerusalem during the 12th and 13th Centuries*, Thesis, University of Pennsylvania, PA.

Pringle, R.D. (1983) 'Two Medieval Villages North of Jerusalem: Archaeological Investigations in al-Jib and ar-Ram', *Levant* 15: 141–77, Plates 14–22a.

—— (1985a) 'Magna Mahumeria (al-Bira): The Archaeology of a Frankish New Town in Palestine', in P.W. Edbury (ed.) *Crusade and Settlement: Papers Read at the First Conference of the Society for the Study of the Crusades and the Latin East and Presented to R.C. Smail*, pp. 147–68, Cardiff.

—— (1992) 'Aqua Bella: The Interpretation of a Crusader Courtyard Building', in B.Z. Kedar (ed.) *The Horns of Hattin*, pp. 147–67, Jerusalem, London.

—— (1994a) 'Burj Bardawil and Frankish Settlement North of Ramallah in the Twelfth Century', in K. Athamina and R. Heacock (eds) *The Frankish Wars and their Influence on Palestine. Selected papers presented at Birzeit University's International Academic Conference, March 13–15, 1992*, pp. 30–59, Bir Zeit.

Richard, J. (1985) 'Agricultural Conditions in the Crusader States', in K.M. Setton (ed.) *A History of the Crusades*, vol. 5, pp. 251–94, WI.

Seligman, J. (1998) 'Jerusalem. The Old City Wall' (Hebrew), *Hadashot Arkheologiot* 108: 138–9.

Vitto, F. and Sion, O. (in press) 'H. 'She'eri (A-Nabi Thari) (2440)', *ESI*.

von Wartburg, M.L. (1995) 'Design and Technology of the Medieval Cane Sugar Refineries in Cyprus. A Case Study in Industrial Archaeology', in A. Malpica (ed.) *Paisajes del Azucar. Actas del Quinto Seminario International Sobre la Cana de Azucar*, pp. 81–116, Granada.

von Wartburg, M.L. and Maier, F.G. (1989) 'Excavations at Koklia (Palaepaphos). 15th Preliminary Report: Seasons 1987 and 1988', *RDAC*: 177–88.

—— (1991) 'Excavations at Kouklia (Palaepaphos) 16th Preliminary Report: Season 1989 and 1990', *RDAC*: 255–62, Plates LXV–LXX.

Watson, A.M. (1981) 'A Medieval Green Revolution: New Crops and Farming Techniques in the Early Islamic World', in A.L. Udovich (ed.) *The Islamic Middle East 700–1900*, pp. 29–58, Princeton.

Castles, urban fortifications, weapons and armour

Aristidou, E. Ch. (1983) *Kollossi Castle through the Centuries*, Nicosia.

Bahat, D. (1989–90) 'Review of Wightman, G.J., The Damascus Gate, Jerusalem', *BAIAS* 9: 61–2.

Bahat, D. and Ben-Ari, M.B. (1976) 'Excavations at Tancred's Tower', in Y. Yadin (ed.) *Jerusalem Revealed: Archaeology in the Holy City 1968–1974*, pp. 109–10, Jerusalem.

Ben-Dov, M. (1969) 'The Excavations at the Crusader Fortress of Kokhav-Hayarden (Belvoir)' (Hebrew), *Qadmoniot* 2.1: 22–7.

—— (1972) 'The Crusader Castle of Belvoir', *Christian News from Israel* 23.1: 26–8.

—— (1974) 'The Fortress at Latrun' (Hebrew), *Qadmoniot* 7.3–4: 117–20.

—— (1975) 'Crusader Fortresses in Eretz-Israel' (Hebrew), *Qadmoniot* 8.4: 102–13.

—— (1986) 'The Sea Fort and the Land Fort at Sidon' (Hebrew), *Qadimoniot* 19: 113–19.

—— (1987) 'The Medieval "Tanners' Gate" and the "Moors' Gate" in Ottoman Times' (Hebrew), *Quadmoniot* 20: 115–19.

—— (1993a) 'Belvoir (Kokhav Ha-Yarden)', in E. Stern, A. Lewinson-Gilboa, J. Aviram, M. Ben-Dov and Y. Minzker (eds) *NEAEHL*, vol. 1, pp. 182–86, Jerusalem.

—— (1993b) 'Latrun', in E. Stern, A. Lewinson-Gilboa, J. Aviram, Ben-Dov, M. and Y. Minzker (eds) *NEAEHL*, vol. 3, pp. 911–13, Jerusalem.

Boas, A.J. and Maeir, A. (forthcoming) 'Blanchegarde Castle (Tell es-Safi)', *Atiqot*.

Boase, T.R.S. (1967) *Castles and Churches of the Crusading Kingdom*, London.

—— (1971) *Kingdoms and Strongholds of the Crusaders*, London.

—— (1977c) 'Military Architecture and Sculpture', in K.M. Setton (ed.) *A History of the Crusades*, vol. 4, pp. 140–64.

Boaz [Boas] A.J. (1990) 'The Fortress: Area Z', *ESI* 9 (1989–90): 129, Figure 120.

Breton, R. (1972) 'Monographie du chateau de Markab en Syrie', *Mélanges de l'Université Saint Joseph* 47, 251–274.

Dean, B. (1927, reprinted 1982) 'A Crusaders' Fortress in Palestine (Montfort)', *Bulletin of the Metropolitan Museum of Art* 22, Part 2: 91–7. Facsimile edition with an introduction by Meron Benvenisti, Jerusalem.

Deschamps, P. (1934) 'Les Chateaux des Croisés en Terre Sainte', vol. 1, *Le Crac des Chevaliers*, 2 vols, *Bibliotheque archéologique et historique* vol. XIX, Paris.

—— (1935a) 'Une gratte-forteresse des croisés au delà du Jourdain: el Habis en Terre de Suète', *Journal asiatique* 227: 285–99.

—— (1935b) 'Le Château de Saone et ses premiers seigneurs', *Syria* 16: 73–88.

—— (1937) 'Les deux Cracs des croisés', *Journal asiatique* 229: 494–500.

—— (1939) *Les chateaux des croisés en Terre Sainte*, vol. 2, *La défense du royaume de Jérusalem*. 2 vols, *Bibliotheque archéologique et historique*, vol. 34, Paris.

—— (1973) *Les chateaux des croisés en Terre Sainte*, vol. 3, *La défense du comté de Tripoli et de la principauté d'Antioche*, 2 vols, *Bibliotheque archéologique et historique*, vol. 90, Paris.

Ellenblum, R. (1996) 'Three Generations of Frankish Castle-Building in the Latin Kingdom of Jerusalem', in M. Balard (ed.) *Autour de la Première Croisade. Actes du Colloque de la Society for the Study of the Crusades and the Latin East (Clermont-Ferrand, 22–25 juin 1995)*, Paris.

Ellenblum, R. and Boas, A.J. (forthcoming) 'Vadum Jacob Final Report for Seasons 1993–1995, *Atiqot*.

Ellenblum, R. and Hartal, M. (forthcoming) 'Metsad Ateret (Vadum Jacob)', *Hadashot Arkheologiot*.

Fedden, R. and Thomson, J. (1957) *Crusader Castles*, London.

Frenkel [Frankel], R. and Gatzov, N. (1986) 'The History and Plan of Montfort Castle' (Hebrew), *Qadmoniot* 19: 1–2 (73–4): 52–7.

Gertwagen, R. (1989) 'Tel Hanaton – 1987', *ESI* 7–8: 71–2, Figs. 59–61.

—— (1993) 'The Fortress' [Bet She'an]', *ESI* 11: 56–9, Figs. 75–81.

Harper, R.P. and Pringle D. (1988) 'Belmont Castle: A Historical Notice and Preliminary Report of Excavations in 1986', *Levant* 20: 101–18.

—— (1989) 'Belmont Castle 1987: A Second Preliminary Report of Excavations', *Levant* 21: 47–61.

Hennessy, J.B. (1970) 'Preliminary Report on the Excavations at the Damascus Gate, Jerusalem, 1964–1966', *Levant* 2: 22–7.

Huygens, R.B.C. (1965) 'Un nouveau texte du traite du constructione castri Saphet', *Studi Medievali 3rd series* 6 (I).

Johns, C.N. (1932–38) 'Excavations at Pilgrims' Castle, 'Atlit', *QDAP* 1–5.

—— (1947) *Guide to 'Atlit: The Crusader Castle, Town and Surroundings*, Jerusalem.

—— (1950) 'The Citadel, Jerusalem', *QDAP* 1–5.

—— (1997) *Pilgrims' Castle ('Atlit), David's Tower (Jerusalem) and Qal'at ar-Rabad ('Ajlun)*, Aldershot.

Kedar, B.Z. and Pringle, D. (1985) 'La Fève: A Crusader Castle in the Jezreel Valley', *IEJ* 35. 2, 3: 164–79, Plates 20a, b, 21a–d.

Kennedy, H. (1994) *Crusader Castles*, Cambridge.

Kloner, A. (1983) 'Bet Guvrin: Medieval Church and Fortifications' (Hebrew), *Hadashot Arkheologiot* 83: 52–3.

Kloner, A. and Chen, D. (1983) 'Bet Govrin: Crusader Church and Fortifications', *ESI* 2: 12–13.

Kloner, A. and Cohen, M. (1997) 'Bet Govrin' (Hebrew), *Hadashot Arkheologiot* 107: 110–12.

Lawrence, T.E. (1936) *Crusader Castles*, 2 vols, London.

—— (1988) *Crusader Castles*, a new edition with introduction and notes by D. Pringle, Oxford.

Marshall, C. (1992) *Warfare in the Latin East 1192–1291*, Cambridge.

Megaw, A.H.S. (1982) 'Saranda Kolones 1981', *RDAC*: 210–16, Plate XLVIII.

Megaw, P. (1994) 'A Castle in Cyprus attributed to the Hospitallers', in M. Barber (ed.) *The Military Orders*, pp. 42–51, Aldershot.

Müller-Wiener, W. (1966) *Castles of the Crusaders*, London.

Nicolle, D.C. (1988) *Arms and Armour of the Crusading Era, 1050–1350*, 2 vols, White Plains, NY.

Oman, C.W. (1898) *A History of the Art of War*, London.

Prawer, J. (1967) 'History of the Crusader Castle Kaukab al-Hawa' (Hebrew), *Yediot* 31: 236–49.

Pringle, R.D. (1984a) 'King Richard I and the Walls of Ascalon', *PEFQS* 116: 113–46.

—— (1985b) 'Reconstructing the Castle of Safed', *PEFQS*: 141–9.

—— (1986a) 'A Thirteenth Century Hall at Montfort Castle in Western Galilee', *The Antiquaries Journal* 66: 52–81.

—— (1986b) *The Red Tower (al-Burj al-Ahmar. Settlement in the Plain of Sharon at the Time of the Crusades and Mamluks A.D. 1099–1516*, London.

—— (1989) 'Crusader Castles: The First Generation', *Fortress* 1: 14–25.

—— (1991b) 'Survey of Castles in the Crusader Kingdom of Jerusalem, 1989: a preliminary report', *Levant* 23: 87–91.

—— (1994b) 'Templar Castles on the Road to the Jordan', in Malcolm Barber (ed.) *The Military Orders. Fighting for the Faith and Caring for the Sick*, pp. 148–66, Hampshire.

—— (1994c) 'Towers in Crusader Palestine', *Chateau Gaillard* 16: 335–50.

Pringle, D., Petersen, A., Dow, M. and Singer, C. (1994) 'Qal'at Jiddin: A Castle of the Crusader and Ottoman Periods in Galilee', *Levant* 26: 135–66.

Razi, Z. and Braun, E. (1992) 'The Lost Crusader Castle of Tiberias', in B.Z. Kedar (ed.) *The Horns of Hattin*, pp. 217–27, Jerusalem and London.

Rey, E.G. (1871) *Etude sur les monuments de l'architecture militaire des croisés en Syrie et dans l'île de Chypre*, Collection des Documents inédits sur l'Histoire de France, series 1, Histoire politique, Paris.

Ronen, A. and Olami, U. (1978) '*Atlit Map*, Jerusalem.

Rosser, J. (1986) 'Crusader Castles of Cyprus', *Archaeology* 39: 41–7.

Seligman, J. (1994) 'Excavations in the Crusader Fortress at Beth-Shean' (Hebrew), *Qadmoniot* 3–4 (107–108): 138–41.

—— (1995) 'Bet Shean: Citadel', *Hadashot Arkeologiot* 103: 38–42.

Seligman, J. (forthcoming) 'Khirbet Ka'qul. Roman Farmsteads and a Medieval Village', *Atiqot*.

Shaked, I. (1997) 'Margaliot Fortress', *ESI* 16: 17–18.

Sinclair, T. (1987–90) *Eastern Turkey: An Architectural and Archaeological Survey*. 4 vols, London.

Smail, R.C. (1987) *Crusading Warfare 1097–1193*, Cambridge.

Wightman, G.J. (1979) *The Damascus Gate, Jerusalem: Excavations by C.-M. Bennett and J.B. Hennessy at the Damascus Gate, 1964–66, BAR* 519.
—— (1993) *The Walls of Jerusalem from the Canaanites to the Mamluks. Mediterranean Archaeology Supplement* 4, Sydney.

Religious architecture

Bagatti, B. (1968) 'Recenti Scavi a Betlemme', *LA* 18: 181–237.
—— (1975) *New Discoveries at the Tomb of the Virgin Mary in Gethsemane*, trans. L. Sciberras, Jerusalem.
—— (1984) *Gli scavi di Nazaret, vol. 2 (Dal secolo XII ad oggi)*, Jerusalem.
Bagatti, B., Piccirillo, M. and Prodomo, A. (1954–55) 'Ritrovamenti nella Nazaret Evangelica', *Liber Annuus* 5.
Enlart, C. (1926–28) *Les monuments des croisés dans le royaume de Jerusalem. Architecture religieuse et civile*, 2 vols, and 2 albums, *Bibliothèque archeologique et historique*, vols 7–8, Paris.
Folda, J. (1991) 'The Church of Saint Anne', *Biblical Archaeologist* 54: 88–96.
Gimpel, J. (1992) *The Cathedral Builders*, trans. T. Waugh, New York.
Harvey, W. (1935) *The Church of the Holy Sepulchre: Structural Survey*, London.
Kenaan-Kedar, N. (1992) 'The Cathedral of Sebaste: Its Western Donors and Models', in B.Z. Kedar (ed.) *The Horns of Hattin*, pp. 99–120, Jerusalem, London.
Negev, A. (1960) 'Caesarea', *IEJ* 10: 127, 264–5.
Orfali, P.G. (1924) *Gethsemani*, Paris.
Piccirillo, M. (1969) 'Basilica del Santo Sepolcro e lintelli medioevali del Portale', *La Terra Santa* 45: 106–17.
Plommer, H. (1982) 'The Cenacle on Mount Sion', in J. Folda (ed.) *Crusader Art in the Twelfth Century, BAR* 152: 136–66.
Pringle, D. (1993a) 'Churches in the Crusader Kingdom of Jerusalem (1099–1291)', in Y. Tsafrir (ed.) *Ancient Churches Revealed*, Jerusalem.
—— (1993b) *The Churches of the Crusader Latin Kingdom of Jerusalem*, vol. 1, Cambridge.
—— (1998) *The Churches of the Crusader Latin Kingdom of Jerusalem*, vol. 2, Cambridge.
Saller, S.J. (1957) *Excavations at Bethany*, Jerusalem.
Schick, C. (1901) 'The Ancient Churches in the Muristan and The Muristan', *Quarterly Statements of the Palestine Exploration Fund.*
de Vogüé, M. (1860) *Les Églises de la Terre Sainte*, Paris.

Art and small finds

Baginski, A. (1996) 'Textiles from a Crusader Burial in Caesarea', *ATN* 23: 16.
Baginski, A. and Shamir, O. (1994a) 'Textiles from Jeriret Fara'un (Coral Island)', *ATN* 18–19: 4–6.
—— (1994b) 'Textiles from Coral Island', *Twentieth Archaeological Conference in Israel*, Jerusalem.
—— (1998) 'Textiles, Basketry, and Cordage from Jaziret Fara'un (Coral Island)', *Atiqot* 36: 39–92.

—— (forthcoming) 'The Textiles, Basketry, and Cordage from Qarantal Cave 38 – The First Medieval Assemblage Discovered in Palestine', *Atiqot*.

Balog, P. and Yvon, J. (1958) 'Monnaies a légendes arabes de l'Orient latin', *RN* 6th series, vol. I: 133–68, Plates XI–XVI.

Barasch, M. (1971) *Crusader Figural Sculpture in the Holy Land*, New Brunswick.

Ben-Layish, D. (1969–71) 'A Survey of Sundials in Israel', *Sefunim* 3: 70–81.

Boas, A.J. (1994) 'The Import of Western Ceramics to the Latin Kingdom of Jerusalem', *IEJ* 44: 102–22.

—— (1997) 'Late Ceramic Typology', in Y. Hirshfeld (ed.) *The Roman Baths of Hamat Gader*, pp. 382–95, Jerusalem.

Boase, T.R.S. (1938–39) 'The Arts in the Latin Kingdom of Jerusalem', *JWCI* 11: 1–21.

—— (1977a) 'Ecclesiastical Architecture and Sculpture', in K.M. Setton (ed.) *A History of the Crusades*, vol. 4, pp. 69–116.

—— (1977b) 'Mosaic, Painting, and Minor Arts', in K.M. Setton (ed.) *A History of the Crusades*, vol. 4, pp. 117–39.

—— (1977d) 'Cyprus: Ecclesisastical Arts', in K.M. Setton (ed.) *A History of the Crusades*, vol. 4, pp. 165–99.

Borg, A. (1969) 'Observations on the Historiated Lintel of the Holy Sepulchre, Jerusalem', *JWCI* 32: 25–40.

—— (1972) 'The Holy Sepulchre Lintel', *JWCI* 35: 389–90.

—— (1982) 'Romanesque Sculpture from the Rhone Valley to the Jordan Valley', in J. Folda (ed.) *Crusader Art in the Twelfth Century*, BAR 152: 97–119.

Briailles, C. de (1943) 'Le droit de "Coins" dans le royaume de Jerusalem', *Syria* 23: 244–57.

—— (1950) 'Bulles de l'Orient Latin', *Syria* 27: 284–300.

Buchthal, H. (1957) *Miniature Painting in the Latin Kingdom of Jerusalem*, Oxford.

Buschhausen, H. (1978) *Die süditalienische Bauplastik im Konigreich Jerusalem vom Konig Wilhelm II bis Kaiser Friedrich II*, Vienna.

—— (1982) 'Die Fassade der Grabeskirche zu Jerusalem', in J. Folda (ed.) *Crusader Art in the Twelfth Century*, BAR 152: 71–89.

Chitty, D.J. (1928) 'Two Monasteries in the Wilderness of Judaea', *PEFQS*: 134–152.

Clermont-Ganneau, C. (1902) 'The Depository of Ancient Arrows in the Castle of David – Archaeological or Epigraphic Notes on Palestine', *PEFQS*: 136–7.

Coupel, P. (1941) Trois petites Églises du Comté de Tripoli', *BMB* 5: 35–55.

D'Angelo, F. (1972) 'Un'ampolla da pellegrino', *Sicilia Archeologica* 17, 58–9.

Dalton, O.M. (1909) *Catalogue of the Ivory Carvings of the Christian Era*, London.

—— (1922) 'On two Medieval Bronze Bowls in the British Museum', *Archaeologia* 72: 133–60.

Davidson, G.R. (1952) 'The Minor Objects', *Corinth XII*, Princeton, NJ.

Davidson Weinberg, G. (1985) 'A Glass Factory of Crusader Times in Northern Israel (Preliminary Report)', *Annales du 10 Congres de l'Association Intern. pour l'Histoire du Verre*.

Edbury, P. and Metcalf, D.M. (eds) (1980) *Coinage in the Latin East*, BAR 77.

Engle, A. (1982) 'Glass and Religious Man', *Readings in Glass History* 13–14.

Flourentzos, P. (1994) *A Hoard of Medieval Antiquities from Nicosia*, Nicosia.

Folda, J. (1976) *Crusader Manuscript Illumination at Saint-Jean-d'Acre, 1275–1291*, Princeton, NJ.

—— (1977) 'Painting and Sculpture in the Latin Kingdom of Jerusalem', 1099–1291, in K.M. Setton (ed.) *A History of the Crusades*, vol. 4, pp. 251–80.

—— (1982a) *Crusader Art in the Twelfth Century*, BAR 152.

—— (1982b) 'Crusader Frescos at Crac des Chevaliers and Marqab Castle', *DOP* 36: 177–210.

—— (1986a) 'Problems of the Crusader Sculptures at the Church of the Annunciation in Nazareth', in V. Goss and C.V. Bornstein (eds) *The Meeting of Two Worlds*, Kalamazoo.

—— (1986b) 'The Nazareth Capitals and the Crusader Shrine of the Annunciation', in *Crusader Art in the Twelfth Century*, pp. 3–8, Pennsylvania University Park and London (Monographs on Fine Arts, 42).

—— (1995) *The Art of the Crusaders in the Holy Land 1098–1187*, Cambridge.

—— (1996) 'Crusader Art. A Multicultural Phenomenon: Historiographical Reflections', in M. Balard (ed.) *Autour de la Première Croisade* pp. 609–15, Paris.

Glücksmann, G. and Kool, R. (1995) 'Crusader Period Finds from the Temple Mount Excavations in Jerusalem', *Atiqot* 26: 87–104.

Gordus, A.A. and Metcalf, D.M. (1980) 'Neutron Activation Analysis of the Gold Coinages of the Crusader States', in D.M. Metcalf and W.A. Oddy (eds) *Metallurgy in Numismatics*, vol. 1, pp. 119–50, London.

Gorin-Rosen, Y. (1997) 'Excavation of the Courthouse Site at 'Akko: Medieval Glass Vessels (Area TA)', *Atiqot* 31: 75–85.

Grierson, P. (1954) 'A Rare Crusader Bezant with the Christus Vincit Legend', *ANSMN* 6: 169–78.

Hanauer, J.E. (1902) 'Julian's Attempt to Restore the Temple, and Other Notes', *PEFQS*: 392–3.

Harden, D.B. (1966) 'Some Glass Fragments, Mainly of the 12th and 13th Centuries A.D., from Northern Apulia', *JGS* 9: 70–9.

Hazard, H.W. (ed.) (1977) 'The Art and Architecture of the Crusader States', *A History of the Crusades*, vol. 4, (gen. ed. K.M. Setton, vol. ed. H.W. Hazard), WI.

Hunt, L.A. (1991) 'Art and Colonialism: The Mosaics of the Church of the Nativity in Bethlehem (1169) and the Problem of "Crusader" Art', *DOP* 45: 69–85.

Jacoby, D. (1981) 'Some Unpublished Seals from the Latin East', *INJ* 5: 83–8, Plate 17.

Jacoby, Z. (1982a) 'The Workshop of the Temple Area in Jerusalem in the Twelfth Century: Its Origins, Evolution, and Impact', *Zeitschrift für Kunstgeschichte* 45: 325–94.

—— (1982b) 'The Impact of Northern French Gothic on Crusader Sculpture in the Holy Land', in *Il Medio Oriente e l'Occidente nell'arte del XIII secolo: Atti del XXIV Convegno internazionale di Storia dell'Arte*, pp. 123–7, Figs. 96–113, Bologna.

Johns, C.N. (1934) 'Medieval Slip-Ware from Pilgrim's Castle, 'Atlit', *QDAP* 3: 136–44, Plates XLIX–LVII.

Kenaan, N. (1973) 'Local Christian Art in Twelfth Century Jerusalem', *IEJ* 23: 167–75, 221–9.

—— (1979)'The Crusader Lintels in the Church of the Holy Sepulchre – Suggestion for a New Reading', in B.Z. Kedar (ed.) *Jerusalem in the Middle Ages*, pp. 316–26, Jerusalem.

Kenaan-Kedar, N. (1992) 'A Neglected Series of Crusader Sculpture: the Ninety-Six Corbels of the Church of the Holy Sepulchre', *IEJ* 42: 103–14.

Khamis, E. (1996) 'The Metal Objects', in A. Ben-Tor, M. Avissar and Y. Portugali (eds) *Yoqne'am 1 The Late Periods, Qedem Reports 3*, pp. 218–35, Jerusalem.

Kirk, G.E. (1938) 'Nen Men's Morris-Morelles-Muehlespiel in Palestine', *JPOS* 18: 229–32.

Kool, R. (forthcoming) 'The Coins of Vadum Jacob', in R. Ellenblum and A.J. Boas 'Vadum Jacob Final Report for Seasons 1993–1995', *Atiqot*.

Kühnel, B. (1977) 'Crusader Sculpture at the Church of Ascension on the Mount of Olives in Jerusalem', *Gesta* 16: 41–50.

—— (1979) 'The Date of the Crusader Church of the Ascension on the Mount of Olives' (Hebrew, English summary), in B.Z. Kedar (ed.), *Jerusalem in the Middle Ages: Selected Papers* pp. 25–6, Jerusalem.

—— (1991) 'Crusader Art in Jerusalem' (Hebrew), in J. Prawer (ed.) *The History of Jerusalem*, pp. 304–52, Jerusalem.

—— (1994) *Crusader Art of the Twelfth Century*, Berlin.

—— (1996) 'Crusader Art Quoted', in M. Balard (ed.) *Autour de la Première Croisade*, pp. 617–24, Paris.

Kühnel, G. (1980) 'The Column Paintings of the Nativity Church at Bethlehem and their Place in the Crusader Decorative Programme of the Church', unpublished Ph.D. dissertation (Hebrew with Engish summary), Tel Aviv University.

—— (1988) *Wall Painting in the Latin Kingdom of Jerusalem*, Berlin.

—— (1997a) 'Das restaurierte Christusmosaik der Calvarienberg-Kapelle und das Buildprogramm der Kreuzfahrer', *RM* 92: 45–71.

—— (1997b) 'Kreuzfahrerideologie und Herrscherikonographie das Kaiserpaar Helena und Heraklius in der Grabeskirche', *BZ* 90: 396–404.

Lane, A. (1937) 'Medieval Finds at al-Mina in Northern Syria', *Archaeologia* 87: 19–78.

Lester, A. (1996) 'The Glass from Yoqne'am', *Yoqne'am I, The Late Periods, Qedem Reports* 3: 207–17, Jerusalem.

Levy, M. (1991) 'Medieval Maps of Jerusalem' (Hebrew), in J. Prawer (ed.) *The History of Jerusalem*, pp. 418–508, Jerusalem.

Macalister, R.A.S. and Duncan, J.G. (1926) 'Excavations on the Hill of Ophel, Jerusalem, 1923–1925', *PEFA* 4.

Malloy, A., Fraley Preston, I. and Seltman, A.J. (1994) *Coins of the Crusader States 1098–1291*, New York.

Mayer, H.E. (1978) *Das Siegelwesen in den Kreuzfahrstaaten* (Bayerische Akad. der Wissenschaften Philosophische-Historische Klasse Abhandlungen), Neue Folge.

Megaw, A.H.S. (1968) 'Zeuxippus Ware', *ABSA* 63: 67–88.

—— (1975) 'An Early Thirteenth Century Aegean Glazed Ware', in G. Robertson and G. Henderson (eds) *Studies in Memory of David Talbot Rice*, Edinburgh.

—— (1989) 'Zeuxippus Ware Again', in V. Déroche and J.M. Spieser (eds) *Récherches sur la Céramique Byzantine*, Paris.

Merril, S. (1902) 'Ancient Arrows in the Castle of David', *PEFQS*: 106.

Meshorer, Y. (1991) 'Coins of the Crusader Kingdom of Jerusalem' (Hebrew), in J. Prawer (ed.) *The History of Jerusalem*, pp. 388–98, Jerusalem.

Metcalf, D.M. (1975) 'A Hundred Stray Finds from Acre', *ANSMN* 20: 141–52.

—— (1983) *Coinage of the Crusades and the Latin East in the Ashmolean Museum, Oxford*, London.

—— (1995) *Coinage of the Crusades and the Latin East in the Ashmolean Museum, Oxford*, London.

Metcalf, D.M., Kool, R. and Berman, A. (forthcoming) 'Coin Finds from the Excavation of 'Atlit (Pilgrims' Castle and its Faubourg)', *Atiqot*.

Morgan C.H. (1942) 'The Byzantine Pottery', in *Corinth* XI, Cambridge, MA.

Pfeiffer, W. (1970) 'Acrische Glässer', *JGS* 12: 67–9.

Piccirillo, M. (1994) 'Uno Stampo per Eulogia trovato a Gerusalemme', *LA* 44: 585–90.

Pijoan J. (1940) *Art in the Middle Ages*, Chicago, IL.

Prawer, J. (1968) 'The Lintels of the Church of the Holy Sepulchre' (Hebrew), *Qadmoniot* 1: 47–51.

—— (1991) 'Crusader Epigraphy in Jerusalem' (Hebrew), in J. Prawer (ed.), *The History of Jerusalem*, pp. 374–87, Jerusalem.

Pringle, R.D. (1982) 'Some More Proto-Maiolica from 'Atlit (Pilgrims' Castle) and a Discussion of its Distribution in the Levant', *Levant* 14: 104–17.

—— (1984b) 'Thirteenth Century Pottery from the Monastery of St Mary of Carmel', *Levant* 16: 91–111.

—— (1985c) 'Medieval Pottery from Caesarea: the Crusader Period', *Levant* 17: 171–202.

—— (1987) 'Pottery as Evidence for Trade in the Crusader States', in G. Airaldi and B.Z. Kedar (eds) *I communi italiani nel regno crociato di gerusalemme*, pp. 451–75, Geneva.

Rahmani, L.Y. (1976) 'The Eastern Lintel of the Holy Sepulchre', *IEJ* 26: 120–9.

Rahmani, L.Y. and Spaer, A. (1965–66) 'Crusader Coinage found in Akko', *INJ* 3:67–73.

Raphael, K. (forthcoming) 'The Metal Finds from Vadum Jacob', in R. Ellenblum and A.J. Boas 'Vadum Jacob Final Report for Seasons 1993–1995', *Atiqot*.

Sandoli, S. de (1974) *Corpus Inscriptionum Crucesignatorum Terrae Sanctae (1099–1291)*, Jerusalem.

Schlumberger, G. (1878) *Numismatique de l'Orient Latin*, Paris. (Republished Graz-Austria 1954.)

—— (1943) *Sigillographie de l'Orient Latin*, Paris.

Sharon, M. (1995) 'A New Fatimid Inscription from Ascalon and its Historical Setting', *Atiqot* 26: 61–86.

Sharvit, K. and Galili, E. (forthcoming) 'Tel Ascalon: Underwater Archaeological Survey' (Hebrew), *Hadashot Arkheologiot*.

Stern, Edna (E.J.) (1995) 'Exports to the Latin East of Cypriot Manufactured Glazed

Pottery in the 12th–13th Century', in N. Coureas and J. Riley-Smith (eds) *Cyprus and the Crusades. Papers given at the International Conference 'Cyprus and the Crusades', Nicosia, 6–9 September, 1994*, pp. 325–35, Nicosia.

—— (1997) 'Acre, Ha-Gedud Ha-'Ivri Street' (Hebrew), *Hadashot Arkheologiot* 107: 12–16.

Syon, D. (1997) 'The Coins of Area TA', *Atigot* 31: 87–90.

Tait, H. (1968) 'European: Middle Ages to 1862', in D.B. Harden, K.S. Painter, R.H. Pinder-Wilson and H. Tait (eds) *Masterpieces of Glass*, London.

Weiss, D.H. (1998) *Art and Crusade in the Age of Saint Louis*, Cambridge.

Weitzman, K. (1963) 'Thirteenth Century Crusader Icons on Mount Sinai', *AB* 45: 179–203.

—— (1966) 'Icon Painting in the Latin Kingdom', *DOP* 20: 49–84.

Wheeler, R.E.M. (1940) *Medieval Catalogue* (London Museum Catalogue no. 7), London.

Yvon, J. (1961) 'Besants sarracénats du roi de Jérusalem', *BSFN* 16, 8: 81–2.

Building techniques and materials

Braun, H. (1968) *An Introduction to English Medieval Architecture*, London.

Ellenblum, R. (1986) 'Construction Methods in Crusader Palestine', unpublished MA thesis, The Hebrew University of Jerusalem.

—— (1992) 'Construction Methods in Frankish Rural Settlements', in B.Z. Kedar (ed.) *The Horns of Hattin*, pp. 168–89, Jerusalem, London.

—— (forthcoming) *Masonry Marks, Quarries and the Management of Frankish Building Sites in Crusader Palestine*.

Kedar, B.Z. and Kaufman, A. (1975) 'Radiocarbon Measurements of Medieval Mortars: A Preliminary Report', *IEJ* 25: 36–8.

Kedar, B.Z. and Mook, W.G. (1978) 'Radiocarbon Dating of Mortar from the City Wall of Ascalon', *IEJ* 28: 173–6.

Maleo, Fr Mariano Morone da (1669) *Terra Santa nuovamente illustrata*, vol. 1, Piacceriza.

Mitchell, C.F. and Mitchell, G.A. (1908) *Brickwork and Masonry*, London.

Pringle, R.D. (1981) 'Some Approaches to the Study of Crusader Masonry Marks in Palestine', *Levant* 13: 173–99.

Burial

Bradley, M. (1994) 'Preliminary Assessment of the Medieval Christian Burials from Tel Jezreel', *Levant* 26: 63–5.

Clermont-Ganneau, C. (1874) 'Letters from M. Clermont-Ganneau', *PEFOS* 261–80.

—— (1876) 'Matériauz inédits pour servir à l'histoire des croisades', *Comptes-Rendus de l'Académie des Inscriptions et Belles-Lettres*, Paris.

Jacoby, Z. (1979) 'The Tomb of Baldwin V, King of Jerusalem (1185–1186) and the Workshop of the Temple Area', *Gesta* 18: 3–14.

Mitchell, P. (1994) 'Pathology in the Crusader Period: Human Skeletal Remains from Tell Jezreel', *Levant* 26: 67–71.

Piccirillo, M. (1975) 'The Chamber Tomb of Mary in the Crusader Period', in B. Bagatti, M. Piccirillo and A. Prodomo, (eds) *New Discoveries at the Tomb of Virgin Mary in Gethsemane*, trans. L. Sciberras, Jerusalem.

Prawer, J. (1974) 'A Crusader Tomb of 1290 from Acre and the Last Archbishops of Nazareth', *IEJ* 24: 241–51.

Smith, P. and Sabari, P. (1996) 'The Human Remains from the Church', *Yoqne'am I, The Late Periods*, *Qedem Reports* 3: 242–5, Jerusalem.

Index